AN INTRODUCTION TO
THE AUSTRALIAN CONSTITUTIONS

First edition	1974
second impression	1975
Second edition	1977
second impression	1979
Third edition	1983
Fourth edition	1987
second impression	1990
Fifth edition	1990
second impression	1993

By the same author

Lane's Commentary on the Australian Constitution
(Law Book Company Limited—1986, with annual supplements)

The Australian Federal System
(Law Book Company Limited—1979)

A Digest of Australian Constitutional Cases
(Law Book Company Limited—1976, 1982, 1988, 1992)

A Manual of Australian Constitutional Law
(Law Book Company Limited—1972, 1980, 1984, 1987, 1991)

The Australian Federal System with United States Analogues
(Law Book Company Limited—1972)

An Introduction to Australian Constitutional Law
(Law Book Company Limited—1967)

The Trade Practices Act: Its Constitutional Operation
(Law Book Company Limited—1966)

Some Principles and Sources of Australian Constitutional Law
(Law Book Company Limited—1964)

Agencies

CANADA AND USA

The Carswell Company Ltd
Ontario

SINGAPORE

Malayan Law Journal Pte Ltd

HONG KONG

Bloomsbury Books Ltd

UNITED KINGDOM

Sweet & Maxwell Ltd
London

MALAYSIA

Malayan Law Journal Sdn Bhd
Kuala Lumpur

USA

Wm W Gaunt & Sons, Inc
Holmes Beach, Florida

An Introduction to the
AUSTRALIAN CONSTITUTIONS

by

P H LANE

BA, LLM, LLD (Syd), SJD (Harvard)
Emeritus Challis Professor of Law
University of Sydney

SIXTH EDITION

THE LAW BOOK COMPANY LIMITED
1994

Published in Sydney by

The Law Book Company Limited
  44-50 Waterloo Road, North Ryde, N.S.W.
  568 Lonsdale Street, Melbourne, Victoria
  40 Queen Street, Brisbane, Queensland
  81 St George's Terrace, Perth, W.A.

National Library of Australia
  Cataloguing-in-Publication entry

Lane, P. H. (Patrick Harding), 1923-   .
  An introduction to the Australian Constitution.

  6th ed.
  Includes index.
  ISBN 0 455 21260 0.

  1. Australia. Constitution. 2. Australia—Constitutional law.
  I. Title.

342.9402

Typeset in Times Roman, 10 on 11 point, by Mercier Typesetters Pty Ltd,
    Granville, NSW
Printed by Star Printery Pty Ltd, Erskineville, NSW

Preface

Who decides whether the Victorian Government must pay payroll tax to the Commonwealth? Or whether the Commonwealth can incorporate companies on a nation-wide basis? If the High Court decides these critical Commonwealth-State issues, who appoints the Judges — the Commonwealth or the States? Why can't Federal Parliament "do something" about prices and incomes in the interest of the national economy? Does Federal Parliament's external affairs power extend to a State's internal affairs, such as Tasmania's preparatory work for the construction of a dam?

What is the role of the Governor-General? The role of the Australian Senate? Should Australia become a republic? Is the Constitution really "badly in need of reform"? What did happen in 1975? How do you answer the question, "What nationality are you?" What is the meaning of this, or of that, parliamentary term, say a "division" or a "Whip"?

Has each State in Australia a Constitution, and can New South Wales make a law that affects Queenslanders? How frequent are State elections, and what happens if the Upper House in Western Australia or Tasmania refuses to pass a bill sent up by the Lower House? What are the different courts in a State?

Does the Australian Capital Territory or the Northern Territory have a "Parliament"? Is the Northern Territory becoming the seventh State?

These are some of the questions answered in this Introduction to the Australian Constitutions, simply and directly. For the Introduction is intended to be an easily read paperback for those who want some general knowledge of the kind of governments we live under.

An up-to-date copy of the Commonwealth Constitution appears at the back of the text, as well as a copy of the *Australia Act* 1986 (Cth).

P H LANE

Sydney,
January 1994

Table of contents

The powers of Federal Parliament

The Federal Government

The Federal Government and Parliament

The federal courts

The States

Prohibitions and guarantees

How the Constitution was made

Table of contents

General matters

1. A federation

Australia is a federation, that is, every Australian must obey two sets of laws . . . can use two kinds of courts . . . elects two different governments . . . and knows two separate Constitutions. These two sets of laws, courts, governments and Constitutions are Commonwealth and State.

The Commonwealth Parliament, courts and Government have special and limited powers only.

Thus, Federal Parliament makes laws on enumerated specific subjects. Many of these are "national" matters, such as interstate trade, customs, defence, immigration and external affairs. Some are not, such as trading or financial corporations, marriage and old-age pensions. But the point is, these legislative subjects are limited and special. In the same way the federal courts mostly deal with special matters, say, cases on the Constitution or on Commonwealth laws, or cases in which the Commonwealth or its officer is a party. And the Federal Government also is concerned with special federal affairs, just as the Federal Parliament and courts are.

The State Parliaments, courts and Governments have wider, more general powers.

Generally, the States deal with matters not usually regulated by the Commonwealth, the kind of "localised" matter you would expect the different States to deal with. So, the States are constitutionally responsible for such matters as education, local government, health, transport and traffic control, general administration of justice and law-enforcement.

Some Commonwealth matters, for example, insurance or bankruptcy, can be controlled by the States as well as by the Commonwealth. Similarly, constitutional cases, for example, can be taken to the State courts or to the federal courts. But if the Commonwealth Parliament passes a law, say, on life insurance or bankruptcy, and a State also passes a law on life insurance or bankruptcy which is inconsistent with the Commonwealth law,

1

then the State law does not operate. (In fact Commonwealth law now controls the special subjects mentioned, life insurance and bankruptcy.)

> "At the time of federation the federating Colonies possessed full powers . . . of legislating for the peace, order, and good government of their people . . . (But the Commonwealth's) power (in s 51 of the Constitution) is not conferred in general terms. It is . . . restricted by the words which immediately follow it. These words are 'with respect to', and then follows a list of enumerated specific subjects . . . None of them relate(s) to that general control over the liberty of the subject . . . "

To sum up, the Commonwealth has the special powers. The States have the general powers. Hence there is no such creature as one Australian Government with national powers. There is a Federal Government with limited powers. The rest of the powers are the States—and that's what "federation" means: a demarcation of powers.

2. The Constitution

The full title of the Constitution is "the Constitution of the Commonwealth". It forms the main part of the *Commonwealth of Australia Constitution Act* 1900 (Imp.), which has a Preamble and eight opening or covering clauses and a ninth clause containing "the Constitution of the Commonwealth".

Strictly, it was the Parliament of the United Kingdom that enacted the overall Act. But, to all intents and purposes, the Commonwealth Constitution itself was not a work produced in the United Kingdom, save for the hand of the Colonial Office in s 74 on Privy Council appeals from the High Court. The Constitution Bill which became the Constitution (and which was to form part of the Act) was despatched from Australia to the United Kingdom only after many Australian conventions in 1890, 1891, 1897-1898 and after several draft bills and then popular referendums on the bills. All of this is discussed in the Chapter on "how the Constitution was made".

The upshot of this Australian endeavour was the passing of the Constitution Act by the United Kingdom Parliament in July 1900. But the Constitution included in the Act did not take effect until 1 January 1901. On this last date also we became "the Commonwealth of Australia".

2

- By this document, in the covering clauses, the former six colonies were replaced by a new form of government—a Federation.

  There were to be six original States and a central government. The States were to be left with their existing colonial Constitutions as modified by the Commonwealth Constitution. The central Government, of course, received a new Constitution.

- By this document also, in the Constitution itself, the special powers of the central government were set out: the special powers of its Parliament, its executive and its courts. And as well, certain guarantees and prohibitions were declared.

The Commonwealth Constitution lays down only broad outlines. After all, it was to be a general charter for the running of the country for many years to come. The Constitution was not intended to go into details we find in an ordinary statute. It tells us especially what the Federal Parliament, the Federal Courts and the Federal Government can do. It does not say a great deal about the States. That is found mostly in their own Constitutions. And the Commonwealth Constitution has a few guarantees, for instance, on religion. It has prohibitions also, for example, against any State attempt to demand customs and excise on goods.

The Constitution is the ever-present measuring rod for what the Commonwealth and the States can do, or not do, in governing Australia. Any law passed by Federal Parliament must be measured against the Constitution. So too, must State laws, but to a lesser extent.

Amendment of the Constitution: The Constitution is a permanent document. It can be amended, but with great difficulty: the main obstacle is the double-majority requirement explained below.

As I mentioned at the outset under this heading, the complete Commonwealth of Australia Constitution Act of 1900 really falls into two parts: first, a Preamble and eight covering clauses (as they are known) and, second, appended to a ninth clause, "The Constitution" itself. The power of amendment in s 128 covers only "This Constitution", as s 128 puts it, that is, ss 1-128, and I will explain this power below.

As for amendment of the Preamble or the covering clauses, the position is complicated. Since it was the United Kingdom Parliament that enacted the overall Constitution Act, you would expect this Parliament to amend the Preamble or the covering clauses. But under the *Australia Acts* 1986 (Cth & UK) the United Kingdom Parliament undertook henceforth not to pass an Act that extends to the Commonwealth. Earlier, under the Statute of Westminster the United Kingdom Parliament conceded the power to the Commonwealth Parliament to amend any United Kingdom Act that is part of Australian law—but not the Constitution Act.

However, the Australia Acts suggest two ways out, for these Acts give power to override the Acts or the Statute of Westminster. Firstly, the Commonwealth Parliament with all the State Parliaments can amend the Acts or the Statute, and then proceed to alter the Preamble or the covering clauses. Alternatively, the Commonwealth Parliament can win this power to amend by holding a referendum under s 128 of the Constitution; and in a referendum only four States are needed for a "Yes" vote, and none of their Parliaments is required to act.

An additional argument may possibly be mounted. When the United Kingdom Parliament totally "abandoned" the Commonwealth of Australia by its Australia Act, it was saying that, from 1986, Australia is to be left to its own devices—that, by implication, Australia is to have complete control of its legislative life. Thus the United Kingdom Parliament gave up its power even over the Preamble and covering clauses, so that these now lie within Commonwealth control through s 128, as much as the rest of the constitutional document.

A proposed amendment to the Constitution (that is, ss 1-128) must first be passed by an absolute majority of each House of Parliament, or at least of one House if the other House refuses. You notice that the *Federal* Parliament must take the initiative—which is a little hard on the States if they want to get through an amendment which benefits them at the central legislature's expense. Then a majority of the "State" electors in a majority of States must approve the amendment. On top of this, a majority of the "national" electors in all the States, and, since July 1977, in the two internal territories must also approve the amendment. So, on the basis of six States (Northern Territory is not yet a State), four small States with less than half the Australian voting population would not be able to get through an amendment. Similarly, the three most populated States, even with more than half the number of voting Australians, would still not get through an amendment.

In their wisdom or otherwise, the Founding Fathers thus opted for a "controlled" Constitution. They deliberately "created obstacles . . . in the path of those who would lay rash hands upon the ark of the Constitution" (*McCawley v R* 1920).

4

(There is no provision in the Constitution for popular initiatives to trigger the amendment process, as there is in Switzerland and some States in United States. But at least our process lets in the electors—the people—unlike most other federations where the amendment process is left to the central and, at times, regional legislators, as in United States, Canada, Germany, India and Malaysia.)

Since Federation in 1901 and up to September 1988 (the latest) there have been 18 referendum days on which the people have voted on 42 Constitution Alteration Bills to amend the Constitution. Because some of these Bills contained several proposed amendments, the people have considered in all something like 50 separate and specific provisions to amend the Constitution. But Australians are referendum-shy. In actual results there have been only eight successful referendums: in 1906, 1910, 1928, 1946, 1967, 1977 (three). The eight Constitution Alteration laws are listed at the top of the Constitution that appears at the back of the book. These laws added **nine amendments** (two were added in 1967) to the Constitution: ss 13, 15, 51(xxiiiA), (xxvi), 72, 105, 105A, 127 and 128.

The latest venture, in September 1988, was the most disastrous attempt since Federation. Despite a two-year education and research program by the 1986-1988 Constitutional Commission and expensive lead-up advertising, the national vote was 2:1 against three of the proposals and nearly the same ratio against the fourth proposal. And the State-by-State vote was the same: to every proposal, "No".

The 1946 referendum put s 51(xxiiiA) into the Commonwealth's catalogue of powers: Parliament can now make laws with respect to "the provision of maternity allowances, widows' pensions, child endowment, unemployment, pharmaceutical, sickness and hospital benefits, medical and dental services . . . benefits to students and family allowances"—whence our national health scheme with Medicare and our Austudy. The 1967 referendum deleted s 127 (on census and Aborigines) and the reference to the aboriginal race in s 51(xxvi) which now reads as a Commonwealth power to make laws with respect to "the people of any race for whom it is deemed necessary to make special laws"—whence such federal laws as the *Aboriginal and Torres Strait Islanders (Queensland Discriminatory Laws) Act* 1975 or the *Aboriginal and Torres Strait Islander Commission Act* 1989 (the "ATSIC"). Since the 1967 amendment the Federal Parliament has become more involved in aboriginal affairs. The States of course continue to pass laws in this area; in fact, every State has a law on aboriginal land, heritage or relics. In July 1977 with unusual enthusiasm the people said "Yes" to three amendments: s 15 (a replacement for a Senate casual vacancy is to be of the same "particular political party" as the casualty), s 72 (High Court Justices and other federal Justices are to be compulsorily retired) and s 128 (territorians are to have votes in a referendum on the Constitution).

It is the Constitution with the people's few additions and the High Court's many additions that makes up constitutional law, the supreme law of the land.

3. The courts

The Constitution gives only a general outline of government. And it was written many years ago in a different age. Therefore, **the High Court of Australia**, especially, fills in the details for the day-to-day running of the country, and it adapts the Constitution to the present day.

> "It is a Constitution we are interpreting, an instrument of government meant to endure and conferring powers expressed in general propositions wide enough to be capable of flexible application to changing circumstances"

> "We should avoid pedantic and narrow constructions . . ."

The High Court was explaining here that the Constitution is a broad instrument of government, as well as an organic instrument of government, and that it is not to be taken too strictly, in a pedantic spirit. So the Court went on to say that the Commonwealth power over interstate trade allows the Commonwealth, not just to control the trade of others, but also to engage in interstate trade itself with its own government airline, the Trans-Australia Airlines (*Australian National Airways v The Commonwealth* 1945). Next, the courts keep the Constitution alive. The High Court, for example, has decided that the Commonwealth's power in s 51(v) over "postal, telegraphic, telephonic, and other like services", given in 1901, now allows the Commonwealth to control broadcasting (*Brislan's* case 1935) and television (*Jones v The Commonwealth* 1965). Thus the High Court has updated the postal power.

And the High Court is continually deciding whether a particular State tax is bad as a forbidden excise duty under s 90 which does

6

not explain "duties of excise". The High Court is continually deciding how "free" interstate traders and travellers can be under s 92 of the Constitution or, to put it another way, what they are to be free from, for the Constitution itself does not explain this freedom guaranteed by s 92. The High Court, too, often expounds on what is meant by a State law that is "inconsistent" with a federal law. The Constitution itself, s 109, just uses the term "inconsistent", without elaboration. The High Court explains when the Commonwealth is making a law "for establishing any religion", a prohibition that is unexplained by s 116 itself.

Not only does the High Court fill in the details, adapt and update. The Court is also the custodian of the Constitution, ensuring that its provisions are kept by Commonwealth and State, say the provisions just mentioned: ss 90, 92 and 116 on excise duties, interstate trade and religion.

Even at this early stage you begin to appreciate the pervasive influence the High Court has in Australia. You begin to realise that *the Constitution means what the High Court says it means from time to time.*

Judicial review is the name given to the special role played by courts in a federation, as expounders of the Constitution (Commonwealth or State) and as custodians of its provisions.

So the courts decide on the constitutionality of a law or action. They decide whether a federal law is a valid postal law or not, or whether a State law attempts to impose duties of excise or not, to take a couple of questions which I just mentioned. With us in Australia, Federal (or State) Parliament does not pass a law and then simply declare that its law is within the Constitution, say, by attaching a Speaker's certificate to the law. In 1950 the *Communist Party Dissolution Act* itself declared that the proscription of communism was necessary for the "defence of the Common-wealth" (see s 51(vi) of the Constitution) and foreclosed any attempt to challenge this legislative opinion in a court. In 1974 the Governor-General's Proclamation itself insisted that all the steps required by s 57 of the Constitution for the double dissolution of April 1974 had been undertaken. But in each instance the High Court—undeterred by these self serving protests of the Federal Parliament in its Act or of the Federal Executive in its Proclamation—examined the documents and the actions to see if they complied with the Constitution, the defence power in s 51(vi) in the first case, s 57 in the second (the *Communist Party* case 1951 and the *PMA* case 1975).

7

Notice the wide surveillance exercised by the courts in our community, especially the High Court, the ultimate custodian of the Constitution.

Thus, the courts may measure a federal law or a State law against the Constitution and throw out the law (there are too many cases to cite). The High Court may measure the Federal Parliament's steps in a double dissolution and find them defective (the *PMA* case 1975), or measure the Federal Executive's steps and find weaknesses (the *Communist Party* case 1951), or check the Family Court of Australia or the Federal Court of Australia, or determine that State jurisdiction stops at the low-water mark, the Commonwealth then taking over (the *Seas and Submerged Lands* case 1975), or allow the Commonwealth, again against State claims, to use its external affairs power to control such internal matters as racial discrimination (*Koowarta's* case 1982) and the conservation of the natural heritage (the *Tasmanian Dam* case 1983 and the *Lemonthyme Forest* case 1988), or to exert its trading and financial corporations power over football clubs (*Adamson* 1979) and Victoria's superannuation board (*State Superannuation Board* 1982) but not to use this power to incorporate companies (*New South Wales v The Commonwealth* 1990) or, leaving Commonwealth powers for constitutional guarantees, the High Court may abruptly end the wholesale freedom that interstate traders once enjoyed under s 92 (*Cole v Whitfield* 1988) or, a different kind of case again, the High Court may advise Queensland to respect the rights of the Meriam people to the Murray Islands (*Mabo's* case 1992).

In a federation with a demarcation of powers between the central government and the State governments and with a Constitution carrying guarantees and prohibitions, a citizen, a State or the Commonwealth frequently goes to the courts for help.

Incidentally, the court does not take it on itself to review some doubtful law or action. Rather, the court must wait till a citizen, or a State, or the Commonwealth brings the law or the action into the court to be challenged. In fact, the court waits for a party with "standing", that is, a direct material interest in the litigated matter. A person could not attack the *National Health Act* on the basis that, if found invalid, administrative machinery will be dismantled and then his taxes might be cut. But he could attack on the basis that he will no longer have to pay a specific health levy or fill in a prescribed form.

And so, we have accepted the doctrine of judicial review—the high role of the courts—as part of our overall government. We have accepted the doctrine as an historical fact, for it is nowhere specifically encapsulated in the Constitution.

The result may be that, in the last analysis, the High Court is the supra-legislature for Australia. But there is no need to be fearful or critical of this almighty office of the High Court. It arises from the necessity of the case. There just must be some independent arbiter between the Federal and State Governments, and between these Governments and the citizen. What other body but the High Court can stop midnight sorties by the States, daylight robberies by the Commonwealth?

Thus, the High Court of Australia in particular is enormously active in the Federation, as is illustrated in the previous paragraphs.

4. Pigeon-holing federal laws

The Constitution gives *special powers only* to Commonwealth Parliament, as I said in No 1 above. This Parliament has a definite list of subjects on which it can make laws. Most of these matters are in s 51 of the Constitution.

- Canberra's laws, then, are special federal laws, not general national laws—a fundamental which even some High Court Justices seem to forget.

- You must be able to pigeon-hole every federal law somewhere in the list of special Commonwealth matters.

There is no use complaining, for example, that "the Commonwealth should do something about moneylenders and moneylending", because the Federal Parliament simply cannot deal with moneylenders and moneylending at large. It is a State matter, just as crime in general is. In fact, take the Commonwealth's own *Crimes Act* 1914. Despite its general title, it deals only with special federal matters. For instance, it penalises obstructions to interstate trade, see s 51(i) of the Constitution, the interstate trade and commerce power . . . it provides against espionage, see s 51(vi) of the Constitution, the defence power . . . it deals with Commonwealth property or Commonwealth public servants, see s 52(i) or, for example, s 51(v) or s 51(vii) of the Constitution, that is, the Commonwealth-property power, the "Government Departments" powers, etc.

9

In the same way the Commonwealth can exercise some control over drugs, pornography or prices although it has no general power over drugs, pornography or prices. For instance, the Federal Government, under its special overseas trade and commerce power, can ban imports of drugs. Under another special federal power, the postal power, the Government can prohibit the mailing of pornography. In the territories the Government can use its special territories power to fix prices, if it wants to. But in these examples on drugs, pornography and prices the Parliament is able to pass a federal law only because each example, as it happens, can be placed somewhere in the list of special Commonwealth matters.

A Commonwealth *Banking Act* is mostly built on the banking power in s 51(xiii)—otherwise it is bad. A Commonwealth *Life Insurance Act* must be based chiefly on the insurance power in s 51(xiv)—otherwise it is invalid, too.

Thus, in every case a federal law can be pigeon-holed somewhere in the list of special Commonwealth matters. Indeed, the law must be filed somewhere in this special list, otherwise it is invalid.

5. Testing laws

And so the courts—and always the High Court particularly—test federal laws to see if they can fit the laws into the Commonwealth's list of subject matters. The courts try to identify the subject matter in a federal law, that is, to characterise the law, as a law with respect to a Commonwealth matter. The courts also test State laws, as well as federal laws, to see if these laws offend some guarantee or prohibition in the Constitution, such as the guarantee of free interstate trade or the prohibition against State excise or import duty, or to see if a State law is inconsistent with a federal law, and so on. I have already referred to this testing by the courts when I explained the doctrine of judicial review in No 3 above.

How does the High Court go about its task of testing a law to see if it is valid? Does the Court examine a law with literal exactitude, or does the Court peer beyond, to what the law is really driving at? Does the Court turn over a law in a technical way, or does the Court insist on how a law "must" operate in practice?

A law is taken at face value by the High Court in many of the cases that it deals with, at any rate, cases where a Commonwealth law-making power (but not a prohibition on power) is the issue.

In 1961 Commonwealth Parliament amended its *Income Tax Assessment Act* 1936. The Act (with the *Income Tax Act*) now taxed trustees of superannuation funds unless they invested in Commonwealth securities and State public utilities, such as water, gas, electricity. In so many words this amending section simply dealt with a tax, just as the other sections in the Assessment Act did. Therefore the High Court in *Fairfax* (1965) could place this amending law in s 51(ii) of the Constitution, the power with respect to taxation. It was then a valid law. Of course, the trustees argued that the law was really meant to force them to invest in public utilities and that the subject of public utilities was not in the Commonwealth catalogue of special powers. But the High Court discounted this imputed aim of the law. Instead, the Act was simply taken at face value and when considered in this way it appeared as a valid federal tax law.

In 1975-76, a company owned a Queensland mining lease on Fraser Island which is annexed to that State. After a Federal Government inquiry into the impact of mining on the Island's environment, the Government was concerned to preserve the Island, but it has no federal power on mining and environment. However, the Federal Government has a special power in s 51(i) of the Constitution on overseas trade. Under this power the Government classified certain mined concentrates—such as those on Fraser Island—as prohibited exports in its Customs Regulations. Thus, the federal Regulation was really designed to deal with mining and environmental impact. Both are non federal areas. Still, the Regulation was allowed by the High Court in *Murphyores* (1976) as a valid federal law on overseas trade since this was what the law dealt with, taken at face value.

Then the High Court in this kind of case examines a law on its face and in its express terms, rather than by some devious purpose which can be read into the law.

The legal rights and duties affected by a law are considered by the High Court, again in the kind of case we are considering.

Take the two cases just given, but looked at from another angle. In the tax example in *Fairfax* the High Court sought out the legal effect of the *Income Tax Assessment Act* with the *Income Tax Act*. The law now imposed a liability to pay tax where there was none before. This change in legal rights and duties was the test of what the law was doing—taxing the subject. So regarded, the Act was valid under the taxation power. Its non legal effect of encouraging trustees to invest in public utilities was not the test. Similarly with

11

the mining-impact example in *Murphyores*. In legal terms the Customs Regulations barred the right to engage in overseas trade. Certainly there were repercussions on a mining proposal. But the measure of the law was its effect on rights and duties, not on consequences.

You will notice, by the way, how Federal Parliament was able to use its legitimate powers in *Fairfax* and *Murphyores* to "invade" non Commonwealth areas—because of the favourable way the High Court looked at what the Parliament had done, or because of the literal and legalistic way the High Court characterised each federal law.

> "The true nature of a law is to be ascertained by examining its terms and, speaking generally, ascertaining what it does in relation to duties, rights or powers which it creates . . . The consequential effects are irrelevant for this purpose. Even though an indirect consequence of an Act, which consequence could not be directly achieved by the legislature, is contemplated and desired by Parliament, that fact is not relevant to the validity of the Act."

In these instances, then, the Court tests a law according to its actual terms. And the Court looks at the direct, legal effect of the law.

I said "in these instances" because there are times when the High Court scrutinises **what a law does "in substance"**. The Court adopts this "practical" review especially when examining a State law, or even a Commonwealth law, and its possible contravention of a prohibition in the Constitution.

For instance, a Victorian pipeline operation licence fee at face value and according to its abstract legal effect seemed to be concerned with the business of operating a pipeline—and so have nothing to do with goods (for a State tax on goods is prohibited by s 90 of the Constitution as an excise duty). But in the particular circumstances before the Court the fees—or taxes as they were found to be—did affect the goods conveyed in the pipelines. Specific licences were granted by Victoria to operate named pipelines carrying hydrocarbons; moreover, this carrying was the link between the initial and finishing processes of the hydrocarbons. So *Hematite Petroleum* (1983) held that the licence fees were bad under s 90 of the Constitution because they were taxes on the hydrocarbons "in practical operation" and "in substance".

The different ways of testing laws reflect the different styles of Justices on the High Court. Some Justices can be labelled conservatives because of their exactness in reviewing laws or their narrow interpretations of prohibitions and federal powers in the Constitution. Some Justices can be labelled liberals because of their latitude in discovering what a law does or their wide interpretations of prohibitions and federal powers in the Constitution.

There is another contradiction. Laws sourced by Commonwealth powers are commonly taken at face value (whereas most of us can see what the laws are driving at). Yet laws, Commonwealth or State, that come up against prohibitions in the Constitution are commonly exposed because of what they are really doing.

Severability: A law may be bad in part only or in some applications only. If a court declares that some law is invalid, it does not follow that the law is bad altogether—in all of its sections and in all cases whatsoever.

- If the High Court had struck down the amending section in the *Income Tax Assessment Act* given above, or the prohibited exports provision in the Customs Regulations also given above, the rest of the sections in the Act or the rest of the provisions in the Regulations could still stand.

- If the High Court strikes down (as a State tax on goods prohibited by s 90 of the Constitution) a tax on the receipt of money because certain taxpayers receive money for goods, the tax will survive in other cases because these taxpayers receive money for services.

So, on some occasions the bad parts or applications of a statute (or a regulation) are treated as severable from the good parts or applications. These occasions arise when what is left of a partly bad statute—that is, its good part or application—still makes sense and still reads, more or less, as the whole statute did before the severance of the invalid part.

But if what is left after the bad parts of the statute have been put aside does not make sense or is a substantially different kind of law from the law put out by Parliament, then the whole statute falls because of the doctrine of "inseverability". Once Parliament took away from the former Arbitration Court its power to deal with industrial disputes, and gave this power to Conciliation Committees. The last part of the law (about the Committees) was bad; in theory it could be cut out. But this would have left no machinery to handle industrial disputes, and Parliament would not have intended this kind of law. So the whole law fell. It would go back to Parliament to re-assess (*ARU v Victorian Railways Commissioner* 1930).

6. Federalism and federations

By now you have some idea of what is meant by "federalism". It has four chief characteristics—namely, a written constitution, especially a distribution of legislative powers between the parties in the federation, an influential court system and a separation of powers (principally the judicial and non judicial powers). Before going into these characteristics in detail, consider the pros and cons of federalism for Australia in particular.

On the credit side:

* Federalism means a division of power, it is true. Yet this very fragmentation between the seven governments, at Canberra and in the six States, thwarts a dictatorial centralist government. The citizen is not at the mercy of the monopolistic few at the centre. The subject is protected by checks from the States. *A fundamental in democracy is division of power*. The same principle of institutional checks and balances, the same principle of power-splitting, operates in a bicameral legislature and in a paid Opposition.

* On-the-spot government is sympathetic government. It is found at seven points scattered around Australia. The alternative is remote government through a scanning screen from Canberra alone. In our huge country Canberra seems a long way off to the people in Queensland, Western Australia and Tasmania.

* Participatory democracy is rather more feasible with seven sets of institutions than with one aloof centrepoint. There is a little more chance of involvement with seven administrations.

* Federalism caters for Australian people as they in fact are. People who think parochially on education or urban development; people who think nationally on defence or external affairs. People who pride themselves, say as Queenslanders or New South Welshmen, with a distinctive way of life, different attitudes and so on.

14

- With multiple States there is competition, and there is experiment in government. A National Party-Liberal Coalition in Queensland might refuse to saddle business with a financial institutions duty in 1983 or a Labor Government there might abolish the Upper House in 1922. A Liberal Government in Victoria might try a mini-income tax in 1968 or random breath tests in 1976. A Labor Government in New South Wales might promote a speedy and inexpensive Australian Commercial Disputes Centre in 1986, or a Coalition Government there might limit itself by a fixed four year term in 1991. These things are possible where there is the diversity found in a federation.

- In the great overseas federations, United States and Canada, the national governments are now decentralising. Power and money are being returned to the States, the provinces and the cities. There are at present about ten federal or near federal systems in the world.

On the debit side:

- Many legislatures mean over-government. There are seven legislatures, as well as two territorial legislatures, and about 850 parliamentarians in Australia for a population of 17.5 m, say one politician for 20,600 people. There is one legislature and there are effectively about 980 parliamentarians (650 in the House of Commons) in United Kingdom for a population of about 57.4m, say one politician for 58,500 people. And a corollary: paradoxically, multi-government is weak government. It also breeds legalism and this bogs down government.

- Not only many legislatures, but duplicated machinery also, say, in education, transport, health and hospital care, and in car registration . . . all this wastes resources. It also explains why one in three employees is either a Commonwealth, State or local government public servant. Better to have economies of scale. The country could be run more efficiently on a single nation-wide basis with regional administration centres, such as we already have in our greater city areas and rural centres.

- In a homogeneous society like Australia there is no call for seven different governments, as well as the Northern Territory Government, the Australian Capital Territory and the Norfolk Island Administration. We have no great blocks of culture, race and religion to be accommodated in the different parts of a federation, as Canada has in Quebec.

15

- In our interlocking communities with frequent interstate passage we can do without diversity in laws on crime, defamation, domestic and industrial relations, public health and traffic. We can also do without different court systems. There should be one body of laws, administered in a national court system.

- *The important thing is not to debate about different areas of jurisdiction, but to carry out government programs well.*

- Since the very essence of federalism is division of power, this must cause conflict between the "partners", or at least give an opportunity for lack of cooperation, point-scoring and buck-passing—and the governed community is not assisted by all this.

- Recognition of human rights, cultural and natural heritage, the environment, consumer protection and the corporate sector have gone international. Australia can join in more effectively with a single national voice than with a babel of federal-State voices.

In the last analysis, it seems to me, our choice lies between two alternatives:

Do we want the checks and balances, the democratic safeguard, of multiple governments against the monolithic few at the centre?

Or do we want the economy and efficiency of centralism? The fundamental option of getting things done?

And there it is . . .

Turn now to the common characteristics of federalism. There are four, the first four that I am about to list.

(i) *A written constitution* lays down the form of a federal government. So, we have the *Commonwealth of Australia Constitution Act* 1900. Canada has the *British North America Act* 1867, renamed in 1982 the *Constitution Act* 1867. United States has the *Constitution of the United States* 1789.

A document may be drawn up by the people themselves who intend to federate, as the people in United States did. This is done in a series of conferences and conventions. Or the document may be drawn up or encased in an Act for a coming federation by a former mother country, as United Kingdom did for some of its dependencies, such as Canada and Australia. However it is drawn

16

up, the document is fairly rigid. It is not easily altered, for it is intended to last in its original form, more or less, for some time; and it is not alterable by the unilateral act of one of the parties in the federation.

The written constitution especially sets down the powers of the governments in the federation, or at all events the powers of the central government. The constitution may also say something of those powers in relation to the subject or citizen, that is, the constitution guarantees certain civil liberties.

Thus, the most important document or the fundamental law in a federation is—"the constitution".

(ii) *A distribution of powers* between the central government, on the one hand, and the member States or Provinces, on the other hand, is found in the constitution.

> *The essence of federation is this division of power. Federalism really means a fragmentation of power, a fact that is unpalatable to the politician in Canberra, Ottawa or Washington.*

The constitution stipulates, for example, which government is to look after defence and external affairs. (It is likely to be the national government, as in Australia, United States, Canada and India.) The constitution stipulates which government is to look after health, education, crime, housing, traffic. (It is likely to be the States or Provinces; for instance, the States or Provinces in the four federations I just mentioned look after the hospitals.)

Commonly, special and limited powers only are assigned to the central government, the wider and general powers to the regional governments, as in Australia, United States, Germany and Malaysia. Uncommonly (and broadly) it is the reverse in Canada.

Of course, the two sets of powers presume the coexistence of two polities—a central or national government and a State or provincial government. These two political entities govern, each in its own right, an overlapping geographical area and a common subject or citizen.

(iii) *The role of the courts* receives more emphasis in a federation, especially the role of the Supreme Court as it is called in United States and Canada, or the role of the High Court as it is called in Australia.

The courts become the independent arbiters to decide conflicts between the governments in a federation. An external affair matter might involve an internal affair matter also, say, desegregation or the construction of a dam. Then the courts must decide which government is to have control over the apparent external affair matter—the central government or some member State or Province. The courts, too, safeguard the citizen against unconstitutional interference either by the national government or by a member State or Province. In fact, without the courts it would be difficult for a federation to operate in practice—whence Dicey's aphorism, "federalism means legalism".

(iv) *A separation of powers* is also found in a federation. At least the Judiciary is kept separate from the legislature and the Executive. The chief mark of federalism, as I have already stated, is a division of powers between the central government and the other governments in the federation. The courts preserve this balance of powers. Therefore, the courts should not be aligned with either government, the central government or a State government. The Executive, too, may be separate from the legislature. Thus, in the United States, members of the Administration (save for one exception) do not sit in Congress. But such thorough-going separation is not necessary in a federation. So, in some federations, certain members of the Executive must sit in parliament, as in Canada or Australia, each with its cabinet system.

(v) *A Bill of Rights* is often found in a constitution of a federation.

Sometimes a Bill of Rights is set out expressly and at length in a constitutional document, as in the United States by way of amendment and, since 1982, in Canada. Other federations too have enshrined rights, say Germany, India or Malaysia. A Bill of Rights guarantees the civil rights of the subject against interference by the several governments in the federation or, to put it another way, a Bill of Rights lays down limits for government action. But in some constitutions a Bill of Rights is not expressly set out. A few Bill-of-Rights provisions might appear scattered throughout the constitution, as in Australia or Switzerland. Otherwise, the protection of the subject's civil rights is left to the ordinary law of the land (say, the law on defamation, sedition, breach of the peace and trespass to person or property) and to understandings in the community. In other words, a Bill of Rights is not a necessary element in a federal constitution.

So much for federalism in general . . . now look at some federations. Our present federal concept hasn't an ancient lineage.

It can be pinpointed at the convention of delegates from the 13 original States in "the Union" (United States). The delegates met to hammer out and sign a draft federal Constitution at Philadelphia on 17 September 1787. Some better known federations, arranged in order of birth, are: United States 1789, Switzerland 1848, Canada 1867, Australia 1901, Germany and India, both 1949, Nigeria and Malaysia, both 1963. But I will focus on two particular federations: Canada and United States.

Our federation, the Australian federation, was modelled partly on the Canadian federation but mostly on the United States federation. The Canadians gave too much power to the centre. The Americans left their States with more independence. See the Chapter on "how the Constitution was made", No 2. Hence our Founding Fathers—many not overwhelmingly enthusiastic about federation at all—did not borrow as much from Canada as from United States.

The Dominion of Canada was created by the *British North America Act* 1867, the "BNA Act", as it is called. Before I describe its provisions—for these were the provisions that the Founding Fathers had before them in the 1890s when drafting our Constitution—I should state the present position.

For 50 years the Dominion and Provincial governments have been at odds on the form of the Constitution that they would like Britain to transfer to Canada (the BNA Act was, of course, an Imperial Act)—whence the phrase, "the patriation" of the Canadian Constitution. The Canadians, or their politicians anyway, debated the possibility of abolishing the BNA Act and replacing it by an Act that would be entirely Canada's in the sense that the new Act would not require United Kingdom amendments, as the BNA Act did, but could be amended in Canada. In November 1981 Prime Minister Trudeau and nine Premiers (Quebec stood out) asked for Britain's help. The United Kingdom Government had been waiting until then for the Prime Minister to gain the concurrence of a substantial number of Provinces. In December 1981 the Dominion Parliament forwarded to the Queen the provisions of the Constitution of Canada which that Parliament asked the Queen to lay before the United Kingdom Parliament, as we had done with our Constitution Bill in 1900. So in March 1982 the United Kingdom Parliament passed the *Canada Act* 1982. On 17 April 1982 the *Constitution Act* 1982—contained in the *Canada Act*, as our Constitution is contained in the *Commonwealth of Australia Constitution Act* 1900—came into force when the Queen proclaimed "the patriation and amendment of the Constitution of Canada".

The *Canada Act* 1982 ends Britain's role in making constitutional amendments for Canada. The Queen remains, however, as the Queen of Canada.

The *Constitution Act*, contained in the *Canada Act*, does three things:

- It lists existing constitutional documents, notably the *Constitution Act* 1867, which is the old BNA. Act renamed, along with its many amendments.

- It provides amending procedures. The main rule requires the resolutions of the two Houses of the Dominion Parliament and of at least seven of the ten Provincial "legislative assemblies"; the latter must represent half the population of the Provinces—that is, the rule is something like the double-majority rule that we have in our s 128, as explained in No 2 "the Constitution" above.

- It entrenches a Bill of Rights, called the "Canadian Charter of Rights and Freedoms", as part of the Constitution, rather as the United States bill-of-rights provisions are part of its Constitution.

For the rest, it is up to the Dominion and the Provinces to sink their differences and set about re-making their own Constitution. But I have to say that even in the 1990s the centre and the regions are sorely pressed, at times seemingly in extremis, with the added complication of separatist Quebec.

Now return to the foundation document of Canadian federalism, the *British North America Act* 1867, as it was then called. The Act, like our Constitution, was passed by the United Kingdom Parliament. It was not a declaration by the citizens of Canada, as the United States Constitution was a declaration by the people of United States. The BNA Act established the Dominion Government or, as it is popularly called, the Federal Government. The Act also converted the existing three colonies—Canada, New Brunswick and Nova Scotia—into four Provinces, namely, Ontario, Quebec, New Brunswick and Nova Scotia. Our Constitution Act, on the other hand, assumed the six existing colonies; moreover, the Australian States did not get new Constitutions in 1900, as did the Canadian Provinces in 1867. Now there are ten Provinces in the Dominion of Canada—the four just listed plus Manitoba, British Columbia, Prince Edward Island, Alberta, Saskatchewan, Newfoundland. There are also two territories: the Yukon Territory and the Northwest Territories.

Throughout the following material I will speak in the present tense, relying on the provisions of the BNA Act, renamed the *Constitution Act* 1867. But remember that the Canadians can now amend this Act for themselves and, indeed, have proposals to do so.

The Dominion has a House of Commons and a Senate. The latter was intended to represent provincial interests as a "States' House", but it didn't work out that way any more than it did in the Australian Senate. Senators are appointed by the Governor-General, not elected directly and regularly by the people as in Australia. With its non elective character, its long tenure—until 75 years—and property qualifications, the Canadian Senate is more like the House of Lords than the Australian Senate.

Like our federation, the Canadian federation took over from Britain the idea of cabinet responsibility to Parliament. Thus, the members of the Dominion Government sit in the Dominion Parliament so that they can be responsible or answerable to this Parliament.

- *This is what we mainly borrowed from the Canadian Federation (and from our own Colonial experience), namely, responsible government, or an Executive determined by and answerable to the legislature through the cabinet system, what is called the Westminster system of government.*

On the other hand, unlike our federation with its single set of specific federal powers, Canada has a threefold distribution of powers. (i) Certain specific powers are given exclusively to the Provinces, such as powers over "property and civil rights" and "matters of a merely local or private nature". (ii) The residual powers remain with the Dominion. Our distribution is quite the reverse: with us, the residual powers go to the State. (iii) In addition, the Dominion has its own list of powers, mostly exclusive. Our Federal Parliament has many powers shared with the States, few exclusive powers.

Canada, like us, insists that trade and commerce between the Provinces must be free. But we do this by an express section, s 92. Canada does it by court doctrine.

The Supreme Court of Canada, the highest court in Canada, was not established by the BNA Act itself, as our High Court was established by the Constitution, and in fact the Dominion Parliament did not create the Supreme Court until 1875. The Court is made up of nine Judges; ours has seven. It takes references for

21

advisory opinions, a useful service to test the validity of legislation before it is put into operation, at times with costly machinery and administration. Our High Court refuses to answer such questions, for there are no specific parties and specific rights.

Unlike our federation where the Commonwealth and the States stand apart, in Canada the Dominion Government may disallow Provincial laws within a year of their enactment—not that this Dominion veto has been used for many, many years. Furthermore, the Dominion Governor-General appoints the Senators representing various Provinces, the Provincial Lieutenant-Governors—the equivalent of our independently appointed State Governors—and the Judges of the superior, district and county courts in each Province. We have none of these centralised controls over the States.

The United States of America, or "the Union", was established by the *Constitution of the United States* 1789. This was a popular compact which proclaimed "We the people of the United States . . . do ordain and establish this Constitution". The Constitution set up the United States Government, the national government. There were 13 original States with their existing Constitutions, just as we had six original States with their existing Constitutions. Now there are 50 States in the United States. Congress, the counterpart of our Federal Parliament, has a House of Representatives and a Senate. The latter is a "States' House", as our Senate is theoretically.

We borrowed heavily from provisions in the United States Constitution, such as provisions on prohibitions and guarantees, on federal court jurisdiction and judicial power, on the machinery of the central legislature and on the enumerated powers. As regards the enumerated powers, the United States federation has a distribution of powers in which certain enumerated specific powers are given to the central government. The residual and general powers are left with the States.

- *This is what we mainly borrowed from the United States Federation, namely, enumerated specific powers are given to the central government, residual powers are left with the States.*

But the United States Constitution differs from ours in the following ways.

(i) The United States Constitution is a more general outline, particularly in the list of powers given to Congress (our Commonwealth Parliament). These legislative powers are more broadly stated than ours and there are fewer of them. For example, Congress has only one power over commerce. But our Commonwealth Parliament has power not only over commerce, but also over bounties, banking, insurance, bills of exchange, foreign, trading or financial corporations and labour disputes in industry. Our Commonwealth Parliament also has power over marriage, matrimonial causes (including divorce) and social services.

Congress is made up of a House of Representatives (elected every two years) and a Senate (elected for six years on a rotation system with one third of the senators being elected every two years). The House of Representatives has 435 members, the Senate 100 (two for each State) for a population of about 258.4m. Our respective figures are 147 members and 76 senators (12 per State and four for the territories) for a population of about 17.5m.

(ii) The United States courts are perforce more active than ours in filling in the gaps in the Constitution, for their Constitution is drafted in broader outlines than ours and it includes a wide Bill of Rights which allows the judges to declaim "philosophies". There is no doubt that the United States courts do take a greater part in law-making than do ours. Without wishing to be sweeping, I would say that the United States courts are more concerned with the spirit and the policy of the law. Our courts attempt to adhere more closely to the letter of the law.

(iii) The United States court system differs from ours. Firstly, there is a separate federal court system. There are innumerable federal district courts, and from these litigants appeal to the circuit courts of appeals. But we make use of the existing State court system for federal law, although since 1976 and 1977 the Family Court of Australia and, increasingly, the Federal Court of Australia have moved into the federal law area. Secondly, the United States Supreme Court, made up of nine Judges, the counterpart of our High Court with seven Judges, takes cases from State courts, but only when there is a "federal question"—broadly, cases under the Constitution, United States treaties or federal laws. The High Court of Australia, on the other hand, takes general cases from State Supreme Courts, as well as federal cases from all kinds of courts, although special leave of the High Court is now the rule with few exceptions.

(iv) The Senate is a more powerful body in Congress than is our Senate in Federal Parliament. For example, the United States Senate must concur before the President can make a treaty. Thus, the Senate refused to ratify President Wilson's ratification of the

Treaty of Versailles. Again, the Senate's consent must be obtained when the President appoints ambassadors, Supreme Court Judges and other high ranking officials. For instance, in October 1987 President Reagan's determined nomination of Judge Bork for the Supreme Court was refused by the Senate. The Senate can try for impeachment civil officers (it has tried Judges) or the President himself, as it did in 1868.

The Senate can even amend (although it cannot originate) bills for raising revenue; with us this amendment (or introduction) of money bills is kept in the Lower House. The United States Senate committees have become extremely powerful inquisitions into the Administration and its policies. We have introduced an elaborate Senate committee system only since 1970.

(v) The cabinet system as we know it—that is, responsibility of the Executive to Parliament—is just not found in the United States Constitution. Still, there are the Senate inquisitions into the Administration, as already mentioned. But the Government is answerable to the United States people who elect it.

The President and his Administration do not sit in Congress. Indeed, they shall not. With us, it is just the opposite: members of the Ministry must sit in Parliament. No person holding any office under the United States shall be a member of either House of Congress; an exception is made for the Vice-President of the United States.

So, it is possible to have a Republican President with his Republican Administration but, on the other hand, a Democrat Congress—whence a lame duck President appears in the White House. In the 1980s Reagan and Bush, Republican Presidents, faced two Democrat Houses, the Senate and the House of Representatives. In November 1992 the newly elected Democrat President Clinton was favoured with Democrat Houses. But "his own" Congress is capable of overriding his recommended laws, taxation and appropriations. The President must argue policies and plead for money before a Congress that may often be an unsympathetic Congress. Remember that a Democrat or a Republican in Congress is not like our Labor or Liberal back-bencher in Federal Parliament, looking for promotion to ministerial rank. Usually, however, a President will have the support of his political party which does sit in Congress.

Contrast the comfortable arrangement at Canberra. There, in practical politics, a Federal Government sits in, and well nigh controls, the House of Representatives and, at times, the Senate as well.

Bills get into Congress on the recommendation of the President or they are introduced simply by the members themselves. United States has no government bills, as we have.

There are other ways, too, whereby United States separates its two arms of Government, the Executive and the legislature. The President cannot dissolve the House of Congress, as our Governor-General can dissolve both Houses of Parliament. Congress cannot bring down an Administration by a vote of no-confidence, as our Parliament can. The Senate cannot force the Administration to advise an election or to resign, as our Senate can by refusing Supply.

The United States Founding Fathers wanted a thorough-going separation of powers. The Judiciary was to be separate, as with us. But the Administration also was to be separate, unlike us. The result: *"the mile between the Capitol (where the Congress sits) and the White House (where the President sits) can be the longest mile in the world."* The President, his Cabinet Officers and his Special Assistants try to run the country as America's Administration. Congress with its innumerable Committees tries to run the country as America's Legislature.

Still, that's how it's been since 1789 . . .

(vi) The President is both the chief of the Executive and the head of the Union in the United States. In other words, in the United States the one person, the President, is at one and the same time the head of Government (cf our Prime Minister) and the head of State (cf our Governor-General as the Queen's representative).

The President of the United States is a more powerful figure than our Prime Minister or our Governor-General. To begin, the President of the United States is the Commander in Chief of the forces. With the Senate he makes treaties. With the Senate, too, the President appoints the high ranking officials in the United States, the Judges of the Supreme Court, the ambassadors, the "Ministers", the top officials—in short, the President has a strong hand in appointing the people who run the country. Especially, the President is *the Executive* in the United States. He must "take care that the laws be faithfully executed." The President is not obliged to act upon, or even seek, the advice of his "Ministers"—in the United States these 14 Cabinet Officers are called "Secretaries" of the various State Departments; for instance, the Secretary of State matches our Minister of State for Foreign Affairs, the Secretary of Defence our Minister of State for Defence. Thus, the President has

25

no influencing and controlling cabinet or ministry as our Prime Minister has. He is not limited by the notion of collective responsibility of cabinet.

Neither is the President answerable to Congress, as we have seen. He does not sit in Congress, as our Prime Minister must sit in Federal Parliament. You may say that in a theoretical sense the President *is* answerable to Congress since the House of Representatives can vote to impeach him and the Senate can then try him. I said "theoretical" because only one President was tried (and he was acquitted) in 1868. As for our different system, the Governor-General dismissed his Prime Minister in November 1975; or to give another analogy, our Parliament has successfully voted against the government of the day on eight occasions. But these analogies are unlike an impeachment which is based on high crimes or misdemeanours.

A bill has to be signed into law by the President. To put it another way, the President may veto Congress' bill, and in the 1980s and 1990s President Reagan and President Bush did just that (the House of Representatives was Democrat, the President was Republican). However, under the "two-thirds rule" the veto can be overridden by two-thirds of the members in each House of Congress.

The President is elected every four years by the people (being limited to two terms; we have no such limit for a Prime Minister); and he is answerable to the people. Strictly, the people vote State by State for delegates who then constitute an Electoral College which actually elects the President. The delegates will, by custom, act in sympathy with their "constituents", and thus the elected President can be said to represent the people's vote.

(vii) A Bill of Rights is found in the first nine amendments to the United States Constitution (added as soon as the Constitution was adopted—in 1789) and in the later 14th amendment (inserted in 1868). We have no such Bill of Rights in our Constitution, only a few scattered guarantees and prohibitions; they are mentioned in the Chapter on "prohibitions and guarantees".

The first nine amendments to the United States Constitution protect the subject against federal action. The 14th amendment safeguards the subject against State action. Thus, the citizen is guaranteed, for example, freedom of religion, speech, press and assembly. He is assured fair play in legal process or proceedings:

26

for instance, there are to be no unreasonable searches or seizures, or delayed trials or absence of legal representation. The citizen shall not be deprived of life, liberty or property without due process of law. His property shall not be taken for public use without just compensation. All citizens are to have equal protection of the laws: for example, there is to be no discrimination on grounds of colour, race or religion.

The Commonwealth and the States

1. Engineers case and Melbourne Corporation

When you look at the Constitution itself you do not find much said about the relations between the Commonwealth and the States. The Constitution does not tell you whether the Commonwealth can use its arbitration power to make a federal industrial award which binds all employers of teachers or professional engineers, including the New South Wales Education Department or the New South Wales Public Works Department. And the Constitution does not tell you whether Victoria can use its quite general power to impose a four cent stamp duty on all receipts, including receipts given by a Commonwealth agency, such as the former Australian Shipping Commission carrying on business in Victoria.

There are only a few sections in the Constitution which expressly say how the Commonwealth and the States can act in regard to one another. For instance, the federal acquisition power in s 51(xxxi) says that the Commonwealth can take property from the States. On the other hand, the federal banking power in s 51(xiii) or the insurance power in s 51(xiv) guarantees that the Commonwealth will not interfere with a State bank or insurance company that operates within the State only; so, the New South Wales State Bank, as long as it operates within New South Wales, is outside the Commonwealth's banking power. Section 114 says that a State cannot tax any Commonwealth property or vice versa.

Since such express provisions on Commonwealth-State relations are scarce in the Constitution, the High Court has had to decide for itself whether the Commonwealth can control some particular State activity or whether a State can control a given Commonwealth activity.

So, you see, the law on Commonwealth-State relations depends to a very large extent indeed on the High Court. *It depends on the High Court's subconscious understanding of our federal system.* Is it to be a balanced federal system, or is it to be a centralised system?

There are two leading High Court cases on the relation between the Commonwealth and the States. They are

- *Engineers* case (1920).
- *Melbourne Corporation* case (1947).

The Engineers case (1920) decided that the Commonwealth could use its arbitration power in s 51(xxxv) of the Constitution to authorise an industrial award which would bind the Western Australian Engineering Works, a State government enterprise. That is, the *Commonwealth* could make the *State* give better pay and working conditions to these State public servants. The federal industrial award, of course, covered engineers employed by private industry as well. In deciding the case, the High Court made two points in particular which are important throughout the whole of constitutional law.

Firstly, we should take the provisions in the Constitution on federal powers at face value without lightly introducing qualifications.

For instance, the federal arbitration power does not say in so many words that this power must not extend to State enterprises. As long as this power is exercised literally, that is, as long as the federal law based on the power deals with arbitration, an industrial dispute and the other elements in the power, that federal law will apply to any State enterprise, operation or agency that comes within the field of the federal law. Later, in 1971, the High Court applied the simple ruling in the *Engineers* case (about reading a constitutional provision on federal powers literally) even to such a power as the Commonwealth's taxation power. This, too, could be used so that a State, Victoria, had to pay pay-roll tax to the Federal Government, along with other employers (*Pay-roll Tax* case). Hence, general Commonwealth laws can certainly control State enterprises and State public servants, as well as the private sector in the State. True, but it is only occasionally, the Constitution makes an express exception for State enterprises, such as a State bank or State insurance company that operates only within the State. So the State Bank of New South Wales, as long as it operates within the State only, is outside the Commonwealth's banking power.

Secondly, we should interpret the Commonwealth's enumerated specific powers in the Constitution fully and effectively before we arrive at the general powers left over for the States—"the depository of residual (State) powers", as the Engineers case put it.

29

For example, the State labour powers over employees in its own enterprises must give way until the Commonwealth's express power over arbitration in s 51(xxxv) of the Constitution has been fully explained.

> "Where the affirmative terms of a stated (Commonwealth) power would justify an enactment, it rests upon those who rely on some limitation or restriction upon the power, to indicate it in the Constitution . . . it is a fundamental and fatal error to read sec. 107 (of the Constitution dealing with residual State powers) as reserving any power from the Commonwealth that falls fairly within the explicit terms of an express grant in sec. 51" of the Constitution, dealing with Commonwealth powers.

For the most part, *Engineers* case told us only what the Commonwealth can do to the States. But the High Court did say that the same principle applied when the States acted, too. So, the Court suggested that a general *State* income tax law could affect *Commonwealth* parliamentarians as much as anybody else. But the States were not in as strong a position as the Commonwealth, at least where the Commonwealth could pass a valid law. If a State law was inconsistent with that Commonwealth law, then the State law would not operate. It would be struck down by the inconsistency-of-laws provision in s 109 of the Constitution.

The Melbourne Corporation case (1947), the other leading case in Commonwealth-State relations, decided that the Commonwealth could not use its banking power in s 51(xiii) of the Constitution in order to stop the private trading banks from dealing with the States or State authorities as customers. The Commonwealth had attempted in its *Banking Act* 1945 to require the banks to obtain the written consent of the Federal Treasurer before they dealt with any State or any instrumentality of the State; and the Treasurer had indicated that he would not be giving his consent to the National Bank of Australasia Ltd so that it could continue to serve Melbourne Corporation (which was, of course, a State instrumentality).

But the High Court denied that Commonwealth Parliament could use any of its powers to single out State activities in this way, and the Court struck down the Commonwealth's *Banking Act*. A State, too, cannot use any of its powers to discriminate against the Commonwealth.

All the members of the Court in the case emphasised that we have a **Federation**, that is, a system in which there must always be two independent Governments—the Commonwealth and the State. Neither party should discriminate against the other.

The Court added another injunction in a Federation. Even a general federal law that impedes the continued existence of the States or their continued capacity to exercise essential functions, such as banking, would be bad. This federal principle applies equally in favour of the Commonwealth against State action.

Subsequently in 1985 the High Court again reviewed a discriminatory law. An amendment to the federal Arbitration Act had attempted to deny to Queensland electricity authorities rights before the Arbitration Commission that were freely available to other employers. The amendment was struck down under the *Melbourne Corporation* ruling against discriminatory laws in the Federation (*Queensland Electricity Commission v The Commonwealth*).

- The *Engineers* case decided that the Commonwealth or the States can control one another's activities to some extent.
- The *Melbourne Corporation* case decided that the Commonwealth or the States must not single out the other party for special treatment, or substantially impede the other party in the exercise of its constitutional powers.

But I should warn you that it is rather the *Engineers* case than the *Melbourne Corporation* case that has the upper hand. Time and again the federal powers have been first and fully interpreted by the High Court. The remnants are the States'. Moreover, State powers are curtailed by the exercise of federal powers, even if this is done indirectly. See the examples of *Fairfax* and *Murphyores* in the previous chapter, No 5. In other words, despite the countervailing doctrine in the *Melbourne Corporation* case, the States have had the worst of it in High Court law.

Thus, under High Court law the Commonwealth is in a stronger constitutional position than the States.

2. Inconsistent federal and State laws

In the Federation there are two different Parliaments, a Commonwealth Parliament and a State Parliament. And so the citizen is likely to find two laws, a Commonwealth law and a State law, each law attempting to control the one action—and these laws seem to be inconsistent with one another. Which of these laws is the subject to obey?

For example, a federal *Navigation Act* (regulating interstate and related shipping which may include intrastate shipping) and a New South Wales *Navigation Act* (regulating intrastate shipping) may each lay down its own right-of-way rule for shipping, including a ship that is in Port Jackson in New South Wales, having just sailed from Victoria. In this situation, in which each Act seems to apply, which one does the ship's captain obey? The captain must comply with the federal law because of s 109 of the Constitution (*Hume v Palmer* 1926). Section 109 says: a Commonwealth law is to be obeyed before an inconsistent State law, and the State law is to that extent invalid. But only "to that extent" invalid, for the State Act may still operate in areas where it is not inconsistent with the federal Act. For instance, the New South Wales Act above may still apply to purely intrastate shipping, whereas the federal Act focuses on interstate and related shipping, and it is only the invalid part of the New South Wales Act that is severed. Severability, to use the technical term, is explained in the first Chapter, No 5.

However, first notice that there may not be an inconsistency at all just because Commonwealth Parliament contemplates and accepts the operation of State law along with its own law. For instance, the Commonwealth's *Trade Practices Act* 1974 explicitly provides that any State law on consumer protection, say, on misdescription of goods, shall operate concurrently with the provisions in the federal Act on consumer protection. A customer can use either the federal Act or some State Act in the same area, such as the Fair Trading Act of Queensland, New South Wales or South Australia, unless the State Act contradicts the federal Act (*R v Credit Tribunal; ex p GMAC* 1977). Again there may not be an inconsistency because the Commonwealth law lays down safety regulations for overseas and interstate air navigation, whereas the State law deals with air navigation only within the State itself. The State law can take over where the Commonwealth law ends (*Airlines (No 1)* case 1964).

But there *is* an inconsistency in the following two kinds of situations at least:

• A federal industrial award *permits* an employer under the federal award to employ females on milling machines in his New South Wales factory. But the New South Wales Minister for Labour and Industry makes an order which *forbids* the use of women on milling machines operated by any employee in New

South Wales. The employer need not obey the New South Wales law. As far as the employer is concerned it is invalid (*Colvin v Bradley Bros* 1943).

- The Commonwealth makes regulations on slaughter houses for export meat which *cover the field*. That is, the multiple regulations deal with all kinds of details and conditions which are to apply to such slaughter houses. A South Australian law cannot trespass on to that field by laying down its details and conditions for these same slaughter houses. The State law would be inconsistent with the Commonwealth regulations if it did so. In such a case a proprietor could not be required to take out a State licence for the slaughter house (*O'Sullivan v Noarlunga Meat* 1954).

> This second kind of inconsistency "depends upon the intention of the paramount (federal) Legislature to express by its enactment, completely, exhaustively, or exclusively, what shall be the law governing the particular conduct or matter to which its attention is directed. When a federal statute discloses such an intention it is inconsistent with it for the law of a State to govern the same conduct or matter."

So, there are two tests for an inconsistent State law which have been devised by the High Court (and there are other less used tests). The State law forbids what the Commonwealth law permits, or vice versa; to put it more widely, there is a direct collision between the State law and the Commonwealth law. Or, the State law trespasses on to a field covered by the Commonwealth law. In either case, under s 109 of the Constitution the Commonwealth law ousts the State law which can then be disregarded.

Thus, because of Constitution s 109, the Commonwealth is in a stronger statutory position than the States, especially through the Court's use of the vague cover-the-field test.

An aside on the politics of the matter—A Commonwealth Government of one political persuasion can bring in its Navigation Act in order to "overrule", through s 109, an earlier Navigation Act brought in by a New South Wales Government of another political persuasion (cf *Hume v Palmer* 1926). In the 1980s-90s the Federal Government "threatened" State Governments with the use of its invasive external affairs power—backed by s 109—to stymie State initiatives unacceptable to the Federal Government.

3. Commonwealth grants to States and other fiscal matters

Through High Court law in the *Engineers* case, the Commonwealth exerts a constitutional control over the States. Through s 109 of the Constitution the Commonwealth exerts a statutory control over the States. Through s 96 of the Constitution the Commonwealth exerts an economic or financial control over the States. Under s 96 the Commonwealth can give money to the States, and it can lay down pretty well any condition the Commonwealth wants to—so far as the States are concerned, the sting is in the tail.

To begin, there are two kinds of federal grants under s 96 of the Constitution:

- general purpose grants or general revenue payments.
- specific purpose grants or tied grants.

General purpose grants or general revenue payments are large money grants given by the Commonwealth to the States each year (and lately to the Northern Territory, as well). No strings are attached, apart from the understanding that the States will keep out of the income tax field; and sometimes the grants are used as political leverage against a State (for example, if a State persists with a tax which Canberra does not want, Canberra will threaten to cut back that State's general purpose grant). The grants are merely used for the States' general purposes. The only complaint the States have here concerns the amount of their grants—huge as they are, the States never find them sufficient. Besides, the States complain, in a Federation, where the Commonwealth and the States are supposed to be partners, the States should not be at the mercy of the Commonwealth for its funds.

Specific purpose grants or tied grants are particular money grants given to the States *provided* the States use the money only for the specific purposes nominated by the Commonwealth. Here the States complain that in a Federation the Commonwealth should not dictate matters of policy to the States, say, priority of State works, or dictate conditions governing spending. At times, the Commonwealth requires its grants to be matched by State moneys, and this is tantamount to interference with State budgeting.

Take some illustrations of Canberra's conditions. South Australia may be given a road building grant with the specific condition that 50 per cent of the grant must be allocated to a Commonwealth-favoured network, whereas the Premier may protest that only 16 per cent of his people will use this network (this happened in June 1974). South Australia, again, may be given a

34

specific purpose grant to construct a standard gauge railway line with the Commonwealth from South Australia into the Northern Territory. New South Wales may be given money to build a "national" coal port where coal can be handled for export. Queensland and Western Australia may be given Commonwealth money to promote "national" mining industries and oil exploration. State water-resource development has been heavily funded by special purpose federal grants. So, too, have State roads, roads to assist export, for example, Queensland beef roads, or roads to form national highways or to become modern urban arterial roads—and all the time under the dictates of the Commonwealth.

By using its grants-on-condition power in s 96 of the Constitution—its conditions are, under High Court law, well nigh unconditional—the Commonwealth has deeply invaded State territory in transport, road building, hospitals, housing, education.

The extent to which the Commonwealth uses its specific grants power will depend on the kind of government the electors have chosen to put in Canberra. Is this government intent on the capitalism of power at Canberra? To carry out at a national level what the Constitution in formal terms puts at the State level? The zenith—from the State's viewpoint, the nadir—was reached in 1975. Between 1973 and 1975 specific purpose grants rose from 36 per cent to 52 per cent of the overall federal payments to the States, and not surprisingly, for in September 1973 the Prime Minister had declaimed, "Section 96 is . . . quite central to all my hopes".

Then a government, newly elected in December 1975, with an opposing ideology announced a "Federalism Policy", promising "a more selective use of such (specific purpose) grants . . . and not to make inroads into the constitutional responsibilities of the States". For a time untied grants were common. However, by January 1982 the Director of the Research Centre on Federal Financial Relations was saying: the practical working of the tax sharing arrangements (under which the States then operated) and other fiscal developments have intensified "fiscal centralisation" in Canberra since 1976. In 1982 specific purpose grants constituted about 30% of the overall federal payments to the States, in 1990 about 44%.

- *Federal revenue has really become federal regulation. The Commonwealth has veered away from federalism towards centralism in its devious use of the State-grants power in s 96 of the Constitution—a use made possible by the High Court's literalism in reading s 96, ignoring the autonomy of viable State units in a federal Constitution.*

Quite often you are puzzled to find that the Commonwealth is involved in some domestic matter which you cannot easily place in the list of special Commonwealth matters which I referred to in the first Chapter on "general matters", Nos 1 and 4. For instance, if you look at the Federal Ministry you are likely to find a Minister for Education or a Minister for Housing or a Minister for Transport. Yet there is no such subject as education, housing or transport in the list of special Commonwealth matters. Usually the explanation for the these Commonwealth ventures into non-Commonwealth matters is found in s 96 of the Constitution. That is, the Commonwealth has appointed a special Minister to administer federal grants to the States under s 96 for education or housing or transport.

State revenue sources: A final remark on federal grants to the State. It may surprise you to learn that a State's internal revenue, revenue from its own sources, is not of a very high order.

A State's revenue comes predominantly from federal funding. First, there are general purpose grants or general revenue payments, as I explained earlier. Second, there are specific purpose grants, also explained above. Then there are various Commonwealth loans or grants, say, equalisation grants (for example, to Tasmania). Roughly, Tasmania might rely on Canberra for 70% of its income, Victoria and New South Wales for 30-40%.

The rest of the State's revenue comes from its stamp duties on legal documents, cheques especially, receipts, hire-purchase agreements, as well as gift duty, death, succession or similar duty, although the States are phasing out death duty. Apart from stamp duty, gift duty and similar taxes, the State draws on other forms of taxation—entertainment tax, gambling tax including poker machine tax, financial institutions duty, land tax, business franchise fees for dealing in liquor, tobacco or petrol, and—a major source of the State's "own" revenue—pay-roll tax since September 1971, when the Commonwealth left this growth tax to the States. Then, turning away from taxation altogether, there are various government fees, such as car registration fees and, generally, charges for services rendered, such as water supply or railway and bus fares. State lotteries, too, bring in much revenue. And there are royalties on minerals.

The Uniform Tax Scheme: As I have already mentioned, each year the Commonwealth makes general purpose grants or general revenue payments to the States. But these grants are given only on

36

the understanding that the States have not imposed income tax themselves. This understanding was at one time a stipulated condition in the *States Grants Act* itself from 1942 to 1959. In those days the High Court said:

> The Commonwealth condition in its *States Grants Act* can "require the exercise of governmental powers of the State and require the State to conform with the desires of the Commonwealth in the exercise of such powers . . . the condition may stipulate for the exercise or non-exercise of the State's general legislative power . . . Why then does this not apply to the legislative power of imposing this or that form of taxation?"

It was largely because of the use of the grants-on-condition power in s 96 of the Constitution that the Commonwealth was able to introduce the Uniform Tax Scheme. (The Commonwealth first imposed federal income tax in 1915 to meet the cost of World War I, 1914-1918.)

The history of the Uniform Tax Scheme began during World War II, 1939-1945. Then the Commonwealth was engaged in heavy spending and needed as much revenue as it could lay its hands on. At that time, in 1942, the Committee on Uniform Taxation recommended that the Commonwealth take over the income tax market for the duration of the War and one year thereafter, that is, from 1942 to 1946. The Commonwealth—the Curtin Labor Government—did this in 1942, persuading the States not to use their income tax powers. In return the Commonwealth reimbursed the States on the basis of their annual average revenues from income tax during 1939-1942. Notice that this Commonwealth scheme only got off the ground because the Commonwealth was able to take over the State tax departments and officers under its federal defence power which could be invoked in those war years.

However, at the 1946 Premiers' Conference the Commonwealth—the Chifley Labor Government—determined to continue the Uniform Tax Scheme. Liberal Governments have been equally centralist. It should be dubbed "the Commonwealth's Tax Scheme".

At the special Premiers' Conference in February 1976 a new federal government, philosophically opposed to Canberra's monopoly of income tax, heralded a Commonwealth-State tax sharing program for personal income tax. In June 1978 the proposal was put into an Act under which a State might grant a rebate to its people or add a surcharge. In this marginal area of a State surcharge there might have been what is loosely called "double taxation". In this marginal area Canberra's monopoly of the income tax market since 1942 might have been broken. I say "might have been" because the 1978 Act was repealed in June 1989; no State had taken up the offer.

It is not that the States ever lost their power to impose State income tax, although back in 1953 Prime Minister Menzies spoke (not quite accurately) of "returning State taxing powers". The small States, Tasmania and Western Australia, retorted: "We do not want our taxing powers back". Presumably they preferred to be subsidised, through Commonwealth tax collection, by New South Wales and Victoria. In January 1970 the States, unanimous for once, asked Prime Minister Gorton to quit a share of the income tax market for them. He said, "No". In October 1991 Prime Minister Hawke conjured up a possible State income tax. This time it was the States who said, "No".

One may claim that the States are not really interested in an exercise of State accountability. Not even States of the same political colour as Canberra are prepared to take up the slack in State revenue by imposing the extra State income tax. Still, it may be politically unrealistic to expect the State to impose income tax when Canberra's existing rates remain high. If Canberra is really anxious to expose State budgeting, it should lower its tax rates to accommodate State income tax, as the Canadian Dominion Government did to accommodate Provincial income taxes.

For the time being, then, there is no "double taxation" in Australia. The Uniform Tax Scheme survives, followed by heavy general purpose grants and, in some matters, specific purpose grants to the States and Northern Territory.

The Australian Loan Council is a supra-Commonwealth, supra-State body that coordinates most of the borrowing by the Commonwealth and the States, an Australian phenomenon centralising and stabilising public borrowing throughout the Federation. The Commonwealth can still borrow independently for "Defence purposes" approved by Federal Parliament, and both the Commonwealth and the States can still borrow for "temporary purposes", to quote the Financial Agreement below.

The history of the matter is that before 1927 the public debt and the interest had swollen, especially since World War I, 1914-1918, out of all proportion to incoming revenue. Moreover, the Commonwealth and the States borrowed independently, as any sovereign government does. They vied with one another in offering competitive interest rates to investors. The Commonwealth-State

Financial Agreement of 1927 ended this self-destroying rivalry and established the Australian Loan Council. Henceforth most of the public borrowing in Australia could be done only with the approval of the Loan Council. I gave the two exceptional cases above. The Commonwealth alone was to be the borrower, offering its resources as security. The 1928 referendum inserted s 105A into the Constitution in 1929 to authorise the validation of existing Commonwealth-State financial agreements (and the making of new agreements). So, a 1929 Commonwealth Act validated the 1927 Agreement.

In May 1936 a Gentleman's Agreement was made by the States on behalf of their local government and semi-government authorities—s 105A literally extends to "States parties" only. This borrowing was gradually deregulated, and in 1985 the Gentleman's Agreement was ended. Instead, a "global approach" to borrowing was initiated, wherein the States volunteered to watch their authorities' borrowing.

In the 1970s and 80s the States contrived ways of detouring around the Council's limits, say by dealings with resource entrepreneurs or by leasing arrangements.

In 1985 the 1927 Financial Agreement seems to have expired: its main provisions were to run for 58 years. Nevertheless, the "States parties" more or less follow the 1927 provisions for the time being—"for the time being" because a Loan Council decision in 1990 assumes that the States and Territories will one day take full responsibility for raising and servicing their government debts.

Until that day, then, each State and the market fix interest rates, terms and conditions, subject to the Council's global borrowing limits.

Every year and at times twice a year, the Australian Loan Council meets in deep secrecy in Canberra, usually for two days. Its members are the Prime Minister and the State Premiers or their nominees, for example, the Federal Treasurer or a State Treasurer. Thus the membership of the Loan Council is much the same as the Premiers' Conference, which is explained below. In fact, the Premiers devote part of the time at the Conference planning tactics for the Loan Council.

The chief function and power of the Australian Loan Council is to oversee and coordinate most of the Commonwealth-State-local-and-semi-government borrowing. And it is here that the Commonwealth's influence intrudes. The Commonwealth has two

39

votes and a casting vote. Hence with these three votes the Commonwealth needs only two State votes to control the decisions of the Australian Loan Council.

The Commonwealth Grants Commission was established by a 1933 Act to look after "the claimant States", also called "necessitous" or "marginal" States. Northern Territory was added in 1978, the Australian Capital Territory in 1989.

Australian States differ in natural resources, profitable secondary industries, population densities, the distances people live from the main cities and revenue-raising capabilities, such as taxes, rates, charges. Consequently, the standard of government services varies, say education, health, law and order, roads and transport. To lift the level of services in the claimant States (these varied from time to time) to those of the prosperous States, viz, New South Wales and Victoria, the Grants Commission was formed. Thus, in effect, the Commission was an equalisation institution, making recommendations to the Commonwealth to use taxes drawn from the prosperous States to subsidise the claimant States.

"Equality in Diversity" was the title of the Grants Commission's 1983 publication. It might well have been its motto.

Even before 1933 the Commonwealth used to make special grants—under s 96 of the Constitution—to claimant States, but only on a casual basis, beginning in 1910-1912 with Western Australia and Tasmania. However, since the special grants ceased to look like temporary measures, the Commonwealth decided to set up a permanent body with its own settled methods and principles governing grants to claimant States. Later, in 1973 and up until 1986, the Commission's role was widened to recommend grants, through the respective States, to local government.

And so, from 1933 to 1981-1982 special financial assistance grants, as recommended by the Grants Commission, were made to the claimant States, and later the Northern Territory and the Australian Capital Territory. Since 1981-1982 the States have stopped lodging applications with the Grants Commission. Instead arrangements are made at the Premiers' Conferences to secure financial assistance, based on relativities.

The Commonwealth Grants Commission takes Federal Government references; it does not initiate its own investigations. For instance, the Commission may be given a reference to assist Commonwealth financing of the States, the Northern Territory or the Australian Capital Territory. The Grants Commission also keeps fiscal data and other data (for example, a State/s own increased revenue or population changes) to answer the Government's references about relativities between the States and the two internal Territories, or about the special financial need of a State or Territory.

So, you can look on the Grants Commission as the Federal Government's ready-to-hand adviser on State and territorial fiscal positions and needs.

A State Premiers' Conference is held for a couple of days each year in camera. It first met as long ago as 1901. There is still an authentic Premiers' Conference attended by the six State Premiers' alone. But what is usually meant by the "Premiers' Conference" is the one that is summoned to Canberra and chaired by the Prime Minister. Hence its full title, "the Conference of Commonwealth and State Ministers", now the Council of Australian Governments.

The Conference is held regularly about June, immediately before the Australian Loan Council (explained above) meets. In fact, the Conference flows into the Council meeting, since the membership is much the same. Occasionally in February or March a special Premiers' Conference is called. The Prime Minister, the Premiers and lately the Australian Capital Territory and the Northern Territory Chief Ministers, federal and State Ministers and especially Treasurers discuss financial assistance grants and generally Commonwealth aid to the States . . . public loans, loan allocations or, to put it another way, public works programs . . . joint State or Commonwealth-State ventures, for instance, health campaigns, education plans, legislative schemes . . . ways to combat inflation or to contain unemployment throughout Australia.

4. The strength of the Commonwealth

In an ideal federation the two parties—the central government and the State governments—would be equal in strength, each in its own sphere. The Commonwealth would not lord it over the States. Neither would the States lord it over the Commonwealth. In short, there would be a federal balance between the Commonwealth and the States.

But in fact there is a federal imbalance in the Australian Federation. There is centralism rather than federalism.

The Commonwealth, the central government, has become the stronger party in the Australian Federation. In 1901 there were

41

seven Commonwealth Departments and seven Ministers (and two unofficial "Ministers"). Now there are many mega-Departments and 30 Ministers. In 1901 there were 17 federal laws. Now there are often 200 laws a year, filling several fat volumes (in 1991 there were 216 laws in five volumes running into 6904 pages).

As I have shown under the three previous headings, the strength of the Commonwealth has risen because of judicial decisions and because of certain provisions in the Constitution (which have been aided by judicial decisions, too). To begin, the *Engineers* case has had a more permanent effect than the *Melbourne Corporation* case: under the ruling in the *Engineers* case Commonwealth powers are interpreted firstly and fully before we arrive at the powers left over—the powers of the States. On top of this, Commonwealth powers have been allowed to be exercised deviously, even if they do curtail the constitutional powers of the States. See the Commonwealth's use of the taxation power, or see its increasing use of the external affairs power to catapult Commonwealth policies into the States; both extensions are explained in the Chapter on "the powers of Federal Parliament", Nos 2 and 6. Next, the Constitution in s 109 requires Commonwealth laws to be obeyed before State laws when State laws are inconsistent with Commonwealth laws—and the High Court has widened the notion of "inconsistent" in s 109. And finally the Constitution in s 96 permits the Commonwealth to make grants to the States on such conditions as the Commonwealth thinks fit—and again the High Court has interpreted the allowable conditions liberally, almost without qualification.

Especially, the Commonwealth catches a huge revenue from taxation, particularly from personal income tax and company tax.

From 1906, the Commonwealth Government distributed its surplus revenue to the States, as it is required under s 94 of the Constitution. Then it set up trust funds in 1908 for future spending—and that ended the distributable surplus for the States with the blessing of the High Court which allowed this device in the *Surplus Revenue* case (1908). From 1901-1910, under the Braddon clause in s 87 of the Constitution, the Commonwealth Government was permitted to take only one quarter of the customs and excise revenue. Thereafter the Commonwealth was authorised to "otherwise provide". It did. It took all the customs and excise revenue including the lucrative sales tax, and made different (less favourable) payments to the States.

Since 1942 the Commonwealth has monopolised the income tax market, as I showed above in No 3, "The Uniform Tax Scheme".

The Commonwealth's tax cornucopia delivers, year by year, four times the quantity that six States and some 850-900 shires and municipal councils combined extract from their taxpayers, say 80 per cent of the national revenue goes to Canberra (that leaves 20% to the States although they carry 40% of all government spending). From this generous yield the Commonwealth makes grants to the States. This means that the Commonwealth itself will not go short, that the States will not care to offend Commonwealth policy, and that at times the Commonwealth will make specific purpose grants to the States on conditions laid down by the Commonwealth.

On the Australian Loan Council the Commonwealth has strong voting power. Finally, the Conference of Commonwealth and State Ministers, ironically known as the Premiers' Conference, is held at Canberra, the Seat of the Commonwealth Government. There the State Premiers hear the views and policies of the main purse-keeper—the Commonwealth.

Federal Parliament machinery

The Federal Parliament, or "The Parliament of the Commonwealth" as it is called in Chapter I of the Constitution, is a bicameral law-making body. The two chambers, the Upper and Lower Houses, are the Senate and the House of Representatives, and the third component of Parliament is the Queen (or the Crown) who acts through the Governor-General. See s 1 of the Constitution on the make-up of Federal Parliament and s 2 on the Governor-General as "Her Majesty's representative in the Commonwealth".

Since May 1927 Parliament has sat in Canberra, the Seat of Government of the Commonwealth. Until that site was determined, Parliament sat in Melbourne from May 1901, as was stipulated by s 125 of the Constitution.

Not that the Parliament's sitting days occupy much time. About half of this limited time is taken up with debates on proposed laws, the other half with electors' petitions, debates on reports (eg from committees), ministerial statements, question time, discussion of matters of public importance. Parliament works on a four-day week, between February to June and August to December, sitting for two weeks, then taking two weeks break, alternately. In the early days the parliamentarians sat for 90 to over 100 days a year. Now Parliament sits for 60-70 days a year. In 1990 Parliament was scheduled to sit a miserly 36 days. In fact, Parliament's sitting days have been decreasing annually. And yet, Parliament now passes 180 or more Acts a year, compared with about 40-80 Acts a year formerly. The rest of a parliamentarian's time is taken up with ministerial duties, including the running of the Government Departments, or—for backbenchers—with hearing and following up electors' grievances. The last task is particularly time-consuming.

In the material that follows I refer to Federal Parliament machinery mainly as found in specific provisions of the Constitution, namely, in Chapter I of the Constitution entitled "The Parliament". But there are also conventions for Parliament, or fairly common practices anyway, as there are for the Federal Government. For instance, usually a pair is arranged in either House when a senator or member is absent, that is, one opposing senator or member refrains from voting. By convention, too, a

Leader of the House is appointed, or a Leader of the Government in the Senate; neither office, indispensable though it may be, is actually created by the Constitution or by any Act.

1. The Senate

- *The Upper House is elected directly by the people*: s 7 of the Constitution. Elections for half the number of the 72 State senators—by proportional representation (I will explain this later)—usually take place every three years. A senator's actual term is six years, but because of a rotation system there are six senators from each of the six States retiring every three years. These retire before 1 July of the third year when the new senators take their seats for their six years: see s 13. So, elections are commonly held, but need not be, in the previous December (the senators-elect do not sit until the following July) and the elections may or may not coincide with Lower House general elections.

What is called "the perpetual succession" of the Senate has been ended, because of a double dissolution under s 57, on six occasions: in 1987, 1983, 1975, 1974, 1951 and 1914. On such occasions the newly elected senator's term begins in July *preceding* the elections. On such occasions also the Senate decides, on the basis of the State-by-State election results, who are the six year term senators, who are the three year term senators. The latter have to suffer a short term (and so meet the electors sooner) in order to crank up the rotation system again. This occurs only for the first term after a double dissolution, of course.

When a casual vacancy arises, for example, because of death or resignation, the Parliament of the State from which the former senator came fills the vacancy for the remainder of the term by a joint vote of the Houses, or a vote of the single House in Queensland. The appointee, however, must be of the same "particular political party" as the former senator: see s 15, inserted into the Constitution in July 1977.

Territorial senators arrived in the December elections of 1975, two each for the Australian Capital Territory and the Northern Territory. They have a three year term tied to the Lower House; but there is no nexus between their numbers and the numbers in the Lower House. (A Commonwealth Government, inimical to the idea of a States' House, could swamp the Senate with territorial senators.) They are given the same rights and privileges as the State senators, even to the extent of voting rights on all matters in the

Senate. All in all, they cut right across our traditional idea of senators. But now the High Court has held by a shaky 4:3 majority (*Territorial Senators* case 1975) that such senators can be created.

The President of the Senate is elected by the Senate: see s 17. In practice the office, almost as of course, goes to a member of the political party or coalition that forms the government of the day, even though that party or coalition may not control the majority vote in the Senate.

A different senator, the Leader of the Government in the Senate matches the Leader of the House (of Representatives), but with the difference that a hostile Senate can outvote the Government Leader in the Senate. The Leader of the Government in the Senate also matches the Prime Minister in the sense that the Leader represents the Prime Minister in the Senate, and answers questions or criticisms that might have been aimed at the Prime Minister in the Lower House.

The President's "body-guard" is the Usher of the Black Rod, who also takes recalcitrant senators or strangers into custody or has them removed. The President has only a deliberative vote—to preserve State equality in the States' House: see s 23. This section also provides that a tied vote goes in the negative. Because the President has a deliberative vote, his voice may be heard in the debates, but not often. During debates the President rules on the Standing Orders which govern the practice and procedure of the Senate. These Orders, by the way, also tell us about the election of officers, meeting times, order of business, questions, petitions, notices of motion and bills.

• *The Senate was intended to be "the States' House"*, to represent the interests of the people of the several States as a federal device, and particularly to safeguard the small States against the States of New South Wales and Victoria. See s 23 of the Constitution which I have just mentioned. Similarly, under s 9 the Parliament of a State may determine the times and places of Senate elections for the State, and under s 12 the State Governor issues writs for elections of senators for his State. Under s 15, casual vacancies are filled by the Parliament of the State of the missing senator. So, too, the six States vote as six separate electorates, and each State has an equal number of senators under s 7 of the Constitution—all of which points up the Senate as the States' House.

But, I must admit, the political fact is that senators barely represent their electing State. They loyally vote along party lines almost invariably: the mavericks are given a low priority on their party's Senate ticket. And now there are territorial senators to distort "the States' House" notion yet further.

• *Each of the six Original States must have at least six senators, the same number each*: see s 7 of the Constitution. In the December 1949 elections the figure became ten senators for each State and, since the December 1984 elections, 12—that is, always the same number for each State. So New South Wales with 5.97m people is still entitled to only 12 senators, while Tasmania with 471,100 people is equally entitled to the same number of senators. The justification for this malapportionment lies in the role of the Senate, as seen by the Founding Fathers. The Senate was designed to reflect the several States as the single vital units in the federal system.

In December 1975, four territorial senators were elected. Consequently, there are now 76 senators in all.

• The Senate has the same law-making powers as the House of Representatives but for one important difference, namely, **"money bills"**, that is, appropriation and taxation bills. Firstly, a bill that appropriates revenue or moneys or that imposes taxation must not originate in the Senates, such as a States Grants or Parliamentary Allowances Bill or a Sales Tax or Income Tax Bill. Secondly, an appropriation bill for the Government's ordinary annual services (that is, for the regular running of government departments) or a bill that imposes taxation must not be amended by the Senate, say, the annual Appropriation Bill (No 1) or one of the tax bills I mentioned. Appropriation Bills are explained in the Chapter below on "the Federal Government and Parliament", No 4 "public money". Thirdly, any bill in the Senate must not be amended to increase charges on the people, say, a Widows Pensions Bill. See s 53 of the Constitution.

This limitation in money matters is one of the chief distinctions between the Senate and the House of Representatives.

Still, the Senate can at least send a money bill back to the Lower House with a "request" for an amendment. And, as a matter of fact, the Senate has done this with some success from time to time over the years. Mind you, the Senate can simply refuse to pass a money bill or defer it until the Government resigns or goes to the electorate: this power is left untouched by s 53. See the closing pages of this Chapter for an example in October 1975. Our first law, Act No 1 of 1901, was a Supply Bill which stated expressly that it was enacted by the Senate, as well as the House of Representatives.

In other words, appropriation bills and taxation bills must go through—and be passed by—the Senate.

"Equal power with the House of Representatives": Putting aside money bills, the Senate can introduce or amend ordinary bills just as much as the House of Representatives can. *"The Senate shall have equal power with the House of Representatives in respect of all proposed laws"*, save for the introduction or amendment of certain money bills. These are the very words of s 53. See also ss 1, 57 par 3, and 58 on the assumed equality of the Senate with the Lower House. So a Minister who sits in the Senate—six to nine have in the last few Ministries, ten in 1993—will introduce a bill affecting his/her Department in the Senate.

The Senate is not to be compared with the House of Lords, another Upper House. The Lords (since 1911) can delay money bills for a month only, then they become law without the Lords' assent. Other bills (since 1949) can be delayed for 12 months, then again the House of Commons disregards the Lords. Our Senate could not be by-passed in either of these ways. After all, remember that the Senate is "directly chosen by the people": s 7 of the Constitution. The Lords are not. Remember, too, that the Senate has its own charter, particularly s 53 of the Constitution with its affirmation, "the Senate shall have equal power with the House of Representatives in respect of all proposed laws", save for the exceptions I mentioned.

By the way, it is misleading to refer to members of the House of Representatives as alone "MPs". Senators are equally members of Parliament.

Even so, about 90 per cent of our laws are in fact put forward in the House of Representatives, and put forward as Government bills. Very few are proposed in the Senate, and even fewer as private members' bills or as backbenchers' bills. (A private member's bill is one that is not sponsored by the government when it is first introduced by any member in either House; since Federation there have been only about a dozen successful private member's bills. A backbencher does not sit on the front benches where the Ministers, the Opposition "shadow Ministers" and the party leaders sit.) This means that the Senate's role is mainly that of a house of review, viz, publicising, amending and at times rejecting bills sent up by the Lower House.

A three-fold committee system came into operation in the Senate in 1970—a reformation based on the Canadian system, notably a system of standing committees. The refurbished committee system stands against Cabinet's control of Parliament rather as the United States Senate Committees probe the Administration there. The committee system also gathers information from experts or interested parties and builds up the senators' expertise so that they can confront a public service junta with *its* expertise. The committee system can scrutinise proposed laws, more leisurely than the full Senate can. Committees are composed of half a dozen or so hawk-eyed Opposition senators, as well as Government senators.

At the time of the 1970 initiative the House of Representatives had not established a similar critical appraisal procedure. The reason may be that when the committee system came into its own in the 1960s-1970s—spearheaded by Senator Murphy "to ensure there is a restoration of parliamentary democracy in Australia"— the Government did not control the Senate, whereas the Government necessarily controls the Lower House.

The three committee systems now found in the Senate, the Upper House, are:

"*Standing Committees*", or permanent committees, maintain surveillance over the administration of all government departments —a kind of watch-dog against bureaucracy. Of course, there has been since 1932 a Standing Committee on Regulations and Ordinances to examine the massive output of regulations and ordinances. To all intents and purposes this Committee is the sole parliamentary examiner of the bureaucracy's principal means of control—regulations. There has also been since 1966 a Standing Committee on Privileges to safeguard the Senate's own privileges, powers and immunities or those of its Committees. But the 1970 Legislative and General Purpose Standing Committees—there are nine now—have wide-ranging briefs to collect specialist knowledge for the full Senate and to scrutinise all kinds of government activities. Furthermore (and this is the new departure) these 1970 Committees are ever-present aids, unlike the earlier ad hoc committees. There is (or has been, for the titles may change from Parliament to Parliament) a Standing Committee on Foreign Affairs and Defence, on National Resources, on Legal and Constitutional Affairs, and so on.

"*Select Committees*", or special inquiry ad hoc committees, have investigated hundreds of matters since 1901, such matters as medical and hospital costs, drug trafficking and drug abuse, securities and exchange, civil rights of migrants. In 1984 two separate Senate Select Committees, each on the Conduct of a Judge (Murphy J of the High Court), were set up.

"Estimates Committees", six appointed as each Parliament begins, look into the Budget allocations of the several government departments. A given Committee collects information for the full Senate, especially information from Ministers in the Senate and from departmental officers, and some uncomfortable exposures show up. Thus, the Senate is in a position to debate the Estimates in the Budget intelligently and speedily when the annual Appropriation Bills come up from the Lower House in August to September, as well as publicise departmental inefficiencies.

So then, speaking broadly, the Senate as the Upper House of Parliament has two functions:

> *It is often a house of review* for the many bills coming up from the main legislative chamber, the House of Representatives.

> *It is an investigating house.* Through its committee system the Senate keeps an eye on the bureaucracy, on public spending and on public matters generally. Through its committee system the Senate gathers source material for good legislation.

There is another role for the Senate, a vital role. It is, indeed, the role that both Houses of Parliament are expected to play. Both Houses are supposed to act the surveillant of Government. For we keep forgetting that Parliament and Government are two different things, and we are in danger of losing the democratic control we have, through Parliament, over Government.

As it is, the House of Representatives is almost by definition a government-run institution. Government directives are forced through the Lower House by sheer weight of government numbers.

But the Senate may be a "hostile Senate", a Chamber in which the non-government members have the numbers. This was the case from 1962 to December 1975, and has been the case from July 1981 to date.

A "hostile Senate", or at any rate a Chamber that is different in outlook from the Lower House, is likely to arise because of certain factors. First, under the Senate's rotation system only a half of the senators goes to the electorate every three years; the other half will have been elected three years behind the present members of the Lower House. Next, under the Senate's proportional representation system the numbers of the major parties become closer to one another, and there may be small-party or independent senators elected; thus, after the general elections of March 1993, the tally was: seven Australian Democrats, two independent "Greens", one independent Tasmanian. Finally, senators are elected on a State-wide basis, State by State (or on a Territory-wide basis).

A "hostile Senate" is more of a Parliament than a House of Representatives is, for a "hostile Senate" keeps Parliament at arm's length from the Government. Another thing, a Senate has as much right to be "hostile" as an Opposition has in the Lower House, since each has been directly elected by the people, each has its own electorate to represent.

The alternative to a strong autonomous Upper House is rule by Cabinet or Caucus or, in Realpolitik, rule by a cadre of senior ministers.

Having said all that, one must admit that a given Senate may indeed make good government unworkable. For there is such a thing as a legitimate government put there by the majority of Australians to run the country, even if it is within the parameters of Parliament. How the present Senate measures up is a matter for judgment.

Incidentally, if the Government did have a mind to end once and for all the Senate's "obstruction"—another pejorative label used by whichever political party controls the Lower House—the Government would need to secure approval of all the States. This safeguard for the Senate can be spelt out of s 128 of the Constitution.

2. The House of Representatives

• *The Lower House is elected directly by the people*, (as is the Senate): see s 24 of the Constitution. General elections—by preferential voting, to be explained later—take place about every three years (as do elections for half the Senate): see s 28. You notice that I said "about" every three years. Unlike the Senate, the House of Representatives has not a fixed term. And, in fact, premature elections are often sought (from the Governor-General) to take advantage of a politically favourable climate, for the Prime Minister of the day carries the electoral times in his pocket, determined to hang on to power, whatever the political ethics of the tactic. On average we have had elections every two and half years. Strictly, the three-year period runs "from the first meeting of the House" (s 28), and this may not happen until a few months after the general elections were held.

51

Between general elections a "by-election" may be held to fill a vacancy, arising from the resignation or death of a member, for example. Then the Speaker, not the Governor-General, issues a writ for the election of a new member, s 33.

The House must sit at least once a year, with less than 12 months between sessions, s 6.

The Speaker, the principal officer of the House, is elected by the House to preside over its meetings: see Constitution s 35. Since 1937 the Speaker has been chosen from two nominees (if there are two nominees), put forward by the two main political parties. Not surprisingly, in practice he—or she, as Mrs Child in 1986-1989—is always a Government member, but he is bound by a tradition of apolitical impartiality. So, he does not usually take part in the debates. For the same reason (of impartiality) he does not cast a vote, unless the count is equal; then the Speaker "shall have" a casting vote: see Constitution s 40.

You may protest that, with us, the office of Speaker is one of the spoils of victory and that the Speaker returns the favour to his political party. The Speaker may protest that Oppositions are by definition rowdy and so seem to attract the Speaker's ire more than his party. All of which suggests the need to neutralise the office. For instance, we might get the services of an impartial Speaker if he is appointed by secret ballot (as in New South Wales), and severs all political affiliations inside and outside Parliament, but continues as a Speaker as long as he is elected as a member of Parliament (as in the English House of Commons).

Long ago the Speaker's predecessor in England acted as the "speaker" or spokesman to the King on behalf of the Parliament. He is still regarded as the spokesman for the House to the Crown; and he is the spokesman to the Senate and to outsiders. It was the former Speaker (the House had just been dissolved), Mr Scholes, who wrote to the Governor-General and then to the Queen on behalf of the House, expressing a no-confidence vote in Mr Fraser's caretaker government in November 1975. As well as ruling on the Standing Orders in debate, the Speaker looks after the general running of the Lower House, its staff, facilities, etc. The Speaker's "bodyguard" is the Sergeant-at-Arms, who also takes obstreperous members or strangers into custody or has them removed from the House.

The Leader of the House is also a Government member, a senior Minister. He is appointed by the Prime Minister as his delegate to arrange the business of the House, for example, the order of government business, when the House will sit, when money bills or new laws will be debated, and when special debates will take place. The Leader of the House, too, settles the daily business of the House with the Manager of Opposition Business.

For a long time the Lower House has not been subjected to a general committee system, as the Senate has since 1970. The Ministers can do without this kind of watchdog on government. But, firstly, in September 1979 the Lower House appointed multiple Estimates Committees to scrutinise and report on the planned expenditure of government departments, as sought in the annual Appropriation Bill (No 1). Secondly, in September 1987 a network of General Purpose Standing Committees was set up to inquire into government operations or any other matter—*provided* the House or a Minister sees fit to refer the matter (and there's the weakness in the "government's House").

What the Lower House really needs is a thorough going committee system—to look closely at the avalanche of bills pouring into the House and to monitor, without inhibition, government operations.

• *The House of Representatives represents the interests of the people of the Commonwealth at large*, whereas the Senate represents, in theory, the people in each of the six States, putting aside the anomalous territorial senators. The number of members (under s 24 of the Constitution), and so the number of electoral divisions or "electorates" (under the *Commonwealth Electoral Act* 1918), for each State varies in proportion to the population of each State. Thus, even the Lower House reflects the federal character of the Constitution. Since the last redistribution of electoral boundaries (in September 1991), New South Wales has 50 electorates for a population of about 5.97m, while Tasmania has only five for a population of about 471,100. At the latest general elections the distribution of electorates—and of members—was: New South Wales 50, Victoria 38, Queensland 25, South Australia 12, Western Australia 14, Tasmania five, Australian Capital Territory two, Northern Territory one (ACT has about twice the population of NT). In all, 147 electorates, 147 members.

As well as the number of electorates (based on population) varying from State to State, the area of the electorates vary. For example, Western Australia has a rural electorate stretching from Kalgoorlie to the north, 2.2m sq km, New South Wales a metropolitan electorate of 17 sq km. The member for a rural electorate may take several days visiting the constituents in a far-flung electorate; the member for a compact metropolitan electorate in the same State may drive around in 30 minutes, covering this electorate. So, it is not surprising to find that the number of voters in the electorates of a given State also vary. Thus, a member's electorate is related to the number of electors in the electorate, not the number of people who would include transients, children, babes in arms. The average electorate has about 70,000 on the electoral rolls.

The *Commonwealth Electoral Act* allows a 10 per cent deviation in any one of these electorates from the average electorate in a particular State. When there are too many deviations in a State because of population fluctuations, a redistribution is effected. Again because of population changes, the number of electorates to which a State is entitled may also be varied. Hence from time to time the independent Australian Electoral Commission, chaired by a current or former Federal Court Judge and with State Redistribution Committees, redraws the electoral boundaries of a State. Since 1984 the redrawn boundaries are beyond Parliament's interference. After the electoral boundaries have been redrawn the electoral chances of the political parties will change.

• *Each of the six Original States must have at least five representatives.* So Tasmania must always have at least five members no matter how small its population: see s 24 of the Constitution. The number of representatives for the whole of the Commonwealth "shall be" about twice the number of the State senators—**"the nexus",** as it is called: see s 24 again. (Territorial Senators are excluded from the nexus requirement.) Thus, when the Senate was increased to 60 at the December 1949 elections and then to 72 at the December 1984 elections, the number in the House of Representatives was increased on each occasion to about twice the number in the Senate.

There are now 147 members in the Lower House. I gave their State-by-State allocation above.

• *The House of Representatives alone can introduce appropriation and tax bills.* It also has almost exclusive power to amend these "money bills", as I explained in some detail when speaking of the Senate. The House of Representatives is given control over money bills because the Government of the day is drawn predominantly from the members of the controlling party in this House; few of the Government's Ministers sit in the Senate. Then, when Cabinet—that is, pretty well the Government—recommends a money bill to the House of Representatives the House will pass the bill. Thus, the Government is sure of its money. And, as well the Government keeps control of the nation's policies on revenue and expenditure.

The more important House: Incidentally, the last remark indicates the special place of the Lower House—viz, not because it is popularly elected whereas the Senate is not (for that's inaccurate); not because the Lower House is, apart from money bills, a stronger law-making body (which is also inaccurate); but because

- *the majority party (or coalition) in the Lower House provides the Government of the day, not the Senate. Moreover, the Prime Minister, the Treasurer, probably the Deputy Prime Minister and most of the other 27 or 28 Ministers—the core of the Government—sit in the House of Representatives whereas, over the years, the Senate has had four to seven Ministers only. And because*

- *the Lower House to a large extent controls money bills, not the Senate.*

Procedure in Parliament usually goes through the following stages before a bill becomes law.

(i) *Initiation and First Reading*: The bill is introduced in the House of Representatives (or in the Senate if it is to originate there, as a non money bill most certainly does from time to time) by the Minister in charge of the bill. This will generally be the Minister in charge of the department affected by the bill. Then the long title to the bill is read—the "first reading"—by the Clerk of the House. There is no comment, no debate. Only the title of the bill is read. But at least the members will get printed copies of the new bill as these are usually available at this stage. For some bills the members also get an "explanatory memorandum" (which, incidentally, can be used in court since 1984).

(ii) *Second Reading*: Even here the particular clauses in the bill are not examined. The members discuss the philosophy behind the bill, its general purpose and principle, whether there should be such a law at all. For instance, in the debate on the first Trade Practices Bill 1965 both sides of the House discussed the desirability of controlling private enterprise when it engaged in restrictive trade practices. In the debate on the Albury-Wodonga Development Bill 1982 members again spoke of matters of principle, such as the wisdom of decentralisation or, on the other hand, the desirability of improving the cities. In the second reading of the Corporations Bill 1988 the flexible regulation of companies and the promotion of efficiency and competitiveness in world markets were canvassed.

(iii) *Committee Stage*: This is a clause-by-clause examination of the bill. The Speaker leaves the Speaker's Chair but remains to take part and vote in the debate. Another member, the Chairman of Committees, then takes control of this important debate by the Committee of the Whole (explained in "Parliamentary terms" below). But otherwise the House in Committee seems no different from the House of Representatives; in other words, "committee" is a misnomer. The Minister who is piloting the bill explains the clauses and even introduces amendments. Other members criticise the bill or submit their own amendments. The various clauses and amendments are either simply agreed to or a vote is taken and then a given clause or amendment is accepted or rejected. *If you want to find out what the parliamentarians meant by a particular section in a Commonwealth Act this is the stage you should look at.* Hence reference in court to Second Reading debates is becoming fashionable to explain legislation. Still, I must admit that, unfortunately for the inquirer, the House more often than not agrees to go, as they say in the House, "forthwith" from the Second Reading to the Third Reading without a Committee scrutiny at all.

Alternatively, since 1978 a non appropriation bill may be referred to one of the legislation committees; a committee's membership does not exceed 20.

(iv) *Report to the House*: The bill with the Committee's amendments is reported to the House. That is, the Speaker returns to the Speaker's Chair and the Chairman of Committees reports on the progress of the bill through the committee stage to the Speaker and the House generally. The House then approves the Committee's report and proceeds at once to the Third Reading.

(v) *Third Reading*: The bill is "read" a third time, usually forthwith. But it is the bill as amended, so that the members now have a better idea of what the law will be like when the bill is passed.

(vi) *Passed through other House*: The bill, certified as passed by the Clerk, with the Clerk's certificate attached, then goes to the Senate for its First Reading, Second Reading and so on. (Or the bill goes to the House of Representatives for its First Reading, etc, if the bill originated in the Senate.)

(vii) *Bill returned to first House*: The bill with the Senate's amendments, if any, is certified accordingly by the Clerk of the Senate and is returned to the House of Representatives which may accept these amendments. If the House of Representatives does not accept the Senate's amendments, this may lead to a deadlock and eventually a double dissolution of both Houses under s 57 of the Constitution.

(viii) *Royal Assent*: And so the bill is presented for the Governor-General's signature below the standard form, "In the name of Her Majesty, I assent to this Act", and the Governor-General declares his assent. At this point the document passes from a mere proposed law or bill to a formal Act of Parliament. Not that the Act always becomes a law in force immediately even if it has been assented to. At times an Act is only to become law binding on Australians at some later date which is fixed by the Act itself or which is to be proclaimed in time by the Governor-General authorised by the Act to do so.

Parliamentary terms: I will briefly explain here some of the common terms associated with Parliament. Other terms were explained above, such as, President of the Senate, Speaker, Leader of the House, money bills, the nexus, first and second reading of a bill, and so on.

Address in reply—When he summons or opens Parliament after general elections or after a recess between sessions (on "session", see below), the Governor-General addresses both Houses, sitting in the Senate chamber. Actually the Governor-General's "Opening Speech" lays down the general policies and proposed laws of the Government, a new Government if there have been general elections. As a matter of fact, the speech is written by the Prime Minister himself. The members of the House of Representatives return to their own House. Then each House debates in the Address in Reply. In this debate the members range over all kinds of matters and the debate may last for a couple of weeks. The Address in Reply has thus become one of the most important "grievance" debates in Parliament.

Adjournment—see "Session".

Adjournment debate—A debate is allowed, usually at the end of the day, when an adjournment (till the next meeting) is moved. Apart from the limits arising from the general rules of debate, any topic may be raised. Backbenchers seize this opportunity.

Backbencher—The Ministers, the Opposition "shadow Ministers" and the party leaders occupy the front benches in each Chamber. Hence the others, whether Government or Opposition, are known as backbenchers.

57

Budget, the debate, the speech—These three terms are explained in the Chapter on "the Federal Government and Parliament", No 4 "public money".

Closure—To speed up matters, any member moves "that the question be now put", that is, that the matter under discussion be put to the vote at once. If this motion is carried—as it probably will be if the member is a Government member in the Lower House— then the House immediately decides the matter without more debate. This is a useful device which the Government can use to "gag" a speaker when the Government controls a House. Thereby the Government can rush through the bills at the end of a weary session. Another such device is the "Guillotine", explained below.

Committee of the Whole—Either House may decide to resolve itself into "a Committee of the Whole" (Senate or House) to consider a particular matter. The President in the Senate or the Speaker in the House of Representatives comes down from the chair but stays in the committee to take part and vote. The Deputy President or Deputy Speaker—the "Chairman of Committees"— then takes the chair. Proceedings are less formal than those in the normal Senate or House; for example, a member may speak more than once, a motion need not be seconded and party lines may or may not be followed. Chiefly this Committee examines the clauses of a bill in detail. See "Procedure in Parliament", "Committee Stage" above.

Dissolution of Parliament—see "Session". On double dissolution, see under "deadlock" at the end of this Chapter.

Division—When a vote is taken, usually the Speaker of the House of Representatives or the President of the Senate simply reckons the "Ayes" and the "Noes" *on the voices*. If this estimate is doubted, division bells throughout the building summon all members within hearing to attend; a sandglass times the ringing for four minutes; each Whip rounds up the members of his party. The members then divide. The "Ayes" pass to the right of the Chair, the "Noes" to the left, and take their seats. Thus a clear count is made and names are recorded by two tellers for each side, usually by the Whips and their deputies.

To "Call for a division" is a favourite delaying tactic. And to speak of a motion negatived or agreed to "on division" suggests that the vote was close.

Free vote—Usually members, in the Senate (supposedly the States' House) as much as in the House of Representatives, vote loyally along party lines. However, at times a political party

58

"allows" a free vote by its members because, for example, the matter concerns Parliament's privileges or the question is one for individual conscience, such as the funding of abortions under the national health scheme.

Gag—see "Closure".

Grievance debate—Once a fortnight, time may be set aside for the question "That grievances be noted". The Government, however, is not always self-denying, postponing the grievance day for the sake of government business. Backbenchers particularly take advantage of a grievance debate.

Guillotine—To speed up matters, especially for an embarrassing bill, a majority of the House of Representatives or the Senate resolves that a time limit be put on the various stages of the bill. At the fag end of its session each House often guillotines an unconscionable number of bills. Compare "Closure" above. Still, with the introduction of the committee system, especially in the Senate, this practice is not quite as irresponsible as it seems.

Hansard—A record of parliamentary proceedings is taken by "Hansard" reporters. Their daily Hansard is followed by a weekly Hansard, then by a permanent volume covering the whole session. Hansard claims to be "substantially" verbatim, that is, obvious mistakes, repetitions and redundancies are edited out—"substantially" causes controversy from time to time. Since 1984 counsel may bring Hansard into court to ascertain the meaning of a federal Act.

Opposition—Her Majesty's Loyal Opposition, to give it its paradoxical title, is considered at the end of the Chapter on "the Federal Government and Parliament", below.

Pair—An arrangement between the Whips in one or other House. When one member will be absent from parliament, a "pair" is arranged, that is, a member in the opposing party will not vote. But, of course, this can only depend upon a gentleman's agreement, not strict parliamentary practice. In fact, the agreement was broken by the Government in the Senate in May 1973, and by the Coalition in December 1988.

Prorogue—see "Session".

Question time—For about an hour on each day on which Parliament sits, the Speaker or the President asks the members of the relevant House, "Are there any questions without notice?" (Questions on notice demand detailed departmental information, in time answered by the responsible Minister, and stored in Hansard.) The members, almost always the Opposition members, seize the opportunity to ask critical questions of the Government Ministers, questions about government policy or about the department administered by the questioned Minister. *Question time is exposure time.* Hence, on such an occasion you may witness a rare sight—a full Chamber. About 1000 questions are asked each year, either questions on notice or questions without notice.

But question time is often abused by Dorothy Dixers, prearranged between members of the same political party to let in ministerial statements, and sometimes constituting as much as 60% of the questions put to a Minister. These self-serving statements can be ten-minute harangues and, combined with fewer questions (dropping from 19-17 a question time in the 1970s to 14-11 in the 1990s) and fewer sitting days, have greatly decreased questions without notice, from 1000 upwards annually in the 1970s to 600 or 700 in the 1980s. The government that allowed this and the government whose Treasurer retorted in November 1988, "Question Time is a courtesy extended to the House by the Executive branch of Government", have a lot to answer—to Australian parliamentary democracy.

In the 1990s the Senate (probably because it was not government run) sharpened Question Time. A certain number of questions must be answered, and time limits were imposed on a question and answer.

Recess—The interval between sessions or between the prorogation of Parliament and its dissolution. See "Session".

Session—After general elections the new Parliament is "summoned" or opened by the Governor-General. Within three years, that is, before the next general elections, Parliament is "dissolved" by the Governor-General, or it may simply and rarely expire by efflux of time. Between the summons and the dissolution or expiry, Parliament does not continually sit. Instead, it is "prorogued" or suspended from time to time by the Governor-General at the end of a "session". There may be only one session or two or three sessions (separated by a "recess") between the summons and the dissolution or expiry. Within a session each House has a "sitting" or "sits" until it is "adjourned"; then it is later "recalled" by the Speaker or the President.

Annually Parliament has two sittings—an Autumn sitting, February to June, and a Spring or Budget sitting, August to December.

The adjournment of Parliament is a less formal affair than the prorogation, and its effect is less drastic. Thus, when the

Governor-General prorogues Parliament, all business, including all bills, lapse and must be re-introduced if still wanted. Committees appointed for the life of Parliament or appointed by resolution cease; committees under standing orders may not meet; statutory committees may meet. In a prorogation the session is ended, not just interrupted as it is by an adjournment. A prorogation (or a dissolution) of Parliament wipes the slate clean.

A given Parliament from summons to dissolution or from summons to expiry is described as the First Parliament 1901-1903 or the Thirty-seventh Parliament 1993-1996. After general elections a new Parliament is summoned into being, and its "life" runs from 1901-1903 or 1993-1996. Of the 37 Parliaments since 1901, only one has expired or run its full term of three years, the Parliament of 1907-1910. In other words, Parliament has not a fixed term, only a maximum term. In fact, most Parliaments have had a life of two and half years and upwards (the life has been voluntarily terminated by the politicians themselves, in the face of their persistent agitation, and their 1988 referendum, for a four year term).

Sittings—see "Session".

Summons—see "Session".

Whip—Each political party has a Whip in the Upper House and in the Lower House. The Whip arranges the order in which the party's members hope to speak in debate, "hope" because the Whip cannot answer for the Chair's order of calling speakers. The Whip brings the party's members into line when a vote is taken, making sure that every member available is in the particular House when an important vote comes up. The Whip also arranges a "pair", and the Whip acts as a teller in a division.

The powers, privileges and immunities of Parliament, its members and committees, are the same as those that the English House of Commons had in January 1901: see s 49 of the Constitution. Under the same section Parliament passed a law in 1986 on the privileged statements of parliamentarians and witnesses before its committees; it was troubled by the views of the judges in the trials of Murphy J on the use in a court of evidence of parliamentary witnesses. In 1987 Parliament made a wider declaration of its privileges, spelling them out and curtailing some of them. Thus, the Bill of Rights (see below) is saved and its extent is made clear; a breach of privilege or a contempt is described: it must be an improper interference either with Parliament's authority or functions or with a member's duties as a member.

On the other hand, a member can no longer be expelled (only one member had ever been expelled, a member in the Lower House in November 1920), a specific limit is put to parliamentary fines ($5,000 or, for a company, $25,000) and imprisonment is limited to six months.

Throughout the debates on the various readings of a bill outlined above, a member has quite an amount of latitude in what he/she says. This privileged position of the parliamentarian in our community—or, more widely, the privileged position of Parliament to manage its "internal proceedings" without interference—goes back to the Bill of Rights 1689 which provides: *"That the freedom of speech and debates or proceedings in parliament ought not to be impeached or questioned in any court or place out of parliament"*.

A parliamentarian's remarks may even be defamatory, false or malicious. But no court action can be taken against the member because the members of Parliament are absolutely privileged in their statements made in the House—hence the jibe, "coward's castle". It may be different if the member takes up a challenge to make the same remarks outside the House. Then the member may be in danger of court proceedings by the person claiming to be defamed. In 1988, however, a victim of a parliamentarian's excesses under cover of privilege got some relief; the victim can now insist on a right of reply, to be incorporated in Hansard. In December 1988 the Senate allowed the first stranger (tagged a "spiv") to have his say in Hansard; and in December 1990 the Senate again tabled and incorporated in Hansard another rebuttal, this time from a member of the Lower House.

Each House of Parliament can discipline its own members by suspension. The member might have breached Standing Orders, or he might have proved himself an "unworthy" parliamentary representative in his conduct outside the House, say, in business transactions or by his conduct in some court case. Each House, too, can take action against non-members, viz, ordinary members of the public. These outsiders might have threatened parliamentary members, or maliciously criticised or libelled them, or leaked confidential matters, or refused to withdraw from the precincts of the House when asked, or heckled from one of the visitors' galleries—in short, they have improperly interfered with Parliament's authority or functions or with a member's duties as a member. The Senate and the House of Representatives, each has its standing Committee of Privileges to supervise and report on matters of privilege or contempt.

Each House may summon persons to the Bar of the House (or the Senate) to give evidence or to produce documents to assist an inquiry conducted by the House (or the Senate) or by one of its committees; the Bar is a brass rod that may be lowered across the entrance to either Chamber. Punishment of obstreperous or uncooperative members of the public may require the offender to attend "at the Bar of the House" (or the Senate) where he may be reprimanded or fined.

In June 1955 Messrs Browne and Fitzpatrick were brought to the Bar of the House, then taken into custody by the Sergeant-at-Arms under the Speaker's warrant and committed to three months imprisonment. They had published newspaper articles, circulated in a member's electorate, and said to be an attempt to influence and intimidate the member in order to discredit and silence him. The House of Representatives found this conduct to be in breach of privilege. This is the only occasion on which either House has used its drastic power of commitment.

And in all these instances Parliament is scarcely controlled by the Courts. Neither the High Court nor the Privy Council interfered with the Browne and Fitzpatrick finding, although asked. Note two things in this connection. First, it is Parliament, not the court, that finds "a breach and contempt of the privileges of Parliament" (although the court lists the privileges and Parliament cannot add to this conventional list). And second, the Speaker's warrant of committal may simply state that a certain person is guilty of a breach and contempt without going into facts, and this general statement is accepted by the court at face value—a kind of lettre de cachet.

Electors—There were about 12m voters at the federal general elections in March 1993. Federal electors must have certain qualifications, the same qualifications whether they vote for the Senate or the House of Representatives: see ss 8 and 30 of the Constitution.

These qualifications are:

- Registration on the roll of a particular electoral district in a State, the Australian Capital Territory or the Northern Territory or other Territory. The person must be 17 years or older, and must have lived at the present address for the last month. Since 1911 registration has been compulsory.

- The voter must be 18 years (lowered from 21 years since the May 1974 elections) before voting.

- The voter must be an Australian citizen (or if a British subject, say from Canada, New Zealand or United Kingdom, the person must have been enrolled as at 26 January 1984).

With these four commonly accepted qualifications—enrolment, residence, age, and citizenship—a person votes in a particular State (usually for six senators) and in a particular electoral district (for one member) in which the voter is enrolled. Similarly for the Australian Capital Territory and the Northern Territory or other Territory (with their number of senators and members).

Besides having the four qualifications given, a voter must not have certain disabilities: the voter must not be unsound of mind, attainted with treason, or under sentence for an offence carrying imprisonment for more that 12 months.

Once a person has the qualifications given, not only may he/she vote in elections or referendums—*he/she must vote*. Compulsory voting was pioneered in Australia, in Queensland in 1915, then at the 1925 federal elections. All States now have compulsory voting. In practice, compulsory voting means for some simply turning up at the booth to have one's name marked off the electoral list—and "voting" informally. (The great democracies of United Kingdom and United States have not thought it necessary to make voting compulsory. Neither does Canada or New Zealand. In fact, most countries don't.)

Another Australian "first" is the secret ballot. It was introduced as long ago as 1856 by Victorian and South Australian Acts. New South Wales followed in 1858. By 1877 the secret ballot was the rule for all elections.

I said above that one of the qualifications of a federal voter is being an Australian citizen. Who, then, is an Australian citizen?

An "**Australian citizen**" is a term brought in by the *Nationality and Citizenship Act* only since 1948. The Act was renamed in 1973 the *Australian Citizenship Act*. The word "nationality", by the way, is misleading. We are not British "nationals", and we are not usually called Australian "nationals". As Australian citizens we used to have the status of British subjects. The *British Nationality Act* 1981 (UK), in force in January 1983, abolishes that status almost entirely and instead introduces a restricted notion, namely, British citizenship. The Act attempts to bring into line nationality and the right of abode. On top of this, Australians owe allegiance to Her Majesty as subjects of the Queen of Australia, and this makes us Australian subjects, not British subjects.

Hence the answer to the misleading question, "what nationality are you?" is now, "an Australian citizen".

An Australian citizen is a person who is in one of the following four classes: (i) A person who was born in Australia: thus an Australian citizen *by birth*. (ii) A person who was not born here, but whose father or mother was an Australian citizen; in addition, the birth was registered at an Australian consulate (or an 18 year old may apply in Australia for registration): thus an Australian citizen *by descent*. (iii) A person who was adopted by an Australian citizen and was present in Australia as a permanent resident when adopted: thus an Australian citizen *by adoption*. (iv) Any other person—even if this person comes from Canada, New Zealand, India, United Kingdom or Eire—who applied for, and received, a grant of a "certificate of Australian citizenship": thus an Australian citizen *by grant*.

In the usual case this last kind of Australian citizen must have lived for a total of 12 months in the two years before the application for citizenship, and a total of two years altogether in the five years before the application. There are other requirements as well—such as an intention to live in Australia, 18 years of age, good character, a basic knowledge of English, a promise of allegiance to the Queen of Australia, and an undertaking of civic responsibilities (for example, to enrol on the electoral register).

In short form, Australian citizenship is obtained in one of four clear-cut ways: by birth—by descent—by adoption—or by grant.

A migrant who obtains Australian citizenship by grant may keep a former citizenship, at least Australian law has nothing to do with this. However, the migrant's former country may take away its citizenship or, quite the contrary, may refuse to allow the migrant to renounce the former citizenship; whence arises dual citizenship. Take a different case: Australian law does not permit its citizens to take up another citizenship deliberately; for example, if an Australian citizen takes up United States citizenship, the Australian citizenship is lost.

Australian citizenship gives at least four advantages: entitlement to enrol for, and so vote at, elections and referendums . . . to stand for public office, including Parliament . . . to apply for a passport (see next paragraph) . . . to be accepted as a non alien, and so not be liable to deportation from Australia or be refused the right to enter Australia.

Most Australian citizens can get a passport. In other words, strictly an Australian citizen cannot say that he/she *must* be given a passport. A passport requests that the bearer be allowed to go on his/her way freely; it identifies a person and vouches his/her respectability; and it shows the citizenship of a person. With a passport an Australian citizen is afforded abroad "every assistance and protection of which he or she may stand in need" (as the passport puts it) by the Commonwealth Government, and especially by its overseas representatives who look after the passport holder as an "Australian citizen".

The method of election to the House of Representatives or to the Senate differs according to the House to be elected.

(i) Election to the House of Representatives is based (since the December 1919 elections; before this it was a first-past-the-post system) on the *preferential voting system* for each of the 147 federal electoral divisions, as there are at present. That is, each electorate is a single-member constituency.

Say there are three political candidates, A, B, and C, for a certain electorate. Each voter in the electorate marks his/her ballot paper, one, two and three, according to his/her preference for the three candidates. Suppose A gets 50 per cent plus one of the formal primary votes or first preferences on the ballot papers. He/she will then have more primaries than B and C together. A will have an absolute majority, and A will then be elected. But suppose A only gets 40 per cent of the primary votes. Candidate B gets 35 per cent of the primaries. Candidate C gets 25 per cent. A then has a mere simple majority, that is, his/her votes exceed the votes of either B or C taken singly. Therefore, the candidate with the least number of primaries, C, is eliminated. Next, the second preferences on "C's" ballot papers are distributed among A and B according to the voter's choice shown on "C's" ballot papers. These second preferences may well favour candidate B, the candidate with only 35 per cent of the primaries, by bringing his/her votes up to 50 per cent plus one. As a result, B then becomes the elected member for that particular electorate.

The process is just the same when there are innumerable candidates—namely, the candidate with the lowest number of primaries has his/her second preferences distributed up the line. Then, the next candidate with the least primaries has his/her second preferences distributed. Eventually, this eliminating and distributing process produces a candidate with 50 per cent plus one of the votes.

You can see, by the way, that *your second preference is your real vote when you give a first preference to a minor party*. You can also see that a small political party with its candidate can rarely obtain sufficient primaries to secure a seat in the House of Representatives. And yet, this minority party on the other hand may assist one of the other political parties to get in, as we have just seen, because of its preferences.

You will also notice that in a first-past-the-post system, or a simple majority system, which is used in the United States, Canada and United Kingdom (but which a New Zealand referendum abandoned for proportional representation in November 1993), A with only 40 per cent of the primary votes would be elected although 60 per cent of the people do *not* want him. C, on the other hand, would never be elected, for C could not rely on B's preferences. (Thus a first-past-the-post system would spell the end of small parties and independents in Australia.) In addition, C's voters could never show a second preference for B. That is, the influence of 60 per cent of the electors, B's and C's voters, would be thwarted in a first-past-the-post system. But here we are dealing with a preferential voting system, a more democratic way of representing people. Of course, if only two political candidates were standing, A and B, then the first-past-the-post system would fairly represent the voters' wishes.

(The system of *optional preferential voting* applies in New South Wales; for the Legislative Council there is the added element of proportional representation. Under the optional preferential voting system the elector, first, *must* vote for as many candidates as there are to be elected for his/her electorate. The elector, secondly, *may* go on to show his/her preferences by voting for all or only some of the other candidates that are standing. In practice this voting system might easily approach the first-past-the-post system because of the laziness or apathy of the voters.)

(ii) Election to the Upper House, the Senate, is based on *proportional representation* combined with preferential voting—since the December 1949 elections—for each of the six States. Each State votes as one electorate every three years, returning six senators on a rotation system, that is, alternate blocks of six senators are voted in for six years. After a double dissolution 12 senators are voted in for each State. Thus, each State is a multi-member constituency. The ballot paper carries far more names than six (or 12)—in the March 1993 general elections there were 66 names in New South Wales—and the voter marks the names in an order according to his/her preference. More simply, the voter can place "1" in his/her political party's box.

There are two things to notice about this kind of voting system. One is the taking of a quota—a quantity of votes that every successful candidate must reach. The other is the transfer of the successful candidate's excess votes over the quota to the second preferences on this candidate's ballot papers. If I may be allowed to over-simplify, I can say that the quota is roughly arrived at by dividing the number of first preference votes in a given State by the number of senators (for that State) plus one, that is, usually by seven.

Assume the quota comes to 20,001. Suppose candidate A gets 30,000 primary votes . . . B gets 25,000 . . . C gets 10,000 . . . D gets 5,000 . . . and so on. A and B, of course, are in as senators for their State. They reached the quota.

Now, A's surplus votes were nearly 10,000. These extra votes are distributed, according to a formula which actually transfers only a fraction of a full surplus vote, among the candidates who were marked second on "A's" ballot papers. (These second preferences are likely to be members of the same political party as A.) Thus, C will pick up some of A's excess votes if C appeared as a second preference on "A's" ballot papers. Indeed, C may pick up enough of these surplus votes to raise his own primary votes of 10,000 to the required quota of 20,001. Then C becomes a senator, too. Suppose at the end of the transfer of the surplus votes of A and B (and others with first preferences over 20,001) there are still only three senators. Then the preferences of the candidate with the smallest lot of primaries are shared out to the other candidates concerned.

Under this kind of voting system—proportional represent-ation—a candidate from a minority party can reach the Senate, as frequently happens in Australia. The candidate gathers in enough surplus votes to build up his/her own first preferences to satisfy the quota. Under this kind of voting system also there is often a near-equality of the two major Australian political parties in the Senate and the likelihood of a "hostile Senate".

(Territorial senators, two each for the Australian Capital Territory and the Northern Territory, come and go with the House of Representatives' elections. Each Territory votes as one electorate, voting under the proportional representation system.)

The Court of Disputed Returns decides disputes about elections or about returns of writs for elections. The Court has been petitioned to decide about 30 disputes and has declared six void. In November 1992 the Court declared Cleary's by-election to the

Lower House void since he held an office of profit under the Crown, the Victorian Education Department, at the time of the election. The Court is usually the High Court (as it was in *Cleary's* case), acting instead of Parliament itself which could have acted under s 47 of the Constitution. The Court may refer the petition to the Supreme Court of the State where the election or so-called election was held; and then this Court sits as the Court of Disputed Returns.

Apart from electoral or writ disputes, the Court of Disputed Returns may decide two other matters: questions about vacancies in either House and questions about the qualifications of a senator or a member.

But first the Senate or the House of Representatives must resolve to refer either of these last two questions to the Court or, in the alternative, answer the question in the Senate or the House of Representatives itself. The House of Representatives has always answered the question in the House. The Senate has not. Thus, in December 1907 the Court of Disputed Returns decided that what the South Australian Parliament had treated as a casual vacancy in the Senate within s 15 was really a vacancy within s 7 (when the people, not a State parliament, vote). And in June 1975 the Court passed (a favourable) judgment on the qualification of Senator Webster under s 44 which deals with government contracts. In May 1988 the Court—again the High Court sitting as the Court of Disputed Returns—found that Senator Wood did not have the required qualification of an Australian citizen when he had nominated for the Senate representing New South Wales; a month later the Court ordered a recount for this unfilled position.

A deadlock—or "disagreement between the Houses" as the marginal note to s 57 of the Constitution calls it—arises when the Senate twice rejects a bill sent up by the House of Representatives. **A double dissolution** may then resolve the deadlock.

What happens precisely is this: The Government introduces a bill into the House of Representatives where it is passed. The bill goes up to the Senate which rejects it, fails to pass it (eg uses delaying tactics as in 1950-1951, see below), or passes it with unacceptable amendments. The Government must then wait for a period of three months before it re-submits the bill to the Lower House, where again it is passed. The bill is once more sent up to the Senate which rejects it, etc, a second time. Then the Prime Minister asks the Governor-General to exercise his discretion to *dissolve both Houses*: whence the phrase "double dissolution".

So far the Governor-General has acceded to the Government's request, although in February 1983 it looked as if the Governor-General might not grant Mr Fraser's request. Thereupon, the electors will "decide" the disagreement between the Houses by electing a new Senate and a new House of Representatives.

However, it is just possible for the electors not to decide the disagreement at all. The electors may return the same Government in the House of Representatives but put in a "hostile Senate". The deadlocked bill now goes through the Lower House and on to the Senate once again. If there is still a disagreement between the Houses, the next move is the Governor-General's. He may convene a joint sitting of all the senators and all the members, and these vote on the deadlocked bill, as occurred in August 1974 (this too is discussed below).

The complicated deadlock provisions have been used on six occasions: 1913-1914, 1950-1951, 1973-1974, 1974-1975, 1981-1983 and 1987. In each instance the deadlock spread over several years, with the double dissolution occurring in the last year.

In 1913-1914 the Fisher Australian Labor party was the Opposition party, but in the Senate it commanded a large majority. This "hostile Senate" twice rejected a Government bill to abolish union-preference in the Commonwealth public service. The Cook Liberal Party Government, through its Prime Minister, advised the Governor-General to dissolve both Houses of Parliament, and he did in July 1914. The electors then decided the issue. They voted in the former Opposition, the Fisher Labor Party, in the House of Representatives and in the Senate.

In 1950-1951 the Chifley Australian Labor Party, again the Opposition party although with a majority in the Senate, opposed Government measures on banking. This Senate amended the Commonwealth Banking Bill unsatisfactorily to the Government and later "shelved" the bill by relegating it to a Select Committee of the Senate. The Menzies Liberal-Country Party coalition in office complained that its banking bill was blocked and that government was becoming unworkable because of the "hostile Senate". And so, Prime Minister Menzies asked the Governor-General for a double dissolution, which was granted in March 1951. The Governor-General was Sir William McKell, appointed straight from Labor politics by the Chifley Labor Government. This time the electors put the Menzies-Fadden Liberal-Country Party Government back into power in the House of Representatives, and gave it control of the Senate as well.

In 1973-1974 it was the Snedden Liberal-Country Party's turn to act as the Opposition in the Senate where it had a majority. In time the Australian Labor Party's leader and Prime Minister, Mr Whitlam, protested to the Governor-General about this "obstruction", as he put it, and he listed six deadlocked bills. The Governor-General, Sir Paul Hasluck, agreed to dissolve both Houses in April 1974. On the same day the Government Leader in the Senate, Senator Murphy, had warned the "hostile Senate" that, if it defeated his motion (that the question be put on the Appropriation Bill before the Senate), this defeat would be treated "as a denial of Supply", and then certain advice would be tendered to the Governor-General. The motion was lost. The Senator left the Chamber—and returned to advise of a double dissolution.

The electors put the Government back into power, in the House of Representatives anyway. In the Senate Labor Party and Liberal-Country Party members were even. Unfortunately for the Government a tied vote in the Senate is counted as a negative vote. In other words, after the elections the Government could still be faced with a "hostile Senate". And this is just what did happen: the Senate rejected Mr Whitlam's six bills. So, he asked the (new) Governor-General, Sir John Kerr, to convene a joint sitting of all the parliamentarians for the first time in Australian history. The joint sitting passed the six bills in August 1974, a likely result since the House of Representatives can drum up twice the number that the Senate can for a joint sitting.

The double dissolution of November 1975 has become so well-known that it deserves a fuller treatment than its predecessors.

The events of 1974-1975 encompass the overseas loan affair in December 1974, the Senate's deferral of Supply in October 1975, the Governor-General's (Sir John Kerr's) dismissal of the Whitlam Government in November, followed by the double dissolution of the Houses of Parliament, and the culmination—the elections in December 1975. The following is my understanding of those events and the constitutional law involved.

Certain articles of faith are overlooked in emotive discussions on 1974-1975. Such basics as:

- The parliamentarians are there only for the people—a forgotten truism that spells out parliamentary democracy.

- The Government is there only as long as Parliament, on behalf of the people, approves of it. Government and Parliament are two different things.

- Parliament, seeing itself as acting on behalf of the people, may register disapproval of the Government by cutting off the Government's money supply—a vital mechanism in parliamentary democracy.

- The Senate, as much as the Lower House, is Parliament in this watchdog role.

- Constitutional principle dictates that the Government, refused Supply by Parliament, should either resign or advise an election.

- If the Government does not comply with the constitutional principle, the Governor-General may intervene by exercising his reserve power to get the Government (as well as the parliamentarians) to the people.

Now to begin at the beginning. As with any historical fact, the dismissal or the double dissolution in November 1975 must be seen as a piece in the context of its time.

For instance, back on 13 December 1974 "the overseas loan affair" started out. The Government's handling of this proposed loan was one of the weapons used by the Opposition party. The Federal Executive Council meeting, late on that night of 13th, was described by Sir John Kerr in his 1978 autobiography as the "purported" Executive Council meeting. (Sir John had been appointed Governor-General in July 1974 by Mr Whitlam. At the time he had been Chief Justice of New South Wales for two years, and from 1966 to 1972 a Judge of the ACT Supreme Court and the Commonwealth Industrial Court—in all eight years as a Judge). Sir John went on to reveal that Government House was not advised of the intended meeting and that neither he nor his deputy, the Vice-President of the Executive Council, Stewart, had summoned the meeting. Yet both of these particulars are normal practice. The Prime Minister, Mr Whitlam, his Attorney-General Murphy and two Ministers, Cairns and Connor, held the meeting which authorised what it called a "temporary purposes" loan. Seemingly, the point of the "temporary purposes" description was to effect a legitimate loan outside the Financial Agreement of 1927. Under the Agreement the Australian Loan Council must approve most loans, but not temporary purposes loans. The Loan Council consists of the Prime Minister and the six Premiers and, at the time, there were four non Labor—and vigorous—Premiers from the three eastern States and Western Australia.

What was contemplated by the Executive Council meeting, it later transpired, was a \$US4000m overseas loan, repayable in 20 years time, for complicated programs such as coping with the "exigencies arising out of the current world situation and the international energy crisis".

Was this a temporary purposes loan, the kind of loan that need not be subjected to Loan Council scrutiny? The Attorney-General, at the time Senator Murphy and later Mr Justice Murphy of the High Court, was present at the Executive Council meeting. Presumably he accepted the loan as one for temporary purposes. But another later High Court Justice, Deane as Queen's Council in an Opinion tabled in the Lower House in July 1975, raised doubts about the proposed borrowing.

Apart from the magnitude of the loan, a huge overseas debt, and apart from the operation beyond Loan Council scrutiny, the loan was to be effected outside traditional and established financial institutions—through a little known broker, one Tirath Khemlani.

This unorthodox and massive attempt to borrow—the overseas loan affair or the Khemlani affair—was exposed piecemeal by the Opposition party in the ensuing months, January to July 1975.

Besides the overseas loan affair, further ammunition was found by the Opposition party in what it proclaimed to be the state of the nation and by the Opposition leader, Mr Fraser, in what he declared to be "extraordinary and reprehensible" circumstances justifying the deferral of Supply. The claims made about the Whitlam administration in office from December 1972 to November 1975 were: that the economy was failing: the inflation figure had arisen from 4.5 per cent to 17.6 per cent (March 1975), the unemployment rate from 2 per cent to 4.5 per cent of the workforce; interest rates were high; investment and business were low, with bankruptcies and liquidations rife—that the industrial front was bad; 6.2m days were lost because of strikes in 1974, the highest in Australian history, and 3.5m days were lost in 1975—that resource development, such as mining and oil exploration, was practically at a standstill—that Commonwealth-State relations were exacerbated, with Canberra taking over State "preserves" and the State system publicly denigrated—that Ministers were fluctuating and resigning; there were six such Ministers and there were three Treasurers between 1972 to 1975.

These were the claims made by the Opposition party—"claims", that is to say, some may have retorted that by world standards, while the inflation figure was a little high, the unemployment rate was not, that Australia could not be insulated from the economic consequences of OPEC oil prices, of overseas highly productive manufacturing industry, of world stagflation, and so on.

In the end, it was for the electors to decide between claims and counter-claims, and to decide rather later, about May 1977—unless they were to be allowed an earlier opportunity, in 1975.

The Opposition coalition, the Fraser Liberal-National Country Party, controlled the Senate, the Whitlam Labor Party, the House of Representatives, 65 in a House of 127. On 16 October the Senate deferred Appropriation Bills (Nos 1 & 2) 1975-1976; on the previous day it had deferred the Loan Bill 1975; and on 5 November it deferred Loan Bill (No 2). The application of s 57 of the Constitution on disagreements between Houses was academic since it stipulated a three-month delay before the Bills would next come up from the Lower House, thereby activating s 57. And yet, we were told before long that the Government was in financial straits; hence it could not hold off for three months.

Another proposal, this one by Mr Whitlam, was to call a half-Senate election. It suffered three defects. First, the blocking of Supply is aimed at responsible Government; in other words, the Government House, the Lower House, is supposed to be accountable, not the Senate. Next, there would be no guarantee that the election would change the "hostile Senate" into a favourable one; the signs pointed the other way. And thirdly, the electoral process would take time, meanwhile leaving the Government without Supply; and it was vital to get Supply through quickly.

As the Senate deferred each Loan Bill and each annual Appropriation Bill, it pronounced upon the state of the nation as it saw it, moving "*That this Bill be not further proceeded with until the Government agrees to submit itself to the judgment of the people, the Senate being of the opinion that the Prime Minister and his Government no longer have the trust and confidence of the Australian people because of . . .*"

The Senate has the sheer power to defer Supply. The key provision in the Constitution is the last paragraph in s 53. This affirms that the Senate has "equal power" with the House of Representatives in regard to "all proposed laws", except for the introduction of money bills and the amendment of certain kinds of money bills. The Senate's power to grant—or refuse or defer—Supply is unqualified. Other sections confirm the Senate's power over proposed laws, and no exception is made in regard to the granting or the refusal of appropriation bills. See ss 1, 57 par 3 and 58. The latter sections, to put it another way, disclose our bicameral system in which the Senate, as the House of Representatives, plays its part. There are associated provisions, ss 56, 81 and 83 on Parliament's control of the Government's access to Supply.

Underlying these express constitutional provisions and giving sense to the express provisions is a constitutional principle—namely, the Government must give way to Parliament if Parliament shows its disapproval of the Government by refusing Supply.

Now the Senate's power over money bills, that is, appropriation or taxation bills, and the purpose of this power—to compel a government to resign or to advise an election—had been previously acknowledged by Mr Whitlam and Senator Murphy.

Mr Whitlam, when in opposition, objected to a money bill, the States Receipts Duties (Administration) Bill, before the Lower House in June 1970, and warned the members: "Any Government which is defeated by the Parliament on a major taxation Bill should resign. The sooner this [Liberal-National Country Party] Government resigns the sooner the people can elect a government . . . This Bill will be defeated in another place [the Opposition-controlled Senate]. The Government should then resign". At the earlier double dissolution in April 1974 Mr Whitlam's Attorney-General, Senator Murphy, seemed to speak and act on the basis of the Senate's power to block Supply in order to force a dissolution of Parliament. Speaking as the Government Leader in the Senate, Senator Murphy cautioned "hostile senators". If they defeated his motion—that the question be put on the Appropriation Bill before the Senate—the defeat would be treated "as a denial of Supply", and then certain advice would be tendered to the Governor-General. The motion was lost. Senator Murphy left the Chamber—and returned to advise of a double dissolution. Any "right to govern" built on the command of a Lower House majority or "the House should be allowed to run its full term" was thus qualified by the Senate's ultimate power over money bills.

Harrison Moore, a 1910 authority on Australian constitutional law, supported Mr Whitlam and Senator Murphy. He too propounded the constitutional principle. "A check upon the Ministry and the Lower House lies in the fact that the Upper House might in an extreme case refuse to pass the Appropriation Bill, and thereby force a dissolution or a change of Ministry. These are the conditions recognised by the Constitution"; and Harrison Moore referred specifically to s 53 of the Constitution.

The black-and-white power of the Upper House to refuse or defer Supply is there. And, of course, no "convention" or lack of use—as was indeed the case with the Senate till 1975—can transform that power into no power.

There were analogies elsewhere of an Upper House refusal of Supply; and the accepted purpose of this drastic action appeared. Colonial and State Upper Houses have operated the mechanism of holding back Supply to show disapproval of a government, and to force the government to resign or to advise an election. For example, in 1948 the Tasmanian Legislative Council refused Supply, and the Labor Premier advised and got a dissolution. The Victorian lesson of 1947-1952 is instructive on the purpose and justification of a refusal of Supply by an Upper House. The non Labor Councillors in 1947 and the Labor Councillors in 1952—each seeing themselves as acting for the people—cut off the Government's access to Supply. Both governments, following the constitutional principle, thereupon went to the electorate. The people seized the midterm opportunity to say which political party they wanted to run the State—and voted out the existing government: in 1947 the Cain Labor Government, in 1952 (in time) the McDonald Country Party Government. But that midterm opportunity was possible only through the mechanism of an Upper House refusal of Supply.

Had Mr Whitlam observed the constitutional principle, there would have been no November 11.

However, in October 1975 Mr Whitlam neither resigned nor advised an election. He had been elected in December 1972 and again in May 1974 and he continued to command a majority in the House of Representatives. Why should he face the electorate yet again?

Since the Government could not get money from Parliament, it held talks with the reluctant private trading banks to provide somehow for its ordinary annual services, seemingly by certificates to be issued to the banks which had to meet government bills. Legal opinions were given on this expedient and ss 81 and 83 of the Constitution; and other action was in train. These sections require that moneys received by the Government shall form one Consolidated Revenue Fund and shall not be drawn "except under appropriation made by law", viz, by an act of both Houses of Parliament, and not by some indirect device.

Tension built up for three to four weeks with no solution immediately apparent. The dailies began to speculate publicly on the likelihood of the Governor-General acting. Dismissal was in the air.

On 11 November the Governor-General, Sir John Kerr, expressly relied on his personal discretion in s 64 of the Constitution, and he dismissed the Prime Minister and the other Ministers from office. Section 64 of the Constitution deals with the Governor-General's power to appoint officers, called Ministers of State, and goes on to provide: "Such officers shall hold office during the pleasure of the Governor-General". As with the Parliament's control of the Government's access to Supply and in particular the Senate's power to defer Supply, so too the Governor-General's power to dismiss his Ministers is in the Constitution.

Sir John wrote later, in 1978, that he first tried on two occasions in October 1975 to persuade Mr Whitlam to advise an election (for recall the constitutional principle that a government refused Supply by an Upper House should either resign or advise an election). But, added Sir John, the "Prime Minister rejected this approach out of hand". In a letter of dismissal to Mr Whitlam accompanied by a statement of reasons, both handed to Mr Whitlam in the Governor-General's study on the 11th, the Governor-General explained: "You have previously told me . . . that the only way in which such an election could be obtained would be by my dismissal of you . . . You have persisted in your attitude." Calling for Mr Fraser, the Governor-General temporarily commissioned him to form "a caretaker government able to secure supply and willing to let the issue go to the people". There were to be no appointments, no dismissals, no new policies. The status quo was to be frozen. Mr Fraser was to recommend immediately a double dissolution. The next move was to be the electors'. Mr Fraser gave the Governor-General an assurance that all these conditions would be carried out.

This was the Governor-General's action to dampen the tension —or to head off chaos—and to circumvent the intransigence of the politicians. Certainly something had to be done to break the deadlock, and the Governor-General had the power, the reserve power, to intervene. In such an extraordinary and uncontemplated situation it seems fatuous to remind the Governor-General of Bagehot's advice: "the sovereign has . . . three rights—the right to be consulted, the right to encourage, the right to warn. And a king of great sense and sagacity would want no others" ("The English Constitution", 1867).

Mr Fraser's coalition party in the Senate had merely deferred Supply, not rejected it. Hence the Appropriation Bills, already passed by the Lower House, were still within the control of the Senate. So Mr Fraser was in a position to guarantee Supply. In fact, the granting of Supply was finalised by the Senate within about an hour after Mr Fraser's appointment as caretaker Prime Minister.

Now, the whole point of Mr Fraser's assurance of Supply and the subsequent grant of Supply was to enable the carrying on of the Public Service and to recommend and be granted at once a double dissolution to get the matter to the people. Consequently, the later House of Representatives no-confidence vote in the caretaker government would have frustrated Mr Fraser's undertaking if that vote had been treated as more than a formal manoeuvre. Moreover, had the Governor-General dismissed the Fraser caretaker government on the basis of this no-confidence vote, he would have deceived the Senate that let through Supply only on the understanding that the issue would now go to the people.

The Governor-General then completed the exercise of his reserve power to get the issue to the people. Acting under s 57 of the Constitution and listing 21 deadlocked bills (which had in fact been introduced by the Whitlam Government), the Governor-General dissolved both Houses on the same day as the dismissal, the new commission and the granting of Supply. Again, as in the earlier double dissolution of April 1974, the deferral-of-Supply deadlock was overcome by a technical device, that is, by using a ready-made s 57 situation.

In documents at the time and in his later autobiography (1978), Sir John Kerr revealed his crisscrossing reasons for dismissing his popularly elected Prime Minister.

• At the head of his statement of claim was: "Mr Whitlam and his colleagues should, I thought, be dismissed because they insisted, contrary to the customary procedures of constitutional government, on governing without parliamentary supply, failing to resign or advise an election." It was this act more than any other that troubled the Governor-General: the refusal of a government to resign or at least to advise an election once Parliament cut off its Supply.

• Second, the impasse: the Senate would not grant Supply, the Government would not go to the people. Mr Whitlam or, if not, Mr Fraser, should let the electorate decide. "It is for the people now to decide the issue which the two leaders have failed to settle",

Sir John explained in his 1975 statement of reasons. The politicians' obstinacy, whichever party was to blame, should not be allowed much longer to frustrate the running of the country. The people—for whom the politicians run the country—should be called on to decide which political party they wanted to run the country.

• Third, the financial straits of the Government. By November money under the Supply Bills, passed as a five months stopgap before July, was running short; and, of course, the Senate had deferred the Loan and Appropriation Bills. The Prime Minister, the Treasurer and other Ministers publicly declaimed their money worries, warning among other things, "social service cheques will stop". Contractors providing goods and services to the Government had to be paid, as well as public servants including the defence forces. A Government cannot run for long without money, and now Parliament—the Senate anyway—was denying the Government access to Supply.

• Fourth, "mounting public anxiety" was growing, wrote Sir John. There was alarmist talk (by a Minister) of civil anarchy, and there were certainly large protest marches in the city streets favouring the dismissed government. Action had to be taken speedily, otherwise the tension might explode if it was bottled up till a post-Christmas election. If the Governor-General waited much beyond 11 November, time would run out for a pre-Christmas election. The writs for an election must go out a month before the election which could not be later than 13 December.

• Fifth, the Governor-General had constitutional and legal doubts about his Ministers at that time. The doubts began with the 1974 Executive Council meeting on the overseas loan described above: "what happened, in fact, about this meeting was a great shock to me. I found it very disturbing . . .". Twelve months later when Supply was deferred, his Ministers, Sir John wrote, "insisted, contrary to the customary procedures of constitutional government, on governing without parliamentary supply". As for the tentative banking plans, the Governor-General protested at the time, "the announced proposals about financing public servants . . . do not amount to a satisfactory alternative to supply"; and he explained more explicitly in his 1978 reflections that he had "regard to its defects and inadequacies and very doubtful legality . . . [furthermore] the dubious banking exercise . . . could not be regarded as fulfilment of the [Government's] duty to obtain supply" from Parliament. Other matters troubled the Governor-General: the belittling of the Senate, seen as somehow less a chamber than the House of Representatives, the treating of the office of the Governor-General as a rubber stamp. At least, this was the Governor-General's appraisal of the constitutionality and legality of those times.

So the issue did go to the people. As a matter of fact, on one of those breathless November evenings in 1975—remember the talk of civil anarchy, the protest marches and the mounting tension— Mr Whitlam himself called upon the electorate: "It must be made plain—by the secret votes of the Australian people—that they decide who will be the Australian Government". Well, on 13 December 1975 the people did decide who was to be the Government.

> The election figures were: six former Ministers from the Whitlam Labor administration lost their seats; 29 members in all from this administration lost their seats. Tasmania did not return a single Labor member. Queensland returned one out of a possible 18, Western Australia one out of a possible ten.

> The figures in the Senate were 27 Labor, 35 Liberal-National Country Party, picking up five new senators (plus one Liberal Movement, one Independent). So, the Senate was lost. So, too was the House of Representatives: 36 Labor, 91 Liberal-National Country Party, giving the new Fraser Government the greatest majority in the House since Federation.

> In percentages: The average swing throughout Australia against the former administration was 7 per cent. The swing in the national vote towards the coalition was 8.6 per cent in the Senate, 7.1 per cent in the House of Representatives.

Two years later the people repeated their sentiments. On 10 December 1977 the Fraser Government brought on a premature election. Labour picked up two extra seats only: 38 to Labor, 86 to the Liberal-National Country Party (in a House of 124 members now), giving the re-elected Government the second largest majority in the House since Federation. The Senate numbers became 35 Liberal-National Country Party, 26 Labor, two Democrats, one Independent: thus Labor lost one of its senators.

What was the matter with the running of the country in 1974 and 1975 that such unique figures were chalked up on the tally board by the people?

Was the state of the nation really as bad as the Opposition declared and were the circumstances as "extraordinary and reprehensible" as Mr Fraser claimed, so that the Opposition-controlled Senate was justified in deferring Supply in order to force the Government to give an account to the electorate? For what certainly emerges from those tempestuous times are the startling election figures, passing a no-confidence vote in the dismissed Government.

If those election figures showed the people's assessment of the state of the nation, would you say that the Government should have been allowed to run its full term regardless—in the interest of government stability? Or would you say that the Government should have been made by the Senate to go to the people even in midterm—in the interest of government accountability?

In answering, keep in mind the fundamentals of our parliamentary democracy. The Government must be approved by Parliament which can show its disapproval by refusal of Supply (or by a no-confidence vote or a negative vote on a vital government bill); and Parliament is answerable to the electorate. Keep in mind too the proper order: the Government is subject to Parliament; Parliament is not subject to the Government. To speak of a Government "toughing it out" in the face of Parliament's disapproval—and the Senate is part of Parliament—is to invert parliamentary democracy.

If you think that the Government should have been made to go to the people, then you turn to the Governor-General and his action.

In the first place, the Governor-General's action was not a capricious action starting out from nowhere. It was follow-up action. Had the Prime Minister adopted his Attorney-General's rule in 1974 and his own rule in 1970—"This [money] Bill will be defeated in another place [the Senate]. The Government should then resign"—there would have been no need for Sir John Kerr to act. *There would have been no November 11.* As it was, his action became part of the logic of events: the asserted state of the nation and the circumstances of the time, the Senate's deferral of Supply, the Prime Minister's failure to resign or advise an election, the Governor-General's dismissal and new commission, the people's election. Second, the Governor-General's action was not an end in itself. It was a means to an end: "to let the issue go to the people", for the people were the ultimate arbiters and they were free to say aye or nay.

In 1936 Dr H V Evatt ("The King and His Dominion Governors") allied those two doctrines: the reserve power of the

Crown and the wishes of the electorate. The 1975 political crisis may well have been one of the "situations" envisaged by Evatt "in which the exercise of the reserve power will be the only possible method of giving to the electorate an opportunity" to say what they want done in a political crisis.

On an earlier occasion the Queensland Governor, Lord Chelmsford, justified the exercise of the Crown's personal discretion in 1907. He, too, had acted against his Ministry's advice (to swamp the Upper House). When this Ministry resigned and another was formed, it was unable to get Supply from the Legislative Assembly. Lord Chelmsford dissolved Parliament, explaining:

"By the exercise of the Prerogative of Dissolution the people are asked to say what they wish done."

After the double dissolution just discussed, the Fraser Liberal-National Party brought on another double dissolution. Since July 1981 the non government senators commanded 33 of the 64 votes in the Senate, and the technical reason invoked to trigger s 57 was the Senate's double rejection of 13 bills in 1981-1982. The Governor-General, Sir Ninian Stephen, dissolved both Houses in February 1983—not without hesitation. General elections were held in March. The electors put the former Opposition, the Hawke Australian Labor Party, in control of the House of Representatives. But the electors did not give the new Government control of the Senate; it remained a "hostile Senate".

The sixth and latest double dissolution occurred in 1987. In June 1987 Prime Minister Hawke, rebuffed by a hostile Senate on "the Australia Card"—it was meant to be a general ID card—protested to the Governor-General, Sir Ninian Stephen. This identification aid, argued Hawke, was "an integral part of the Government's tax reform package" for Australia's economic recovery. Sir Ninian granted a double dissolution. At the July polls Hawke was returned to the Lower House, but still did not gain control of the Senate.

A Joint Sitting to pass the Australia Card Bill was never held. The starting date for the Bill, had it become law, hinged on the making of regulations, and the Opposition-controlled Senate threatened to disallow the regulations (as it could) if the Bill got through the Joint Sitting. The Bill was dropped in October 1987.

The powers of Federal Parliament

Federal Parliament has **special powers only,** as I explained in the first chapter, while the State Parliaments have general powers over the Australian citizen. So, Federal Parliament has power to deal with particular matters only, such as defence or external affairs or bankruptcy. It has not power to deal with any kind of matter at all, such as labour or health, prices or drugs or even the national economy, just because control of that matter might be for the good of the Commonwealth.

Some of Federal Parliament's powers—in fact, most of Federal Parliament's powers—are shared with the States: they are concurrent powers. Therefore, either a State or the Commonwealth can pass a law on this kind of subject—at least, until the State law conflicts with the federal law. Then the State law does not operate because of the inconsistency-of-laws provision in s 109 of the Constitution. This has happened in such fields as banking (apart from State banking within the State), bankruptcy, bills of exchange and cheques, broadcasting and television, copyright, marriage, divorce and matrimonial causes—now respectabilised as "family law"—life assurance, patents, postal and telephone services, trade marks, restrictive trade practices. In these various matters Commonwealth Acts now alone cover the field.

But some of Federal Parliament's powers are not shared with the States: they are exclusive to the Commonwealth. The power to impose customs duties on goods coming into Australia is one of these exclusive Commonwealth matters. A State just cannot pass a taxation law on this kind of matter at all. Neither can a State pass a law that taxes goods already in Australia, what is called an excise duty; a sales tax is a common example. Section 90 of the Constitution gives to the Commonwealth alone the power to impose customs and excise duties.

So, then, Federal Parliament has two kinds of powers under the Constitution. *"Concurrent powers"* are powers that are shared with the States. The power to impose tax, however, is what is called a "concurrent and independent" power, for the Commonwealth imposes federal tax for federal purposes, while the State impose State taxes for State purposes. *"Exclusive powers"* are powers that are not shared with the States.

I will now discuss a few of the special powers (whether concurrent or exclusive) given by the Constitution to Federal Parliament. Most of these powers to make laws are in Ch I s 51 of the Constitution. But not all of them. For example, Parliament's powers in regard to the federal courts are in Ch III ss 71 et seq., and in regard to territories in Ch VI s 122.

1. Trade and commerce power

Federal Parliament can make laws "with respect to . . . Trade and commerce with other countries and among the States". See s 51(i) of the Constitution.

"Trade and commerce" is a wide phrase. It includes the buying and selling of goods, of course. It also includes the transport of goods or passengers, the supply of gas or electricity, the services of radio and television or banking; in fact, anything that is popularly understood as trade or commerce. But if trade or commerce is to be controlled by Federal Parliament under this power, it must be interstate or overseas trade or commerce, or at any rate related to this kind of trade or commerce, and certainly not trade or commerce wholly confined within one State.

So, a federal law can control, say, shipping companies or airline companies which run interstate services. Thus Parliament has brought in a *Navigation Act* 1912 to impose safety regulations on interstate ships, or a *Seamen's Compensation Act* 1911 to require the payment of workers' compensation to seamen, again on interstate ships. (Both Acts also extend to ships trading overseas or with Australian territories.)

Apart from regulating the trade and commerce of others, the Commonwealth can itself engage in trade and commerce. It can set up a government enterprise. For example, under its trade and commerce power, Commonwealth Parliament has set up or did set up a shipping line and an airline service—namely, the Australian National Line, run by ANL Limited (to be privatised) and operating interstate coastal vessels and overseas container ships, and the former Australian Airlines run by Australian Airlines Limited and flying planes interstate. Each of these government enterprises has or had its own legislation built on the Commonwealth's trade and commerce power. Again, the Australian Wheat

84

Board, a Commonwealth-State agency, sells wheat on the Australian and overseas markets; it, too, has legislation built on the trade and commerce power.

Under the overseas trade and commerce power the Federal Government has created statutory bodies, as we have just seen. It has also promoted and controlled the trade and commerce of others where this trade and commerce is "with other countries", as s 51(i) puts it.

For instance, the Australian Meat and Live-stock Corporation promotes and controls meat sales in Australia and overseas markets, just as the Australian Wool Corporation promotes the use of Australian wool at home and abroad. Both are federal statutory bodies established under the trade and commerce power. To take other examples, Parliament can authorise regulations which lay down conditions for the export of fruit from Australia to other countries, or Parliament can require importers to obtain a licence from the Commonwealth Government before they import their goods from overseas into Australia.

It is in this roundabout way that the Federal Government can control drugs and obscene literature, viz, by using its overseas trade and commerce power to catch the drugs and obscene literature as they come into the country from overseas. (But once the drugs and obscene literature become part of the general mass of goods within Australia they fall within State jurisdiction.) It is in this devious fashion too—that is, by an astute use of the trade and commerce power—that Parliament enacted the unlikely *Protection of Movable Cultural Property Act* 1986. The Act is built on Parliament's legitimate control of exports and imports, in this case heritage items.

Extra-territorial laws, Statute of Westminster: Extra-territorial laws, by the way, are certainly possible for Federal Parliament. These are laws that have an operation on conduct and persons outside the territory of the Parliament that makes the laws, in this instance, outside the Commonwealth of Australia.

To begin, a law passed by the United Kingdom Parliament, namely, the *Statute of Westminster* 1931, declares that Dominion Parliaments have full power to make extra-territorial laws. A "Dominion" includes the Commonwealth of Australia. And in 1942 Federal Parliament adopted the relevant sections of this

Statute, as it first had to, retrospective to 3 September 1939. So, a federal industrial award, authorised by the arbitration power, can regulate labour conditions on ships, even if the ships are running between Australia *and Japan* (*R v Foster; ex p Eastern & Australian SS Co* 1959). Again, federal legislation can apply to the export and sale of dried fruits abroad, that is, the legislation can apply to dealings in Australian dried fruits *in United Kingdom*, for example (*Crowe v The Commonwealth* 1935).

While on the *Statute of Westminster* I might mention its other consequences for Federal Parliament. The Statute abolishes the application to the Commonwealth Parliament of an Imperial Act, the *Colonial Laws Validity Act* 1865. This means that Common-wealth Parliament can now enact laws repugnant to Imperial laws that would otherwise extend to the Commonwealth. Finally, under the Statute an Imperial law used to extend to the Commonwealth only if the law expressly declared that the Commonwealth had requested and consented to the law; (but this section of the Statute no longer applies to the Commonwealth; instead, henceforth, no United Kingdom Act shall extend to the Commonwealth at all— that is, there is now an abdication by United Kingdom of the little law-making power that it did have in regard to the Commonwealth: see the *Australia Acts* 1986 (Cth & UK)).

In other words, the Statute of Westminster acknowledged the political realities that were being formulated by the Imperial Conferences of 1926 (adopting the Balfour Report on Dominion relations with Great Britain), 1929 and 1930—namely, that the members of what was then the British Empire were autonomous communities, equal among themselves, none being subordinate in its affairs to any other. So, the Statute conceded extra-territoriality and parliamentary autonomy to what were already in fact Dominions, the Commonwealth of Australia, New Zealand, Canada and the rest.

But the Statute does not extend to the Australian States which deliberately stood out, unlike the Canadian Provinces. Neither does the Statute touch the internal arrangements in Australia, that is, the existing division of power between the central Government and the six States. This federal distribution of power remains the same after the enactment of the Statute. (However, the States have now been, in effect, given the benefits of the Statute by the *Australia Acts* 1986 (Cth & UK) which are explained in the Chapter below on "the States", No 2 "Constitutional Documents".)

Intrastate trade: Return to the trade and commerce power. Literally, this is a federal power over interstate and overseas trade and commerce, as we have seen. Hence, generally speaking, the States control trade and commerce that stays within a State. Still, some intrastate activities are so closely connected with interstate or overseas trade that Commonwealth Parliament can control these intrastate activities also.

In the first place, it is true that the High Court held in 1976 (*Ansett Transport Industries*) that the trade and commerce power would not support the Federal Government's airservice, TAA (now defunct), between two places in Western Australia just because this intrastate airservice would make TAA's concurrent interstate airservice economically viable.

On the other hand, the former federal *Stevedoring Industry Act* used to deal with the registration and deregistration of watersiders. Yet, strictly speaking, these watersiders were engaged in intrastate activities, activities on the wharf, when they loaded and unloaded overseas or interstate ships. Tugs and line boats that berthed and deberthed overseas ships in Australian ports were also, strictly speaking, engaged in intrastate activities. But the High Court allowed federal laws on both of these activities (*Huddart Parker v The Commonwealth* 1931 and *Seamen's Union v Utah Development* 1978). The Court explained that the activities were "connected with" or "related to" the overseas or interstate trade that does come squarely within the trade and commerce power.

Similarly, federal legislation on trade practices could catch restrictive trade practices associated with manufacturing by private individuals. The manufacturers, of course, would be making their goods and engaging in the restrictive practice *wholly within a State*. Nevertheless, the legislation would be valid as long as the manufacturing process was a special process just because the goods were going overseas or interstate. For example, the goods might be frozen and packed in a special way for the overseas or interstate market. It was in this way that the Commonwealth's *Commerce (Meat Export) Regulations* were found valid by the High Court in 1954 (*O'Sullivan v Noarlunga Meat*). They laid down health regulations for a slaughter house in South Australia where lamb was prepared, packed by a special process and deep frozen especially for the overseas market.

> The High Court concedes "that there are occasions—and the safety procedures designed to make interstate and foreign trade and commerce, as carried on by air transport, secure, are a ready instance—when it can be no objection to the validity of the

Commonwealth law that it operates to include in its sweep intrastate activities, occasions when, for example, the particular subject matter of the law and the circumstances surrounding its operation require that if the Commonwealth law is to be effective as to interstate or foreign trade and commerce that law must operate indifferently over the whole area of the relevant activity, whether it be intrastate or interstate".

Thus, even some intrastate trade can be controlled by Commonwealth Parliament. Interstate and overseas trade is, of course, well within Parliament's control.

However, truth to tell, the trade and commerce power has not made a court appearance for many years. The reason is that the trading corporations power is more reliable: it is not hobbled by an interstate or overseas chain.

2. Taxation power

Federal Parliament can make laws "with respect to . . . Taxation; but so as not to discriminate between States or parts of States". See s 51(ii) of the Constitution.

Whatever the taxpayer may think, taxation is temperately described by the courts as the raising of money for the purposes of government by means of contributions from individuals, companies or even States. Commonly, there are three elements in a law which imposes taxation: a compulsory exaction of money— by a public authority—for public purposes.

Anyone who complains that a federal tax law is bad is not likely to be concerned about the first two elements. The plaintiff is more likely to argue that the so-called tax law is not interested in getting in revenue for the running of the country, but that it is really interested in forcing the plaintiff to do something which the Commonwealth cannot usually control. That is, the Commonwealth "tax" law seems to be dealing with something not included in the special list of Commonwealth matters.

Suppose investment in State service utilities, such as gas, water or electricity, is falling off. Thereupon Commonwealth Parliament adds a new section to its *Income Tax Assessment Act*. This section, along with the *Income Tax Act*, now taxes for the first time the income from superannuation funds whenever they are invested— unless the funds are invested in the service utilities of gas, water or electricity. The trustee of a superannuation fund might complain that this so-called "tax" amendment is really concerned with making "taxpayers" invest in State service utilities. That this is not one of the subjects in the special list of Commonwealth matters. And that therefore this "tax" law is bad. But the High Court would simply say that this tax law is to be taken at face value. It speaks of income tax and it imposes tax. Therefore it is tax. The motive or purpose of Federal Parliament would not alter this fact. (See *Fairfax v Commissioner* 1965.)

In July 1990 the *Training Guarantee Act* (Cth) came in force. It attempts to make employers pay for their employees' training—otherwise the employers must pay a "charge". Another Act explains that this is a debt due to the Commonwealth and is to be collected by the Taxation Commissioner. The Taxation Commissioner also administers the Act. I suppose the Commonwealth thinks it is "doing a *Fairfax*" although, really, the law seems nothing less than an elaborate employee-training scheme (another subject not in the Commonwealth's special list of matters). Nevertheless, the High Court did not strike down this law with its hidden agenda (*Northern Suburbs Cemetery Trust v The Commonwealth* 1993).

> "It must not be forgotten that . . . persons may be taxed in any class, at any rate, for any reason. Manufacturers may be taxed at one rate, for one reason, at another for another, or exempted for a third. How can a Court step in and say the employment of labour at low rates is not a reason which the legislature may select, and adjudge that such a reason converts the Act into one of penal regulation?"

Notice that the Commonwealth can in fact single out this or that class for a special tax. What the Commonwealth cannot do with a discriminatory tax is explained in the beginning of the Chapter on "prohibitions and guarantees".

Notice, too, that the Commonwealth can use its taxation power to carry out its economic, social or other policies.

Hence with a change of government you will notice a change in tax incidence, deductions, rebates and exemptions on your income tax return. This change in the tax scheme is not so much concerned with revenue as with political ideology. One government will favour small businesses and primary producers, another the low-income earners. Home insulation may attract a deduction. Treasury bonds may attract a rebate.

National control of the economy is in many ways open to the Commonwealth Parliament, although it has no specific power "with respect to the Australian economy".

What follows is a lesson on the circuitous use of federal powers. The Commonwealth may be a government of enumerated specific powers, as I was at pains to emphasise at the outset in Chapter 1. Yet Commonwealth Parliament can exploit its limited powers to achieve indirect consequences. Thereby the Commonwealth Parliament, in effect, increases its controls beyond the areas in its enumerated specific powers.

The taxation power in s 51(ii) has just been mentioned. By increasing the rate of personal or company tax the Commonwealth can dampen inflation; or it can freeze extra income by provisional tax. Sales tax and excise duties can be used to control the economy: so, tariff rates are adjusted up or down to regulate inflation or deflation. The overseas trade and commerce power in s 51(i) can be used. Imports can be cut back to manipulate supply and demand or to make up for a fall in overseas reserves. The currency power in s 51(xii) can control gold or regulate exchange rates. The banking power in s 51(xiii) can also be used to dictate monetary policies, to exert credit control or to promote expansion. For example, banking loan purposes, overseas borrowing or bank interest rates can be restricted; or interest rates can be increased to staunch the flow of credit. The note issue is controlled. Private trading banks can be called on to place large statutory reserve deposits with the Reserve Bank of Australia. The corporations power in s 51(xx) can regulate the prices for goods and services, charged by foreign corporations and local trading or financial corporations. Thus, the Prices Surveillance Authority, established in March 1984, can inquire into and report on the prices of declared goods and services supplied by the three corporations described in s 51(xx).

Under the States-grant power in s 96 the Commonwealth can reduce money for State public works, housing or transport. Or, on the contrary, it can stimulate spending in these public sectors by increased grants to the States. Through its strong voting influence on the Australian Loan Council, the Commonwealth can put a ceiling on overall State and semi-governmental borrowings.

But there is one power over the national economy that the Commonwealth lacks, even in its arbitration power, and that is a Federal control of wages and income. A referendum in December 1973 refused this control to the Commonwealth. Still, even here, the Commonwealth has its own large labour force where the

Commonwealth may act as a pacesetter or as a restraining influence. The complementary power over prices generally is also lacking, and referendums in May 1948 and December 1973 said "No" to this power. But again, the Commonwealth can control the prices charged by certain companies, as I pointed out above. Yet it remains true that the Commonwealth cannot freeze all wages and income and all prices across Australia, say to combat inflation.

Return to the taxation power. Under this power Commonwealth Parliament imposes income tax, including "company tax"—that is, tax specifically directed at companies; the company tax rate may not be stepped (as the several steps in personal income tax) and may be as high as 33 cents in the dollar. The Commonwealth imposes excise duties, for instance in the form of sales tax on liquor, petrol and tobacco, and the Commonwealth imposes customs duties on imports. As a matter of fact, these duties of excise, especially in the form of sales tax, and duties of customs on imports are the Commonwealth Government's second best revenue-raisers, next to income tax.

Excise duties or customs duties are, therefore, simply special kinds of Commonwealth taxation. They are paid, for example, by a manufacturer or by an importer just because either of these deals in goods.

Since the States are prohibited by s 90 of the Constitution to impose this type of taxation, Commonwealth Parliament can use excise duties and customs duties to carry out its trade policies for Australia as a whole and without interference from the States. For instance, when cars are imported into Australia from Japan, the Commonwealth Government taxes—or imposes customs duty on—the Australian importer-dealer. So, the Government receives revenue, it is true. But the Government may have additional reasons for imposing the customs duty on the Japanese cars. It may want to protect the Australian manufacturer against the cheaper Japanese cars. At the same time, the Commonwealth Government might lower the tax—in this instance, the excise duty—on the local sale of the Australian car. And so, the Australian manufacturer is further helped by the Government.

Thus, customs duties and excise duties complement one another. Furthermore, they are methods of trade control, as well as tremendous sources of revenue—for the wealthy

Commonwealth, not the States. This form of taxation is considered later, in the Chapter on "prohibitions and guarantees".

Tacking—When the House of Representatives introduces a bill which imposes taxation it cannot "tack" on to that bill sections which do not deal with the imposition of taxation. See s 55 of the Constitution.

Thus, the House of Representatives cannot put into the one bill a section imposing tax and a section penalising tax evasion—and this explains why we have, for example, the *Income Tax Act* 1986 with the *Income Tax Rates Act* 1986 and a separate *Income Tax Assessment Act* 1936 dealing with incidentals, such as tax evasion. The point of this no-tacking provision is to ensure that the taxation bill (one kind of money bill) goes up to the Senate without any subterfuges. You recall that the Senate has restricted powers over money bills, but not over other bills. See the Chapter above on "Federal Parliament machinery", No 1 "the Senate".

There is another paragraph in the same section of the Constitution which also deals with the form of Commonwealth taxation laws. This paragraph states that a law imposing a tax must deal with one subject at a time. For instance, an *Income Tax Act* must only deal with tax on income; it cannot deal also with tax on deceased estates. But a law imposing an excise duty can deal with many items which are subject to this kind of duty. For example, cars, tractors and electrical goods can all be put into the one law. So, too, a law imposing a customs duty can set out many items in the schedule subject to this particular duty.

But such tax laws also must continue to deal with one subject of tax. The Sales Tax Act that attempted to tax a swimming pool in the ground (a tax on a fixture, and so a land tax), as well as a swimming pool in the factory (a tax on goods and so an excise duty) was bad (*Mutual Pools v Commissioner* 1992).

Both these provisions—on tacking and on one subject of taxation—are merely concerned with *the form of a federal taxation Act*, the kind of document which passes through Parliament. The provisions say nothing about the limits of Parliament's underlying taxation power.

3. Defence power

Federal Parliament can make laws "with respect to . . . The naval and military defence of the Commonwealth and of the several States". See s 51(vi) of the Constitution.

One of the first things to realise when considering the Commonwealth's defence power is that it varies according to circumstances. It seems a larger power in war-time than in peace-time. In peace-time, Parliament can do certain things to secure Australia against aggression . . . in a state of international tension Parliament can step up its defence program . . . during actual war-time Federal Parliament almost acts as if it were a State Parliament in sole command of the whole Australian community . . . as the country gradually settles down to peace again, the Commonwealth Parliament can assist the process until the Commonwealth's assistance is no longer justified to restore normal conditions.

> The operation of the defence power "depends upon facts, and, as those facts change, so may its actual operation as a power enabling the legislature to make a particular law . . . The existence and character of hostilities, or a threat of hostilities, against the Commonwealth are facts which will determine the extent of the operation of the power."

• *In peace-time* the Commonwealth, of course, can maintain a regular army, navy and air force. Conscription or compulsory enlistment, even for combatant duties, is within the defence power. The Commonwealth can set up a Weapons Research Establishment and a Woomera Rocket Range, as it has. The Commonwealth can maintain ASIO, an espionage and counter-espionage organisation. A Commonwealth clothing factory, which operates at full strength during war-time manufacturing uniforms, can be continued as a going concern in peace-time, by taking in some civilian orders. Then, when a war does come, the factory can switch over wholly to war production.

"Call in the Army" is a plea made at times—say, during a prolonged industrial strike or when there is threatened violence in some State. What use can the Federal Government make of the Army in such circumstances?

In the first place, the Commonwealth can rely on its express defence and executive powers in s 51(vi) and s 61 of the Constitution to use the forces to maintain the Constitution and Commonwealth law. There is also an inherent self-protecting power in the Federal Government, as in any sovereign state, and the government could rely on this power to use the armed forces to maintain law and order and the running of the government. Presumably this includes the maintenance of essential services to the community. So, Prime Minister Chifley was on safe ground when he "called in the Army" to break the disruptive coal strike in 1949.

93

In special circumstances—that is, when a State applies under s 119 of the Constitution for Commonwealth protection against "domestic violence"—the Federal government could also make use of the Army. No State has yet made a formal s 119 application. However, on six occasions States have agreed to Commonwealth intervention with its Army to deal with strikes, terrorist activities or, as in New South Wales in February 1978, to safeguard international dignitaries meeting in a State.

• *In a state of international tension* Commonwealth Parliament can grow more active in its defence preparations. For instance, to assist its own defence program the Commonwealth might restrict the programs of non-defence enterprises, by checking the issue of capital and the floating of loans by these enterprises.

• *During actual hostilities* Commonwealth Parliament practically runs the country alone. It can control clothing and food production, fix prices, restrict the distribution of motor cars, lay down general conditions of employment. During World War II, 1939-1945, Federal Parliament was able to zone bread carters so that manpower and resources would be conserved for the war effort. The Federal Government even took over the State income tax departments and officers—and has kept them ever since—as machinery for the Uniform Tax Scheme which was initially justified as part of the war effort in 1942.

• *At the end of war* Commonwealth Parliament assists its servicemen, and Australians generally, to settle down to normal conditions. For example, it introduces rehabilitation and training schemes for ex-service personnel or requires preference in housing and employment for ex-service personnel.

But as the days and dislocation of war recede the community will more or less regain its normal way of life. Then Parliament can no longer interfere, under its defence power, on the plea that it is unscrambling the chaos caused by the war. Of course, if international tension begins to build up again, Federal Parliament will once more prepare the community for the defence of the Commonwealth.

Thus what the Commonwealth can do under its defence power waxes and wanes according to the international danger.

4. Corporations power

Federal Parliament can make laws "with respect to . . . Foreign corporations, and trading or financial corporations formed within the limits of the Commonwealth". See s 51(xx) of the Constitution.

For almost 60 years this power had *not* been used by the Commonwealth Parliament. Its use in the *Australian Industries Preservation Act* 1906 was rejected by *Huddart Parker v Moorehead* (1909). Worse: five views of the power were given by the Court, most of them restrictive.

Then in 1971 the corporations power was resurrected by a High Court decision on the Commonwealth's *Trade Practices Act* 1965—the now notorious *Concrete Pipes* case. It held that the power could be used to penalise foreign corporations and local trading or financial corporations when they made agreements to restrain trade. In other words, Federal Parliament could now use its corporations power to regulate the trading activities of the three kinds of companies described in the power. The current *Trade Practices Act* 1974 makes great use of this case to prohibit the companies within s 51(xx) from engaging in restrictive trade practices and to introduce consumer protection provisions when those companies are implicated.

> Laws "regulating and controlling . . . the trading activities" of the named corporations are within the Commonwealth's power . . . a law "governing the conduct of its business by a trading corporation formed within the limits of the Commonwealth is within the power" of Federal Parliament . . . this Parliament can "govern and regulate the trading activities of corporations . . . for the purpose of preserving competition in trade."

In the *Actors Equity* case (1982) the High Court held that the *Trade Practices Act* could regulate the conduct of others, such as a trade union and its officials, if this conduct damaged the trading activities of a trading corporation by hindering the supply of services by a third party to that trading corporation—what is called a secondary boycott. In the *Tasmanian Dam* case (1983) the High Court took another step—outside the trading area for the first time. The Commonwealth can now regulate the general activities of a trading corporation, provided those activities are undertaken for the purposes of its trading. For instance, the Commonwealth was able in this case to prohibit preparatory work on dam construction (for the generation and eventual sale of electricity) by the Tasmanian Hydro-Electric Commission.

And perhaps in time the Commonwealth will be allowed (by yet another High Court case) to regulate the general activities of a trading corporation—say its impact on the environment—even if those activities could not be shown to be undertaken for the purposes of its trading.

Incorporation and internal management: The incorporation of trading and financial companies and their internal management, such as the conditions of company employees, are controls that may be pushed by Commonwealth Parliament under the corporations power. In fact, in July 1989 Commonwealth Parliament bit the bullet, passing the Corporations Act and the Australian Securities Commission Act. These laws, both relying on the corporations power, provided for the national incorporation of companies and their general control, as well as for the regulation of the securities and futures industries. The first Act was invalidated in its attempt to incorporate nationally; incorporation must continue, as before, mostly on a State-by-State, territory-by-territory basis. See *New South Wales v The Commonwealth* (1990). The general corporate control and regulatory provisions were not reviewed. Certainly, Commonwealth Parliament can punish company directors or employees who are knowingly concerned in their company's false advertising, contrary to the consumer protection provisions in the *Trade Practices Act* 1974 (*CLM Holdings* 1977).

But after the failure of its 1989 Act mentioned above, Commonwealth Parliament, using its general territories power, had to work with the States and Northern Territory to pass a joint Corporations Law: see the Chapter on "the Federal Government", No 2.

In special areas Parliament can deal with the incorporation or liquidation and the domestic affairs of companies, and these need not be just the three classes of companies listed in the corporations power.

For example, Commonwealth Parliament can, and has, set up its own corporation in overseas and interstate shipping. It also runs a government airline (which may become privatised). But Parliament has been able to do this only by using its particular power over overseas and interstate trade. Under another special power, the express banking provision, Parliament is able to incorporate banking companies. It has set up its own bank, the Commonwealth Banking Corporation, the Commonwealth Bank of Australia, and the rest. And under the arbitration power Parliament provides for the creation of federal industrial unions or employers' associations. It is true, too, that Commonwealth Parliament can incorporate, liquidate and manage companies in territories, just as much as the New South Wales Parliament can in New South Wales. In fact, the Parliament fell back on this general power to overcome the decision in *New South Wales v The Commonwealth*, as explained above.

Three kinds of corporations only: The *Trade Practices Act* 1974, mentioned above, or any law built on the corporations power has two limitations. It can deal only with corporations, not private traders or individuals, not firms or partnerships. It can deal only with three kinds of corporations: foreign corporations, local trading corporations and local financial corporations. So, to speak of "the corporations power" is really to speak loosely.

"*Foreign corporations*" are, quite simply, companies formed outside Australia, or overseas bodies that have an existence independently of their members, whatever they are called and however they are "formed" in their own countries.

"*Trading corporations*" include manufacturing-distributing companies, wholesalers and retailers, transport services such as airline companies, shipping and road transport companies, broadcasting and television enterprises . . . in short, any company that we would call a "trading company", relying on the ordinary understanding of the phrase.

In *Adamson's* case (1979) the High Court adopted a loose test for a trading corporation, focusing on the on-going activities of a corporation. If a "significant" part of these activities are trading activities, then there is a trading corporation within Federal Parliament's corporations power. In this case the High Court described as trading corporations a football promotion league and club that engaged professional footballers and ran fixtures. Hence, the league and the club were caught by the *Trade Practices Act* when they attempted to restrict the transfer of a player from one club to another. The Tasmanian Hydro-Electric Commission generated electrical power (hence its proposed dam), then sold the power in bulk and by retail. Even if the Commission was a State body, it was an example of a trading corporation caught by a federal law built on s 51(xx), the corporations power (*Tasmanian Dam* case 1983).

There are other trading corporations that we might not have thought of, such as a cricket association (*Hughes v WA Cricket Assn* 1986) or the Red Cross Society (*E v Australian Red Cross Society* 1991).

"*Financial corporations*"—the other kind of local companies that are within Federal Parliament's corporations power—include merchant banks, hire-purchase companies, building societies. The building societies, of course, must be corporations, not just unincorporated associations. Even some statutory superannuation bodies, such as Victoria's State Superannuation Board with its financial activities (eg its substantial investment portfolio) are financial corporations (*State Superannuation Board v TPC* 1982).

Then, in company matters the Commonwealth can control foreign corporations, as well as the trading or financial activities of local trading or financial corporations; or the Commonwealth can control the conduct of others that affects those trading or financial activities; or the Commonwealth can control the general activities of local trading or financial corporations if those activities are directed to the trading or financial activities of the corporations; or the Commonwealth may come to control the general activities of local trading or financial corporations, as much as it controls the general activities of foreign corporations.

5. Immigration power

Federal Parliament can make laws "with respect to . . . Immigration and emigration". See s 51(xxvii) of the Constitution.

At the outset I should warn you that the kind of migrant that the Commonwealth can control under its immigration power is not only the kind of migrant we usually think of. We usually think of a migrant as a person who leaves a home in some foreign country in order to settle permanently in Australia. As well as this "normal migrant", Commonwealth Parliament can also control visitors to Australia. For example, once the Federal Government acted—with the High Court's blessing—under its immigration power to deport a couple of Irishmen who had no intention of settling in Australia and who merely visited Australia to stir up support for an Irish cause (*R v Macfarlane; ex p O'Flanagan & O'Kelly* 1923). A migrant may come from a British country as well as from a foreign country. A migrant may have even been an Australian at one time who has since made a home abroad and now wishes to enter Australia.

These, then, are the kinds of persons for whom Commonwealth Parliament can make immigration laws. The laws themselves may deal with the adoption of infant-migrants, or with the migrants' applications filled in overseas, their transport, their entry into Australia, their temporary housing and assistance, their conduct as long as they remain migrants and, if desired, their deportation.

Of course, the Commonwealth is not obliged to let a would-be migrant into Australia at all.

And even when it does permit a migrant to enter, the Commonwealth may issue a *temporary* entry permit only. At the end of the temporary period the Commonwealth authorities may ask the migrant to leave the country. The Commonwealth may issue a series of temporary permits and thereby stop the migrant from becoming absorbed into the Australian community (*R v Green; ex p Cheung Cheuk To* 1965). When the Commonwealth does issue an *ordinary* entry permit to a migrant, the Commonwealth can place the migrant on a kind of probation for a period, say, of five years or three years. During these five or three years the migrant may be threatened with deportation under the Commonwealth's *Migration Act* 1958 if the migrant commits certain crimes, or becomes a charge on the community by entering a mental hospital, for example.

A migrant, who enters and remains in Australia and passes through the probation period (and is accepted by Australia), may eventually cease to be a migrant any longer, that is, the former migrant now becomes part of the Australian community—at any rate, High Court law seems to be accepting this proposition nowadays.

> "Those who 'originally associated themselves together to form the Commonwealth and those who are afterwards admitted to membership' cannot thereafter, upon entering, or crossing the boundary of, Australia, from abroad, be regarded as immigrating into it unless in the meantime they have in fact abandoned their membership. They have never been within, or else have passed beyond, the range of the (immigration) power". So, there are some "persons whose 'permanent home is in Australia' and who therefore are 'members of the Australian community' ".

Accordingly, to become part of the Australian community two things are necessary:

* the community must "accept" the migrant, and

* the migrant must become "absorbed" into the community.

In the first place, the Commonwealth, acting through its immigration authorities and on behalf of the community, "accepts" a migrant when it issues to the migrant an ordinary permit to enter and remain in Australia. Secondly, the migrant becomes "absorbed" into the community when the migrant does some of the following kinds of things: marries or sets up home here . . . takes up permanent employment or holds public positions here . . . becomes an Australian citizen by grant.

99

In time, the migrant thus passes beyond the control of the Commonwealth's immigration power. At any rate, this is the direction that present High Court law is taking.

An alien differs from an immigrant; an alien comes under the alienage power in s 51(xix) of the Constitution. For example, there were once two immigrants: Pochi who was born in Italy but had lived in Australia for 20 years, Nolan who was a citizen of the United Kingdom but had lived in Australia for 18 years. One might have thought that by now each was accepted by, and absorbed into, the community. Yet both were liable to deportation as aliens since neither had become an Australian citizen (*Pochi's* case 1982, *Nolan's* case 1988).

Even a British subject, you notice incidentally, is an alien from the Australian viewpoint.

6. External affairs power

Federal Parliament can make laws "with respect to . . . External affairs". See s 51(xxix) of the Constitution.

The Constitution itself uses the term "external" affairs. But since 1970 our Department and Minister have been renamed the Foreign Affairs Department and the Minister for Foreign Affairs.

• At the international level it is the *Commonwealth Government*, not Parliament, that actually carries on external relations with other countries. And in world affairs other nations deal only with the Commonwealth Government, not with the State Governments. States are not international persons and do not represent Australia in the world at large. It is true that the States send their Agents-General or Commissioners to some of the large capitals in the world, say, Washington, London or Tokyo. An Agent-General promotes investment in his State and trade with his State and he disseminates information about his State. However, an Agent-General is not a diplomatic representative as the Commonwealth's overseas ambassadors are in foreign countries, or as the Commonwealth's High Commissioners are in Commonwealth countries.

• After the Commonwealth Government has completed its international arrangements, *Commonwealth Parliament* then takes over. It is the Parliament, under its external affairs power, that puts into detailed effect the international arrangements so as to affect the rights of Australian citizens.

Until the Parliament does act in this detailed way (or authorises the making of detailed regulations), the rights of Australians are not affected by the Government's international undertakings. For instance, the *Charter of the United Nations Act* 1945 merely repeats the Charter without implementing its provisions in detail, such as setting up machinery and personnel to administer the provisions in the Charter. Hence this federal act does not give private rights to Australians or impose duties on them. The Charter remains an international ideal.

"*External affairs*" include: treaties for the extradition of fugitives to or from Australia . . . the prevention of sedition against a member of the Commonwealth of Nations, such as Canada or United Kingdom . . . defence pacts, for example, SEATO or ANZUS . . . agreements on the trafficking of narcotics to and from Australia . . . a convention on civil aviation . . . or simply a matter external to Australia whether in a convention or not, such as Commonwealth sovereignty in the territorial sea from the low-water mark to three nautical miles seawards and sovereign rights in the continental shelf beyond . . . or even an internal affair which is in an international convention, such as the protection of human rights or Australia's cultural and natural heritage, for example, the Great Barrier Reef or Tasmania's south-western area.

On any of these matters, then, Federal Parliament can make laws even though some of the matters seem quite general matters or domestic matters, matters we would normally associate with State Parliaments, apart from the territorial sea and the continental shelf which we might have assumed were federal domains.

Notice, by the way, that the *Seas and Submerged Lands* case (1975), the case on the territorial sea and continental shelf, stopped a State's maritime border *at the low-water mark*. However, in 1980 a Commonwealth Act conceded to each State a power to make laws in its adjacent territorial sea, for instance, laws on petroleum and minerals, shipping and shipwrecks. Another Commonwealth Act conceded to each State a limited title to the seabed under the territorial sea.

A matter outside Australia supports an external affairs law, as I said above. A literal example was allowed in *Polyukhovich's* case (1991). A 1988 war crimes law applied to any person who was an Australian citizen or resident at the time of the charge and who did certain acts in Europe, back in 1939-1945. Just because the law dealt with actions outside Australia, the external affairs power could be used.

When there is a treaty or international agreement or convention covering an external affair, the federal law that translates the treaty (etc) into Australian law so as to affect the rights of Australians must match the treaty "in substance". Otherwise the federal law is bad under the external affairs power.

> " 'Hence, federal legislation to implement a treaty may be constitutional even though, independently of the treaty, federal legislation as to the same subject matter would be unconstitutional . . . There may be a general limitation on the treaty-making power which would prevent its exercise in such a way as to change the nature of the government.' "

> "To secure the performance of an international convention (it is necessary) that the particular laws or regulations which are passed by the Commonwealth should be in conformity with the convention which they profess to be executing . . ."

Now for some other examples of the use of this wide power, the external affairs power in s 51(xxix) of the Constitution.

The Chicago Convention on International Civil Aviation of 1944 dealt with uniformity in regulations, standards and procedures and with safety and efficiency in air navigation. At the international level the Commonwealth Government became a party to the Convention. At the domestic level the Commonwealth Parliament authorised the making of regulations which prescribed uniformity, safety and efficiency in air navigation throughout Australia, even for an air route between Sydney and Dubbo, wholly within New South Wales. Apart from using its external affairs power, Federal Parliament could not easily regulate such an intrastate air route. (This is how civil aviation throughout Australia has come under the Commonwealth's control.) The High Court sustained this "internal use" of the external affairs power: *Airlines (No 2)* case (1965).

The International Convention on the Elimination of All Forms of Racial Discrimination of 1965 was signed in 1966 and ratified in 1975 by the Commonwealth Government. Then the Federal Parliament passed the *Racial Discrimination Act* 1975 based on the Convention—and the High Court upheld the law in *Koowarta's* case (1982). The United Nations Convention on the Elimination of All Forms of Discrimination Against Women of 1979 was signed by the Commonwealth Government in 1980, then fed by Federal Parliament into its *Sex Discrimination Act* 1984—and the Federal Court sanctioned the exercise in *Aldridge v Booth* (1988).

Yet the "external affairs" in these Conventions dealt with human rights, the kind of internal affairs or domestic matters that are usually within State competence.

The *Tasmanian Dam* case (1983) upheld the *World Heritage Properties Conservation Act* 1983 (Cth). The Act was built on the Convention for the Protection of the World Cultural and Natural Heritage of 1972. As well as dealing with heritage protection, the Convention made provision for a World Heritage List. The renowned Western Tasmanian Wilderness National Parks had been recommended for listing. Under the Act and because of the recommended listing, the Commonwealth was able to stop the Tasmanian Hydro-Electric Commission's preparatory work on a dam in the National Parks.

In the case the High Court propounded a simple test for an external affairs law. It is sufficient for validity to have a Commonwealth Government's international undertaking followed by a Commonwealth Parliament's matching law. That is all.

In a follow-up (*Lemonthyme and Southern Forests* 1988), more elasticity was given to the external affairs power. As seen already, there was a general Commonwealth Government commitment to preserve world heritage. But there was no specific obligation to do anything about any area in Tasmania outside the listed area. Yet Commonwealth Parliament was allowed to put four and half per cent of Tasmania on hold until an inquiry should see if any of it was worth world heritage listing.

In *Kirmani v Captain Cook Cruises* (1985) an external affairs law was able to control a Sydney Harbour cruise since the law regulated the relations between Australia and the United Kingdom (whose law, extending to intrastate shipping in Australia, was now repealed by the federal law).

> "(T)he treaty itself is a matter of external affairs, as is its implementation by domestic legislation . . . there are virtually no limits to the topics" in the government's international undertakings, and so virtually no limits to the topics in Parliament's external affairs laws.

Since Koowarta's case and the Tasmanian Dam case the external affairs power has come into its own—or, to put it paradoxically, has come into internal affairs. And "there are virtually no limits to the topics" within this wide power if the Commonwealth wants to use it (Mason J Tasmanian Dam case 1983).

Encouraged by the simple test constructed in the *Tasmanian Dam* case, the Commonwealth Government can now enter into a whole range of treaties—on civil liberties, traffic lights, seals, environment—and does make many treaties, as many as 30 a year. Armed with these grenades, the central government can force its politics on the States, overrunning inconsistent State laws (with the aid of s 109 of the Constitution) if the States refuse to capitulate. For example, in February 1992 Western Australia passed drastic measures to combat juvenile crime, and Canberra threatened to pass *its* law if the State measures breached any of Canberra's treaties. In October 1992 a Victorian Government was elected to pursue industrial law reform, and within two months Canberra threatened to use international labour conventions to stymie the implementation.

And that is the sobering lesson on the enormous influence High Court Justices have on the government of Australia, in the *Tasmanian Dam* case by a teetering 4:3 majority.

7. Acquisition power

Federal Parliament can make laws "with respect to . . . The acquisition of property on just terms from any State or person for any purpose in respect of which the Parliament has power to make laws". See s 51(xxxi) of the Constitution.

When you read the words of the acquisition power just quoted, you see that Commonwealth Parliament cannot simply take property from a State or a person. It must give the State or the person fair compensation in return. You also see that Commonwealth Parliament cannot take property for any use it thinks fit. It can take the property only for one of the special purposes in the list of Commonwealth matters, such as postal purposes or defence purposes. Thus, there are two limits in Commonwealth Parliament's acquisition power (the States have neither of these limits in their acquisition powers):

- Parliament must always give just terms to the former owner, and
- Parliament can take property only for one of the special purposes in the list of Commonwealth legislative matters.

Now, whenever Commonwealth Parliament acquires property (apart from property in a territory) it can do so only under its acquisition power. And therefore, whenever Parliament acquires property, it must give just terms (but again this does not apply to property in a territory). The former owner must be given a fair compensation, the kind of price he would have received had he simply sold his property to an ordinary buyer, more or less. He does not always get full compensation from the Commonwealth, but he must get a pretty fair price.

On top of this, Commonwealth Parliament cannot take property because it needs it for the good of the Commonwealth or because it needs it for some public purpose. No, Federal Parliament can make a law with respect to the acquisition of property only because the property is required for, or is connected with, one of the purposes in the special list of Commonwealth matters. For instance, the Commonwealth can take property for its overseas and interstate shipping line if it has one . . . for its Taxation Department . . . for its defence rocket range or for its ex-service personnel . . . for the Immigration Department . . . for the Foreign Affairs Department . . . and so on. For these are some of the special matters on which Federal Parliament can make laws: see s 51(i), (ii), (vi), (xxvii) and (xxix) on overseas and interstate trade and commerce, taxation, defence, immigration and external affairs.

> "The condition 'on just terms' was included to prevent arbitrary exercises of the power at the expense of a State or the subject . . . perhaps the test may be whether the provisions made might reasonably be regarded as just."

> "Before the restriction involved in the words 'on just terms' applies, there must be a law with respect to the acquisition of property (of a State or person) for a purpose in respect of which the Parliament has power to make laws . . . a purpose comprised in some other legislative power."

The "property" which the Commonwealth cannot take unless it gives just terms covers any kind of proprietary interest. For example, the Commonwealth was unable to take exclusive possession of a car park on vacant land for an indefinite period without giving the operator just terms (*Army Minister v Dalziel* 1944).

I should point out that under its acquisition power the Parliament is required to make a law that is merely "with respect to", or about, acquisition. The law need not acquire property for the Federal Government itself. Once, in fact, Parliament's law was merely a law about the acquisition of property to be acquired *by New South Wales* (which is not required to give "just terms") in order to settle Commonwealth ex-service personnel (*Magennis v The Commonwealth* 1949). Equally, Parliament's law need not require that the Commonwealth or its Departments use the property. As in the example given, the Parliament made an acquisition about property for the use of ex-service personnel. In short, the acquirer or the user of the property may be someone who is not the Commonwealth or its agency.

All that the Commonwealth has to show is that its acquisition law is for some purpose in the Commonwealth catalogue of powers. In the example I have given that purpose was the purpose in the defence power.

There are some takings by the Commonwealth which are just not "acquisitions" in the sense in which I have used the term in these pages. And so, in these takings the Commonwealth is not obliged to give any compensation in return.

For instance, under its defence power the Commonwealth can take over enemy property in wartime (*A-G v Schmidt* 1961), or under its overseas trade and commerce power the Commonwealth can simply confiscate prohibited imports, or unlicensed pistols on overseas planes—and the former owner cannot expect to get any compensation. Provisional tax was once attacked under the just terms requirement. The argument was that the Government had the use of the taxpayer's money interest-free and that the money at times was returned to the taxpayer. But the High Court ruled (*Clyne's* case 1958) that there was simply no acquisition as understood in the acquisition power, and so no compensation for the temporarily dispossessed taxpayer.

Again a restriction of rights need not be an acquisition. An owner of copyright in video cassettes protects the right by infringement actions. When the Commonwealth limited the right (by amending the Copyright Act), allowing home copying of videos, the owner's right was diminished; but no one acquired the right—and no compensation was due (*Australian Tape Manufacturers v The Commonwealth* 1993).

Lastly, Commonwealth Parliament can take property on just terms even when a State owns the property. This was one of the reasons for giving Commonwealth Parliament the acquisition power. Otherwise, it might have seemed strange for the new government, the Commonwealth, to have power to take property from one of the States, no less.

Another reason for the acquisition power was to guarantee that the former owner, a private person or a State, received just terms, otherwise the acquisition law would be invalid.

8. Arbitration power

Federal Parliament can make laws "with respect to . . . Conciliation and arbitration for the prevention and settlement of industrial disputes extending beyond the limits of any one State". See s 51(xxxv) of the Constitution.

Under this special power Commonwealth Parliament does not control employer-employee relations in a general way as do State Parliaments with their wide powers over labour. A State Parliament may pass a *Long Service Leave Act* or a *Workers' Compensation Act* or a *Factories and Shops Act*, and any one of these State Acts applies to *all* employers and employees within the State, whether or not they are in dispute, whether or not they are in an industrial dispute that extends beyond the limits of any one State.

Again, for instance, the many State Conciliation Committees can make a binding "common rule". That is, the rule is common to *all* employers and employees in a given industry, whether or not they were in dispute and whether or not they appeared before the Committee. There are other industrial authorities which deal with labour conditions *in a general way*, such as Industrial Courts, Commissions or Boards—and they are all State industrial authorities.

(Incidentally, if any of these State industrial authorities attempts to deal with an industrial dispute that is within the cognisance of the federal Industrial Relations Commission, the Commonwealth's *Industrial Relations Act* 1988 requires the State authority to desist; and the inconsistency-of-laws provision in s 109 of the Constitution supports the federal Act against the State authority.)

While these State laws and these State industrial authorities can deal with labour conditions in a general way, this is not the case with the Federal Parliament under its arbitration power. The Commonwealth can control labour conditions in a special way only.

Before going into the limitations on the Commonwealth's control of labour (through the arbitration power), I should show the two points where Federal Parliament exerts its control of labour. Firstly, Parliament authorises the Industrial Relations Commission *to settle industrial disputes* that fulfil the conditions in the arbitration power. Secondly, Parliament authorises the Commission with the Registrar *to set up federal associations and unions* to carry out the objects in the arbitration power; that is, the

Commission with the Registrar ensure registration of employers' and employees' organisations, which thereby become incorporated bodies.

Now look at the five limitations on the use of the power. These are

- conciliation or arbitration
- industrial dispute
- dispute
- industrial matter
- extending beyond the limits of any one State.

conciliation or arbitration—The Australian Industrial Relations Commission does not make an award on conditions and pay for *all* the workers in a particular industry. It can make an industrial award only for those workers who are in dispute with their employers and who, in addition, come before the Commission to ask for an award—it is only in this way that the Commission can "conciliate" or "arbitrate" (*Whybrow's* case 1910).

For example, the Commission might make an award for the members of the Meat Industry Employees' Union who are disputing with their employers throughout Australia. And, of course, these particular employers and the Union must appear before the Commission when it makes its award. At some later date, however, the Commission could not simply extend this award to other employers in the meat industry, for these employers were not in the earlier dispute with the Employees' Union and did not appear before the Commission on the previous occasion when the Commission made the award (*R v Kelly; ex p Victoria* 1950, following *Whybrow's* case 1910).

In other words, the Industrial Relations Commission cannot make a common rule for all in a given industry.

> "The constitutional power is limited to conciliation and arbitration between disputing parties, and to make a common rule is to go outside the scope of conciliation and arbitration and to assume a function of general industrial legislation."

> "Any parties so joined (before the Australian Industrial Relations Commission) would not be bound by an award made in relation to the dispute unless they were parties, not only to the proceedings, but also to the dispute."

Still, an industrial award binds a union of employees or an association of employers rather than the individuals (*Burwood Cinema* 1925). Consequently, when an award is made it has a wide coverage. Consequently, too, when an employee or an employer, at some time after an award has been made, joins the union or association the employee or employer becomes bound by the award, and receives rights under the award.

On top of this, even non-unionists can be given practical benefits under an award. For example, a union serves a log of claims on employers in the metal trades industry. It demands better work conditions for *all* employees in the metal trades. Then, under its award the employers must give better conditions even to the non-unionists, otherwise the union (or the Registrar or an industrial inspector) will take action against the employers to enforce the award (the *Metal Trades* case 1935).

This gradual expansion (under High Court law) of federal industrial awards over unions, employers' associations and even employers' associations in regard to non-unionists has enabled the Industrial Relations Commission to control 40-50% of the Australian work force. In this figure we should include the Commonwealth public servants who come under the ordinary public service powers, not the limited arbitration power, and workers including watersiders in overseas and interstate airlines and shipping industries who come under the trade and commerce power.

And the Commission's influence does not stop there. Workers under State awards are often affected because the State industrial authorities mentioned at the outset frequently model their awards on federal awards. So, there is a "flow-on" from federal awards to State awards (as well as from the key federal metal trades award to other federal awards).

industrial dispute—Before 1983 one used to find, firstly, something called an "industry", and then find in this industry a dispute. However, in 1983 the High Court gave a simple description of an industrial dispute (*CYSS* case). Industrial disputes include "disputes between employees and employers about the terms of employment and the conditions of work". An industrial dispute also takes in a demarcation dispute. The point being made by the High Court was that industrial disputes extend to disputes between all kinds of employers and employees, even employers in such community services as the Community Youth Support Scheme ("CYSS"), whether this occupation can be described as an "industry" or not.

But the *CYSS* case suggested that an industrial dispute does not include a dispute in the administrative services of the States, say a dispute between a State public service board and its State public servants generally. In fact in 1993 the High Court hinted that the arbitration power might not extend to an industrial dispute that attempts to rope in State public servants as a class (*State Public Services Federation*).

And certainly an industrial dispute includes a dispute between State education institutions and lecturers or teachers (*Teachers' Associations* case 1986).

dispute—Of course, you have a dispute where the employees go out on strike because their employers will not give them better pay or conditions. And you have a dispute where the employers lock their employees out because the employees will not agree to a reduction in their wages, a chimera these days.

But a "paper dispute" is the most common dispute in the federal sphere. Suppose the secretary of some federal union simply sends a log of claims, with a letter demanding these claims, to the employers of the unionists. The employers refuse to grant these claims. There is a quiet exchange of letters. There is no great industrial upheaval, but at least there is a *demand and a refusal*. When the union and the employers go before the Industrial Relations Commission, the Commission can then make an industrial award to settle this dispute—even if it does seem to be only on paper.

industrial matter—It is true that the arbitration power itself does not in so many words speak of an industrial matter. Yet, I don't suppose that we would say that employers and employees had an industrial dispute on some matter when they were only arguing politics or religion. An industrial matter, then, is a subject that concerns the employers, the employees and their work. For instance, employers and employees dispute about full production or higher wages, workers' compensation, working hours, annual leave and similar matters, but not the trading hours of proprietors of butcher shops, whether employers or not (*R v Kelly; ex p Victoria* 1950), or nuclear conventions or green bans.

extending beyond one State—For example, there is no mere State dispute, but an Australian dispute, when the general secretary of the Waterside Workers' Federation of Australia serves a log of claims on the Commonwealth Steamship Owners' Association, demanding better work conditions for those watersiders who load and unload ships around Australia, or ships between Brisbane and Darwin. Similarly, there can be a dispute "in the building trade . . . (as long as the dispute is) extending over an area comprised in more than one State" (*Builders' Labourers'* case 1914).

All that one concentrates on is the geographical area of the dispute. Is the dispute in one State and extending outside the State? There is then an industrial dispute extending beyond the limits of a State, and Commonwealth Parliament can call in aid its arbitration power, exercised through the Australian Industrial Relations Commission, to settle the dispute, even compulsorily.

9. Other powers

Apart from the eight powers I have particularly discussed above, Commonwealth Parliament has about another 40 special powers. Two increasingly important federal powers I did not discuss above. I will leave them to the Chapter on "the Federal Courts", No 3 "the Family Court of Australia", for what can be done under these powers commonly arises in proceedings in the Family Court. These related powers in s 51(xxi) and s 51(xxii) of the Constitution are the "marriage" power and the "divorce and matrimonial causes" power. As can be seen, both are found with the eight powers I just explained in the Commonwealth's main catalogue of powers in s 51 of the Constitution.

The power over territories, however, is found elsewhere. It is in s 122 of the Constitution, and reads: "The Parliament may make laws for the government of any territory."

The nine territories are: Ashmore and Cartier Islands; Australian Antarctic Territory; Australian Capital Territory including the Seat of Government at Canberra and (since 1915 to provide a port) Jervis Bay Territory; the Australian Capital Territory was set on the road to self-government in May 1989; Christmas Island; Cocos (Keeling) Islands; Coral Sea Islands; Heard Island and McDonald Islands; Norfolk Island which received a representative Legislative Assembly with competence to make laws, an Administrator and an Executive Council in August 1979 with a view to internal self-government; for the time being it is known as "the Administration of Norfolk Island"; and Northern Territory which also set out towards self-government in July 1978. Nauru celebrated its Independence Day in January 1968, and Papua New Guinea celebrated its Independence Day in September 1975. Nauru had been a joint "trust" territory under Australia, New Zealand and United Kingdom, New Guinea a "trust" territory under Australia, and Papua an Australian territory.

111

(Lord Howe Island, by the way, is attached to New South Wales, as King or Macquarie Island is part of Tasmania, or Fraser Island part of Queensland.)

- The Australian Capital Territory (surrounded by New South Wales, population c 296,400) and the Northern Territory (north of South Australia, population c 168,600) are the Commonwealth's two main territories. They are the internal territories.

The Australian Capital Territory—"ACT"—was transferred by New South Wales and accepted by the Commonwealth as from 1 January 1911. Then in May 1927 Parliament first sat at Canberra in the Territory—the city of Canberra is the Federal Capital and the actual Seat of Government of the Commonwealth. All of this was authorised by s 111 and was required by s 125 of the Constitution.

In 1973 the Territory got its first Legislative Assembly with 18 part-time elected members, re-named in June 1979 the House of Assembly, and allowed to expire in June 1986. Then in October 1986 an Advisory Council was created to advise the Minister for Territories. For that matter, the earlier "legislatures" were merely advisory, too.

In 1976 the Federal Government proposed to move the Territory along the road to self-government, but in November 1978 nearly 64% of the Territory's voters protested "No" in a referendum. Probably they preferred to remain administered by apolitical government departments, and certainly they feared locally imposed charges and taxes.

In December 1988 the Federal Government said "Enough coddling". Disregarding a supposed "people's right to self-determination" (that is, without holding a referendum), the Commonwealth imposed the *Australian Capital Territory (Self-Government) Act* 1988 on the Territory, granting it a measure of self-government. This Self-Government Act is the nearest thing to a Constitution that the Territory can claim. But it is an ordinary Commonwealth Act, not protected against amendment as the Commonwealth Constitution is by s 128.

Under the Self-Government Act the Territory acquired an Executive consisting of a Chief Minister (like a State Premier) and three other Ministers, drawn from the Assembly and answerable to it. But there is no Governor (as in a State) or Administrator (as in the Northern Territory), and so there is no Executive Council either. There is a Treasury and a power to raise taxes, and an administration and a public service.

The Territory now acquired for the first time a true Legislative Assembly with a general State-like "power to make laws for the peace, order and good government of the Territory".

Certain matters are excepted, such as acquisition of property on unjust terms, interference with trade, commerce and intercourse into and out of the Territory, raising a defence force and coinage. You have similar provisions in the Constitution, binding the Commonwealth and/or the States: see s 51(xxxi), s 92, s 114 and s 115 respectively. In fact, one provision in the Constitution—s 90 that gives the Commonwealth exclusive power to raise excise duties, such as sales taxes—applies to the Territory also. So the Legislative Assembly was not able to tax videos (*Capital Duplicators v ACT* 1992).

The Crown is *not* an element in the legislature, as is the case in the Commonwealth and State Parliaments (although the Territory is constituted "a body politic under the Crown by the name of the Australian Capital Territory"). Hence the Assembly passes an Act in the simple form: "The Legislative Assembly for the Australian Capital Territory enacts as follows", etc, and the Chief Minister gives notice in the Gazette that a proposed law has been passed (in lieu of the Crown's assent). Likewise, after each general election, the Assembly elects a Chief Minister (in lieu of the Crown's commission). However, the Crown does emerge through the Governor-General. See what follows.

The Governor-General—that is, in Realpolitik the Commonwealth Government—can disallow an Assembly law within six months after it has been passed. He can even dismiss an Assembly by dissolving it if he thinks that it is "incapable of effectively performing its functions or is conducting its affairs in a grossly improper manner". It is because of these retained Commonwealth powers to veto laws and to dissolve an Assembly that I said at the outset, the Territory has "a measure" of self-government. It has not yet grown to full statehood.

On 4 March 1989, 17 members were elected (through an extraordinarily complicated quota system) to the Assembly for a three year *fixed* term. The term can be cut short by the Governor-General's dismissal of the Assembly (see above) or by a no-confidence vote in the Chief Minister. The members do not represent single-seat constituencies, but they represent the whole Territory as one electorate, just as a New South Wales Senator, for instance, is elected to represent New South Wales. The Assembly first sat on 11 May 1989, the day of self-government, when the Commonwealth formally handed over power to the Australian Capital Territory.

Additional material on the Australian Capital Territory which is common to this Territory and the Northern Territory is given below, after the material on the Northern Territory.

Northern Territory, the other internal territory, has been a bit of a wanderer. Some of it, then most of it, came within the western boundary of New South Wales: in 1788 then in 1825. In 1846-1848 it was proclaimed a separate Colony, and then returned to New South Wales. In 1863 it was annexed to South Australia. In 1901 clause VI of the Commonwealth Constitution defined one of the States of the new Commonwealth as "South Australia, including the northern territory of South Australia".

This "northern territory" was transferred from South Australia and accepted by the Commonwealth, as from 1 January 1911, each party acting under s 111 of the Constitution. The Territory, like the Australian Capital Territory, is progressing towards self-government.

The saga began when the former partly elective, but mainly nominated, Legislative Council (so constituted in 1947) was replaced by a Legislative Assembly. In October 1974 the Assembly's first 19 members were elected from 19 electorates. Next, on the passing of the *Northern Territory (Self-Government) Act* 1978, operative on 1 July 1978, "a body politic under the Crown by the name of the Northern Territory of Australia" was established, *politically and administratively separate from the Commonwealth*—and that's the point to grasp.

The 1978 Act is a kind of Constitution for the Territory. But that is as much as you can say, since it is an ordinary Commonwealth Act, not protected against amendment as the Commonwealth Constitution is by s 128.

An Administrator was appointed (and is also dismissible) by the Governor-General. The Administrator is like a State Governor, representing the Crown, exercising its prerogatives and advised by an Executive Council. The Administrator is part of the Assembly, assenting to and enacting its laws. And it was the Administrator who swore in the first Ministry to run the Territory.

The Ministry of nine is headed by a Chief Minister (who is like a State Premier), and it includes a Treasurer. All Ministers are Executive Councillors. Whence the Government of the Northern Territory, a government drawn from and answerable to the Legislative Assembly, arose—and a new flag appeared in Australia.

114

So there are now nine governments in Australia: the Commonwealth, the six States, the Northern Territory and the Australian Capital Territory. Norfolk Island has a degree of self-government also.

The term of the Northern Territory Legislative Assembly runs for a maximum of four years. At present it has 25 members.

The Assembly's general law-making power reads: "to make laws for the peace, order and good government of the Territory", but not laws on an acquisition of property on unjust terms, or laws interfering with the freedom of trade, commerce and intercourse into and out of the Territory: compare s 51(xxxi) and s 92 of the Commonwealth Constitution. Some matters were not transferred by the Commonwealth to the Territory, notably uranium and other prescribed substances; neither were rights respecting Aboriginal land. The Assembly passes Acts with the assent of the Administrator or the Governor-General. However, the Governor-General—once again, in practical terms, the Federal Government —may withhold assent to a proposed law (reserved by the Administrator for the Governor-General's pleasure) or, within six months, recommend amendments or even disallow a proposed law which is then, in effect, repealed.

So, this Territory, as the Australian Capital Territory, has merely "a measure" of self-government.

Yet the Northern Territory can be established as a State under s 121 of the Constitution. But there is some doubt whether the Australian Capital Territory could ever become a full-blown State since s 125 demands that the Seat of Government be within this Territory. And, in fact, the Northern Territory has advanced further towards statehood than the Australian Capital Territory. For example, the Northern Territory has its own Administrator, police force and flag. Its Ministry of nine approaches the size of some State Ministries. Its Assembly cannot be dissolved by the Governor-General. Its Supreme Court decisions are taken, first, to its own Full Supreme Court, then they are appealable directly to the High Court. Hence a Commonwealth law often places the Northern Territory alongside the States as though it is a seventh State.

When will the Northern Territory really be the seventh State? That depends on Canberra's continued interest in the Territory's resources, such as uranium. Besides, as long as it remains a mere Territory, the Commonwealth can acquire any property in it without having to give compensation on just terms.

In each of these two internal Territories there are Small Claims Tribunals. There are also magistrates, constituting a Magistrates Court (ACT) or Court of Summary Jurisdiction (NT, criminal matters) and Local Court (NT, civil matters). There is a Supreme Court (ACT and NT). Norfolk Island also has a Supreme Court and inferior courts. Cocos (Keeling) Islands and Christmas Island are to use Western Australian courts (and laws) under a Commonwealth Act of June 1992. Appeals now lie from the Australian Capital Territory and Norfolk Island Supreme Courts (they used to go to the High Court), as well as from the Western Australian Supreme Court when used under the 1992 Act, to the Federal Court of Australia; and appeals go from the Federal Court to the High Court, but only with the High Court's special leave. Appeals from the Northern Territory Full Supreme Court go, once again, to the High Court, but only with the High Court's special leave.

The jurisdictions and powers of the territorial courts are like those of the State courts—wide and plenary. "Wide", because territorial courts can take all kinds of (territorial) matters; they are not restricted to certain matters, as federal courts are. "Plenary", because territorial courts can exercise judicial and non judicial powers; they are not restricted by a separation of powers doctrine, again as federal courts are (*Spratt v Hermes* 1965). In addition, territorial Supreme Courts can now take State matters and some federal matters under the 1988 cross-vesting scheme: see the Chapter on "the federal courts", No 3 "cross-vesting of jurisdiction".

For each of the two main Territories there are members in the House of Representatives; two members for the Australian Capital Territory voting as two electoral divisions, one member for the Northern Territory voting as one electoral division—the Australian Capital Territory has almost twice the population of the Northern Territory. Then at the general elections in December 1975 each of these Territories gained two senators. These members and senators enjoy the same voting rights, powers, privileges and immunities as ordinary members and senators. They are not restricted to territorial matters, for instance.

This election of territorial senators to "the States' House", the Senate, was barely approved by the High Court's 4:3 decision (*Western Australia v The Commonwealth* 1975). The decision was followed for territorial members in the Lower House (*Queensland v The Commonwealth* 1977).

Federal Parliament can make general laws for any of its territories (not excluding the Australian Capital Territory and the Northern Territory) in much the same way as the New South Wales Parliament, for example, can make general laws for New South Wales. In fact, Federal Parliament, the national Parliament with Australia-wide jurisdiction, can go further: its laws can operate freely even outside a given territory, provided the laws remain connected with territorial matters.

Hence Parliament can make laws for its territories in an altogether general way, laws on such matters as labour conditions, public health, education, local government, prices and rents, property, wills, contracts, and the rest. These laws can operate even outside the given territory. For instance, a Commonwealth law with respect to Northern Territory was able to guarantee freedom of access into the Territory, and so (with the help of s 109 of the Constitution) override a South Australian law which attempted to restrict a road haulier driving from Adelaide to Alice Springs (*Lamshed v Lake* 1958). Again in a liberal mood the High Court held that land in a territory can be acquired by the Commonwealth without the need to concede just terms (*Teori Tau* 1969); contrast a law under the acquisition power that affects a State.

> The power over territories in "s. 122 is dealing with laws relating to the Government of a territory. It is not a power directed to a matter of private law as for example, bills of exchange, marriage and so on . . . What is in view is the establishment of a part of Australia (to speak in terms of the Northern Territory) as a distinct area for purposes of administration and government. The Territory . . . (is) governed only by one legislature", that is, Commonwealth Parliament.

But now, as we have seen, the Northern Territory, as well as the Australian Capital Territory and Norfolk Island, have gained local legislatures.

Still, as long as these places remain territories, they will also remain within the general territories power of Commonwealth Parliament. For example the *Jurisdiction of Courts (Cross-vesting) Act* 1987 (Cth) "interferes with" the Supreme Courts in the Australian Capital Territory and Norfolk Island by authorising them to take State-vested jurisdiction and by vesting their jurisdiction in certain courts. (Northern Territory passed its own cross-vesting Act.) And if a Territory law is inconsistent with a Commonwealth law, the Commonwealth law is treated as fundamental (*A-G (NT) v Aboriginal Affairs Minister* 1989).

117

Under its **appropriation power** Commonwealth Parliament can allocate money in a general way, too. It can earmark money simply "for the purposes of the Commonwealth", to repeat the wide phrase in Constitution s 81.

These Commonwealth purposes need not be the narrow purposes as exactly found in the special list of Commonwealth matters. Indeed, the *Australian Assistance Plan* case (1975) has left these purposes to Parliament's say-so.

> " '. . . it is for the Parliament to determine whether or not a particular purpose shall be adopted as a purpose of the Commonwealth' " within s 81 of the Constitution.
>
> "Parliament may determine that the purposes of the Commonwealth include promotion of scientific research . . . cultural activities, sport, education and health.
>
> It may determine that the purposes include the general management or the economy . . . To that end it may appropriate for expenditure where it wishes, and is not restricted to spending in confined areas such as . . . banking, insurance or interstate trade and commerce."

To be sure, in some cases Federal Parliament can justify its spending by pointing to one of its special powers. For example, money spent on a Department of Primary Industry with a Forestry and Timber Bureau (since the names of some of these departments etc, change although the substance and the point made remain, I use "a", not "the"), or money spent on a Department of National Resources with a Bureau of Mineral Resources, etc, helps to build up Australia's national resources. These resources then become a stockpile ready for the defence of the Commonwealth. And so, the defence power in s 51(vi) of the Constitution can support this kind of Commonwealth spending.

But in other cases Federal Parliament cannot point to one of its special powers. For instance, consider a Department of Health with a Commonwealth Serum Laboratories Commission. There is no precise power in the Commonwealth list of special powers (apart from a limited quarantine power) that can be called upon to support this kind of Commonwealth spending. Similarly, Federal Parliament has set aside money for national development in forestry or agriculture, for the Commonwealth Scientific and Industrial Research Organization, for the Australian Atomic Energy Commission or for backing up the *Industry, Research and Development Act* 1986 and many other research Acts—although it is difficult to find these precise subjects in the special list of Commonwealth matters that are principally given in s 51 of the Constitution.

If challenged on its involvement in these strange areas, the Commonwealth Government could now pull out the following High Court decision.

In 1973-1974 the Federal Government instituted an Australian Assistance Plan, and funds were appropriated by Commonwealth Parliament for Regional Councils for Social Development throughout Australia. Social and community welfare projects and agencies, not necessarily run by the Commonwealth itself, were financed and coordinated nationally. Although the subject of general "social and community welfare" does not appear in the Commonwealth list of special powers, in the *Australian Assistance Plan* case (1975) the High Court permitted even this kind of appropriation and expenditure as one of "the purposes of the Commonwealth" referred to in s 81 of the Constitution.

But notice that I am talking about federal *appropriation and expenditure of money* in such seemingly non federal matters as general social and community welfare. The case would be different if the Federal Parliament attempted to *regulate the conduct of the citizen* in these non federal areas. Such a federal regulatory law would be invalid, for there is no wide power in s 51 or anywhere else comparable to the wide spending power assumed in s 81.

The power over Commonwealth-acquired places is exclusive to Federal Parliament, that is, the "exclusive power . . . with respect to . . . all places acquired by the Commonwealth for public purposes", as s 52(i) of the Constitution puts it.

For instance, New South Wales cannot expect its *Scaffolding and Lifts Act* to apply to building operations on the Commonwealth's Royal Australian Air Force base at Richmond, even if it is in New South Wales territory. The New South Wales Act may be quite general, not directed against "Commonwealth places". Yet it will not apply. So, a workman injured during building operations on the base cannot rely on the State Act to claim damages, and the High Court so held in *Worthing's* case (1970).

But Federal Parliament can bring down its own *Scaffolding and Lifts Act*. Or Federal Parliament can simply adopt the surrounding State law, as it did by passing the *Commonwealth Places (Applications of Laws) Act* 1970 which adopted the law of New South Wales for Commonwealth places in New South Wales, the law of Victoria for Commonwealth places in Victoria, and so on for each State.

Such Commonwealth-acquired places—or what are loosely called federal enclaves—include defence installations such as the

RAAF base given above, a General Post Office, a Commonwealth Bank building, the Commonwealth-owned airfields, say at Eagle Farm, Mascot or Essendon, quarantine stations, federal court buildings.

- A State law enacted *before* one of these places was acquired by the Commonwealth just ceases to apply once the Commonwealth has acquired the place (*Phillips* case 1970).

- And a State law enacted *after* one of these places has been acquired by the Commonwealth, even a perfectly general State law such as the New South Wales *Scaffolding and Lifts Act* above, does not apply to the Commonwealth place either—only Commonwealth law does (*Worthing's* case 1970).

Even State laws on general criminal law, which seem to be not in the least concerned with Commonwealth places, still cannot control conduct and activity in those places. Thus, a Western Australian law on offences against male persons ceased to apply in a site when the Commonwealth acquired the place for a RAAF base (*Phillips* case 1970).

If the Commonwealth transfers its former property to the State or to any other person, Commonwealth laws cease to operate in that area. Earlier State laws are not automatically revived. Instead, the State must then make fresh laws for the former Commonwealth-acquired place (*Stocks & Holdings* 1970).

The incidental power is one of the other federal powers that I should at least mention.

This incidental power is an ever-present weapon for the Commonwealth to ward off attacks on its legislation. The Commonwealth can always argue that its legislation may not be spot-on taxation or spot-on interstate trade, but that the legislation is still valid because it deals with something "incidental" to taxation or interstate trade. There is an express incidental power in s 51(xxxix) of the Constitution. But there is also an implied incidental power attached to each one of Parliament's main powers, and this is the power I am considering here.

- *Under an implied incidental power Parliament can do "all things necessary or proper to make effective the purpose in the main grant"* (cf *BMA v The Commonwealth* 1949).

So, Parliament was able to set up the Australian Coastal Shipping Commission to engage in interstate shipping. Here Parliament was relying on its interstate trade and commerce power, the main grant. Then, under its incidental power, Parliament proceeded to free the Commission from any State taxes—and the High Court upheld Parliament's action under the incidental power, together with the inconsistency-of-laws provision in s 109 of the Constitution (*Australian Coastal Shipping Commission v O'Reilly* 1962).

Or again, Parliament can impose taxes under its express taxation power. Then, under its incidental power, Parliament has gone on to require the registration of tax agents or to impose penalties for tax evasion. The registration of the tax agents and the imposition of the penalties are not taxation laws so much as incidental laws, incidental to taxation. They go beyond the sheer exaction of taxes. Nevertheless the measures are valid as incidental provisions (*Stuckey v Iliff* 1960, *Trautwein* 1936).

And this is what the incidental power does. It expands the interstate trade and commerce power, the tax power, or some other main power to get control of incidentals.

The matters-referred power is a federal power that is in fact not often used, although it does seem to be a useful device for the States to get the Commonwealth to make laws for them, or for the States to make use of Commonwealth Australia-wide machinery.

The power, in s 51(xxxvii) of the Constitution, depends upon a State referring some State matter to the Federal Parliament. On this reference the Federal Parliament then makes a Commonwealth law which will extend to the State that made the reference, or to another State that adopts the law.

For example, Queensland in 1950 and Tasmania in 1952 referred the matter of air transport to the Federal Parliament. Then the Federal Parliament brought down *its own Commonwealth law* which authorised the Government's airline, Trans-Australia Airlines (now defunct), to fly in Queensland and Tasmania without waiting on any State law to do so. In other words, by using its reference power the Federal Parliament was able to act in purely intrastate trade, a thing Parliament could not have done under its interstate trade and commerce power. In 1986-1987 four States, and in 1990 Queensland, referred some matters on children (their maintenance, custody, etc) to the Federal Parliament which could then make a law about children, even those quite unconnected with a marriage. In this way the Family Court of Australia was authorised to deal with children who did not come within its ordinary "marriage jurisdiction", say certain extra-marital children. Again under s 51(xxxvii) in March 1993 the Federal Parliament initiated an Australia-wide mutual recognition scheme: a State or Territory is encouraged to accept another State's or Territory's standards for goods or occupations.

The Federal Government

1. Governor-General and the Government

Actually the Federal Government, or what we call "the Government", is not clearly described in the Constitution. Chapter II of the Constitution is headed "The Executive Government", and it goes on to speak in formal terms of the Governor-General and his Federal Executive Council rather than the Government made up by a Prime Minister, the Ministers and Cabinet. And yet we usually think of the Prime Minister, the Ministers and Cabinet as "the Government".

Furthermore, when we speak of the Governor-General or of the Government we need to be aware of certain accepted understandings, or conventions, as well as the provisions in the Constitution itself.

For instance, the Governor-General almost invariably *acts* on the advice of his Ministers; he doesn't merely listen to that advice. A Prime Minister who is dismissed (as Mr Whitlam was in November 1975) or who submits his resignation (as Mr Fraser did in December 1977) takes with him, by convention, the whole Ministry (and so Mr Fraser was then able to request the Governor-General for a commission to form a new Ministry). Again, the office of Prime Minister or the institution of Cabinet is in no explicit provision in the Constitution; each is convention-driven, as is the doctrine of Cabinet solidarity. And again, the Government is supposed to resign or go to the electors if Parliament refuses it Supply or if the House of Representatives does not support it. The Federal Government has in fact resigned or gone to the polls because of what was treated as a no-confidence vote in the House of Representatives on eight occasions: in 1904 (twice), 1905, 1908, 1909, 1929, 1931 and the last successful no-confidence vote, October 1941; (in Tasmania Premier Gray resigned in June 1989 after the House of Assembly passed a formal no-confidence vote).

You will not find these practices regulated by the Commonwealth Constitution at all. They are simply accepted understandings in our political life, constitutional usages and practices.

Now, turn first to **the Governor-General**. I can make three points about the Governor-General. He is the representative of the Queen who is the head of State, in this instance, the Commonwealth of Australia. He has functions associated with the Federal Parliament. He has functions associated with the Federal Government or Executive.

Consider each of these three roles of the Governor-General in turn.

- *The Governor-General, as the representative of the Queen who is the head of State, acts as the authentic spokesman for the nation as a whole.*

Thus, outsiders know that the Governor-General speaks on behalf of the nation when he declares war, or when he appoints ambassadors, consuls and High Commissioners or when he accepts the credentials of similar dignitaries from foreign or Commonwealth nations. People within the nation, too, acknowledge the Governor-General as the resident head of State, a person of stature and one highly regarded in the community. People take oaths of office before the Governor-General, again acting on behalf of the nation. They expect him to commission a Prime Minister on behalf of the nation. They may even expect him to dismiss a Prime Minister in extreme circumstances, still acting on behalf of the nation, or technically, on behalf of the electorate. And see the last Chapter on "changing the Constitution—a republic in Australia". There examples are given showing how a Governor-General (or a Governor) may be a useful institution in political crises.

The Governor-General on behalf of the Australian community confers awards or honours, say for bravery or services to the community, and encourages attitudes that are seen to be worthwhile in the Australian community, for example, by exhortation and by granting patronage to voluntary organisations.

In all of this, the Governor-General is outside and above party politics. Parties may come and go, but the Governor-General remains and stands apart as the nation's resident head of State. Hence the controversy when a Governor-General comes up from the political ranks, as McKell and Hayden did (both Labor and appointed by the Labor Party), and Hasluck (Liberal and appointed by the Liberal-Country Party). Isaacs and Casey had also been politicians, but not immediately before their appointments.

The Governor-General represents the Queen or Crown in Australia (see s 2 of the Constitution) or, more accurately, the "Queen of Australia", for the Commonwealth Parliament assented to the Queen's adoption of this title in October 1973. And so, the Governor-General's powers are the kinds of powers which the Queen had in 1900 when the Commonwealth Constitution was passed. For example, the Governor-General has the power to pardon—the prerogative of mercy, it is called—or the power to set up a royal commission to inquire into Commonwealth matters.

There have been 21 Governors-General since 1901. Eight have been Australians: Isaacs 1931-1936, McKell 1947-1953, Casey 1965-1969, Hasluck 1969-1974, Kerr 1974-1977, Cowen 1977-1982, Stephen 1982-1989, Hayden 1989 to February 1996. Since Casey's appointment it looks as if the Governor-General from now on will always be an Australian. Of course, it is true that the Governor-General is in theory appointed by the Queen, but the Queen makes the appointment on the recommendation of the Australian Prime Minister. And from Isaacs' appointment in 1931 that Australian "recommendation" has really been non-negotiable.

In other words, especially since the Imperial Conferences of 1926-1930, the Governor-General's position has become Australian rather than British.

The 1926 Imperial Conference declared that the Governor-General should hold "the same position in relation to the administration of public affairs in the Dominion as is held by His Majesty the King of Great Britain and that he is not the representative or agent of His Majesty's Government in Great Britain". The 1930 Imperial Conference declared that the Governor-General should be appointed by "the King, whose representative he is, and the Dominion concerned", the King being advised by "His Majesty's ministers in the Dominion concerned". So, in November 1975 when the Governor-General dismissed his Prime Minister, Mr Whitlam, the Queen insisted that the Governor-General is "the representative of The Queen of Australia". She refused to intervene in those days, leaving it to "the Governor-General . . . (to take decisions) in accordance with the Constitution" of Australia.

Since Isaacs (1931), the average term of office of the Governor-General has been almost five years and, in fact, the usual appointment is for five years.

- *The Governor-General has duties particularly in connection with the Federal Parliament.*

Thus, the Governor-General summons and dissolves Parliament, or prorogues Parliament, that is, suspends it at the end of a session: s 5 of the Constitution (and compare s 28). He is part of the legislature, see ss 1 and 2 of the Constitution. The Governor-General alone (that is, without the Executive Council) declares his assent to Parliament's bills and they then become an "Act of Parliament", s 58 of the Constitution. The Governor-General in Council causes writs to be issued for elections to the House of Representatives, s 32 of the Constitution. Once the writs have been issued, by convention no major policy matters are decided, and no appointments to high office are made.

It is the Governor-General, too, who dissolves both Houses of Parliament on the advice of his Prime Minister, usually backed by Cabinet. This double-dissolution power under s 57 of the Constitution was discussed in the closing pages of the Chapter above on "Federal Parliament machinery". An associated—but rare—power is the Governor-General's power in s 64 to dismiss a Ministry and so usually dissolve Parliament as well. The sole instance of this, in November 1975, was also discussed in the Chapter mentioned.

(Another instance occurred, but this was at the State level. Sir Philip Game, Governor of New South Wales, dismissed his Labor Ministry led by Lang on 13 May 1932, although Lang had a large majority in the Legislative Assembly, 55 in a House of 90; the Opposition controlled the Legislative Council. The Governor believed that his Ministry flouted federal law ensuring the repayment of government loans from overseas bondholders. Sir Philip then called Stevens, the leader of the Opposition in the Assembly, to ask him if he could form a new Ministry. Stevens formed a Ministry and recommended the prorogation of Parliament. During the prorogation the Governor dissolved Parliament. At the ensuing elections the people confirmed Sir Philip's action by voting in a new Government, that 'nominated" by Sir Philip.)

As regards the Crown's "interference" with Parliament, that is, the Crown's action on the Ministry, reflect on what Dr H V Evatt—High Court Judge and later Labor Leader—wrote in 1936 in "The King and His Dominion Governors". The theme of this 324-page book continually stresses the reserve power, or personal discretion, of the Governor-General or the Governor, citing many instances, such as the Governor-General or the Governor refusing to accept his Minister's advice to dissolve the House of Representatives (1904, 1905, 1909) or the Assembly (Victoria 1872, Tasmania 1879, 1914). On an early page Evatt warned: "it cannot be taken for granted . . . that the King's personal view of what is a just and proper exercise of the royal prerogative does not count". On a later page Evatt explained that the Crown can exercise its discretion to side with the people, for they are the ultimate governors, against the parliamentarians:

"Yet situations may arise in which the exercise of reserve power will be the only possible method of giving to the electorate an opportunity" of expressing its will in a given case.

- *The Governor-General also has duties in connection with the Federal Government or the Federal Executive.*

Here I will discuss, among other things, the Governor-General and the **Federal Executive Council**, the formal Executive. Then I will go on to discuss the Ministry and Cabinet, what we regard as the Executive or Government in practice.

It is the Governor-General who sends for the person who is the leader of the majority party or of the main party in a coalition in the Lower House and commissions him to act as his Chief Adviser or Prime Minister. He commissions others who with the Prime Minister then constitute the "Federal Executive Council to advise the Governor-General in the government of the Commonwealth": s 62 of the Constitution. See also s 63 which provides that whenever the Constitution refers to "the Governor-General in Council" the Constitution means the Governor-General acting with the Federal Executive Council's advice. This does *not* stipulate that the Governor-General must always act with the Executive Council's advice. It will depend on the particular provision. For example, under s 64 par 1 the Governor-General acts on that advice to set up departments, but under s 64 par 2 without that advice the Governor-General could dismiss—and has dismissed—a Prime Minister.

Each of the Executive Councillors receives a second commission from the Governor-General as he appoints them to administer the great public service departments: see s 64. Thus arise the Ministers. The seniority of the Ministers is determined by the order of their swearing in, as recommended by the Prime Minister, not by the holding of a particular portfolio.

While all Ministers are Executive Councillors (as well as Parliamentary Secretaries and Assistant Ministers), it does not work the other way. For example, a dismissed or resigned Minister almost invariably keeps his/her commission as an Executive Councillor for life but, in practice, he/she will not be an "Executive Councillor under summons".

At the Executive Council meetings—lately about 40 a year—the quorum consists of three members: the President (the Governor-

General) or his deputy, the Vice-President (a specially appointed Minister, already with a portfolio) and two Executive Councillors (also Ministers). "The counsels of the Crown are secret", the High Court explained in 1951 (*Communist Party* case), usually at any rate, for the Court later ordered the production of some Executive Council material in connection with "the overseas loan affair" (*Sankey v Whitlam* 1978). So, generally we do not know what is said at Executive Council meetings. Certainly, Executive Council Minutes are approved, then signed by the Governor-General at a meeting. The Minute is a short recommendation with an explanatory memorandum, prepared and signed by the interested Minister, dealing with some Executive matter. Proclamations, Orders, Regulations and appointments also come from "the Governor-General in Council". Usually Executive Council meetings are formalities. But an able Governor-General can trigger further deliberations; for example an alert Governor-General may ask, "where is the statutory authority for this course of action?" At this level, at least, the Governor-General's Executive Council meetings serve some purpose.

In a few words, the Federal Executive Council *advises* the Governor-General and gives *formal legal authority* to acts of the Executive, acts taken elsewhere, for example, by the Ministers, by Cabinet or (for the Labor Party) by Caucus. This practical side of government, the Ministers, etc, in contrast to the formal side, the Governor-General with the Executive Council, is discussed below. For formally and technically it is the Governor-General who, as the Queen's representative, constitutes "the Executive Government" of the Commonwealth and who wields "the executive power of the Commonwealth", that is the power to execute and maintain the Commonwealth Constitution and the federal laws. For all this see s 61 of the Constitution.

Another role of the Governor-General is to procure supply for his Government from Parliament. In a message to the House of Representatives he recommends the purposes for which the House should appropriate money in the same session: see s 56. Thereby the Government, through the Governor-General, controls the expenditure of public money—"the financial initiative of the Crown", as it is called. So, a private member or even a Minister cannot get an expenditure bill through either House unless the Governor-General, in other words, *the Government*, has recommended its purpose to the Lower House.

The Governor-General is the Commander-in-Chief of "the naval and military forces" of the Commonwealth, as s 68 puts it. No doubt, this extends to the air force.

The Justices of the High Court of Australia, the Judges of the Federal Court of Australia and the Family Court of Australia, are all appointed by the Governor-General. Equally, these federal Justices and Judges can only be removed by the Governor-General on certain grounds in s 72 of the Constitution, not that this has ever been carried out fully. Since 1977 the Justices and Judges must in any event retire at a certain age: see the Chapter below on "the federal courts", No 1 "a fixed tenure".

So much for the Governor-General and his duties in connection with the Federal Executive and especially his relation to the Federal Executive Council. Turn now to the **Federal Government and Ministry**, although this is understood in the light of what I wrote about the Governor-General with the Federal Executive Council (for it is the latter combination that constitutes the formal Executive Government).

Begin with the electors who vote in a party, such as the Australian Labor Party or a coalition of parties, such as the Liberal-National Party. This party or coalition will command the majority vote in the House of Representatives. And, as a consequence of its majority vote, this party or coalition will ensure the Government's access to Supply through Parliament and will ensure the passing by Parliament of the bills necessary for workable government. The chief of the party or of the main party in a coalition will have been elected by his own party members. By convention the Governor-General accepts him as Prime Minister and, as we have seen, the Governor-General commissions other Ministers who with the Prime Minister are appointed "to administer such departments of State of the Commonwealth as the Governor-General in Council may establish": s 64 of the Constitution. The permanent head of one of these government departments is a public servant, commonly called the Under Secretary. As well as running the department assigned to him/her, a Minister administers certain Acts related to his/her particular portfolio.

These are the people whom we regard as forming the Federal Government, namely, the members of the Ministry.

For instance, at election time when a particular party is not returned to government we simply speak of a change of Ministry. True, the formal and technical "Executive Government" is the Governor-General, usually with the Federal Executive Council, as

I explained above when dealing with the Governor-General. But I also explained that the Ministers (the practical side of the Government) are at the same time Executive Councillors (the formal side of the Government). Through this link of Ministers-Executive Councillors the government in practice is given outward formal authority through the acts of the Governor-General.

The Ministry has up to 30 members; the number is fixed by the *Ministers of State Act* 1952, passed under s 65 of the Constitution. The Liberal Party of Australia allows its parliamentary leader to select his own Ministers and allocate portfolios. The Australian Labor Party parliamentary leader is merely permitted to allocate portfolios among the Ministers given him by Caucus, which has used an elective system for its Ministry since 1908; but a strong leader can pretty well dictate whom he wants to have as Ministers. ("Caucus" is the Parliamentary Labor Party in Caucus, either State or Federal. Thus the Federal Caucus is composed of all the Labor senators and Labor members in Federal Parliament.)

There are "lesser Ministers" and officials associated with the Ministry: an Assistant Minister is sworn in as an Executive Councillor and is in the Ministry to deputise for the plenary Minister and to assist in routine matters, but is not one of the Ministers of State who are appointed to administer one of the great departments of State (whence the alternative description, a Minister without portfolio); a Parliamentary Secretary to a Minister of State is, lately, also sworn in as an Executive Councillor, and assists the Minister with correspondence, consultations and delegations (and gains subministerial experience, as well as extra staff and allowance); there were an unusually high number after the elections of March 1993, ten.

The Cabinet may mean an inner circle of the Ministry, or it may be used as a synonym for the Ministry.

In January 1956 Liberal Party Prime Minister Menzies set aside a core of senior Ministers, known as the Cabinet, following the pattern in Britain. The Labor Party broke with its past practice in March 1983 when it too formed a Cabinet (of 13 in a Ministry of 27; 20 in a Ministry of 30 after the 1993 general elections). The Cabinet, chaired by the Prime Minister, meets in private. Even so leakages occur, and we read about them in the newspapers. *It is this body, this Cabinet, that is the body that hammers out government policy.* Under the convention of "Cabinet solidarity" or collective ministerial responsibility (see below), the policy is presented as a united policy, the policy of the Cabinet and not the policy of some member of the Cabinet. By the same token, if a member of the Cabinet refuses to accept the common policy of the Cabinet he must, by convention, resign. Bury did so in the Menzies-McEwen Ministry in July 1962, a rare act indeed. Kerin, returning from abroad, publicly criticised the decision of the Hawke Cabinet in October 1989 but, significantly, soon apologised.

Responsible government: The Commonwealth Government is responsible to Federal Parliament through the ministerial system. There is an individual ministerial responsibility and a collective ministerial, or cabinet, responsibility.

This ministerial responsibility—Ministers sitting in Parliament to be accountable to Parliament—is the essence of "the West-minster system of government", the kind of government at Westminster, London, where the British Houses of Parliament sit. Thus, in the Westminster system the government is associated with and dependent on Parliament. In the United States presidential system the President with his Administration stands apart from Congress and is responsible, not to Congress, but directly to the people. (Other elements in the Westminster system are: a head of State, the Crown, that does not also act as the head of government running the country (the Prime Minister does), and a judiciary that is independent of the other two arms of government.)

As I have explained, under the Constitution the Commonwealth Government may be the Governor-General with the advice of his Executive Council in formal terms. But for all practical purposes the Commonwealth Government is the Ministry or the Cabinet. It is the Ministers who are in charge of the Commonwealth departments. It is the Ministers who actually run the country.

But remember that these Ministers must also sit in Federal Parliament. *The Constitution itself in s 64 expressly states that officers are to be appointed by the Governor-General to act as Ministers of the Government—and that these Ministers must be senators or members of the House of Representatives.* The Prime Minister sits in the House of Representatives, and always has. So Prime Minister Gorton, 1968-1971, quit the Senate to join the Lower House when he became Prime Minister. About 21-24 Ministers sit in the House of Representatives. The remaining nine to six are senators; indeed, a Minister with a sensitive portfolio can be sheltered in the Senate, away from the turbulence of the Lower House. Notice that it is not quite accurate to boast of the House of Representatives as the House of Government: s 64 speaks of (Government) Ministers in the Senate, as I just pointed out.

Of course, in the Upper and Lower Houses the Government backbenchers and the Opposition sit, too. In fact, that's the whole point of the cabinet system, viz, to require the government of the day to sit in Parliament and there be accountable to Parliament. In practice, this means that the government of the day sits in Parliament to be exposed by the Opposition, which is then given a public forum by the press, radio and television to address the electorate.

- And so, Government backbenchers and Opposition members are given the opportunity to examine and criticise the Ministers—the government of the day—especially in "question time". Since 1970, over 1000 questions have been asked annually. It used to be 2500 to 3000. Questions are asked almost daily when Parliament sits, closely watched by the press. "When Parliament sits" is the weakness. Parliament sits only 60-70 days a year, and a sly government takes advantage of the non sitting time to bring in controversial measures.

  When Parliament does sit, the Ministers can be exposed on their individual administration of government departments and on their collective running of the country. Ministers can suffer a no-confidence vote in either House, which may not mean a resignation these days, but it remains a political embarrassment, just the same.

Thus, *each individual Minister* answers for his/her particular department and related bodies. He will try to explain the alleged shortcomings of his department. For example, a Minister for Transport can be blamed in Parliament for the alleged bad administration in his department and the state of affairs in our airports. Even the Prime Minister can be taken to task in Parliament for mistakes alleged to be in his department. He also reports to Parliament for the Australian Public Service Board. As a corollary of this ministerial responsibility, a Minister who deliberately misleads Parliament should, by convention, resign from the ministry or be dismissed. In the 1970s three Ministers, Labor and Liberal, resigned or were dismissed for allegedly misleading Parliament. In December 1987 Brown resigned from the ministry, as did Richardson in May 1992; each denied the allegations made, gave their own explanations and resigned.

And, as well, *the Ministers collectively* or as a single group are criticised in Parliament for their united running of the country— say, for their policy on combating inflation, their relations with trade unions, their overseas defence commitments. In this way, the Commonwealth Government is made answerable to Federal Parliament.

The responsibility of Government to Parliament does not stay at the level of examination and criticism. Parliament can put teeth into its disapproval of the Government by a House of Representatives no-confidence vote, or by a Senate refusal to grant Supply (by either Chamber's censure of a Minister by a no-confidence vote or by a Senate refusal to pass a government bill). The first two acts of disapproval can lead to the Government losing office.

Responsible government or ministerial responsibility is used in a third sense, that is, apart from individual and collective ministerial responsibility—in the sense that the Crown, with us the Governor-General, will almost invariably act on the advice of his Ministers, and that his Ministers in turn will accept responsibility (to Parliament) for those actions.

- But, not only have we responsible government, we have also **representative government**.

For, the Commonwealth Government is drawn from the popular political party (or parties in a coalition) in the House of Representatives, that party which represents most of the electors. Then, just as we have gone from the Government to Parliament, so we can go from Parliament to the people, or more precisely, the electors. In the first place, every three years the people as electors decide who is to sit in Parliament, that is, in effect who is to go into the Ministry or the Government. In the second place—although this is an unlikely occurrence with our strict party political alignments—if the House of Representatives passes a vote of no-confidence in the Government, the Government should by convention resign. Then the Governor-General would dissolve the House of Representatives (although at times he has been able simply to call upon an alternative government). Next, the people will elect a new Parliament and therefore a new Government, too.

> "The rule that the powers of the Crown must be exercised through Ministers who are members of one or other House of Parliament and who 'command the confidence of the House of (Representatives)' . . . , really means, that the elective portion of the legislature in effect, though by an indirect process, appoints the executive government; and, further, that the Crown, or the Ministry, must ultimately carry out, or at any rate not contravene, the wishes of the House of (Representatives) . . . But as the process of representation is nothing else than a mode by which the will of

132

the representative body or House of (Representatives) . . . is made to coincide with the will of the nation, it follows that a rule which gives the appointment and control of the government mainly to the House of (Representatives) . . . is at the bottom a rule which gives the election and ultimate control of the executive to the nation.''

Thus, the Government—through its Ministers who sit in Parliament—is responsible to Parliament.

And Parliament is responsible to the people.

These two fundamentals are not spelt out in so many words in the Constitution, although the High Court was prepared to find responsible government (see ss 61, 62, 64) and representative government (see ss 5, 7, 24, 128) in the specific provisions I have given: see the *Political Advertising Ban* case 1992.

2. Powers of the Executive

- *The Governor-General* has powers which have been mentioned already—his powers to summon Parliament, to assent to its bills, to appoint Ministers, and so on.

- *The Federal Executive* keeps law and order, Commonwealth law and order including the preservation of the Constitution, the Parliament, the Government itself and the Federal Judiciary.

The Director of Public Prosecutions conducts Commonwealth prosecutions since March 1984. (Victoria appointed a DPP in June 1983; Queensland and New South Wales followed a few years later.) As well as instituting a prosecution, the DPP or his Office is able to stop a prosecution begun by some other public official, say a police officer, or by a private individual. In exceptional cases the Attorney-General must consent to a prosecution, otherwise the DPP does. The DPP also takes civil actions to thwart criminals who squirrel away assets: for example, actions to recover unpaid taxes, to compel the disclosure of assets or to freeze assets.

The Federal Executive relies partly on the State police, although from 1979 to a less extent than formerly. And it uses State prisons, as is provided in s 120 of the Constitution.

The Federal Executive also relies on the Australian Federal Police, a 1979 amalgam of the earlier Commonwealth Police Force (with its origin during the 1914-1918 War when Prime Minister Hughes found State police uncooperative), the Australian Capital Territory Police Force and the federal narcotics squad. So, we now have two police forces, rather like United Kingdom with its metropolitan police and its county constabulary.

The Australian Federal Police assists in anti-crime work. Apart from the general control over crime in the Australian Capital Territory, the Federal Police watch international and federal crime, such as drug trafficking and smuggling, customs and taxation offences, fraud and forgeries, counterfeiting of money and illegal entry into Australia. The offences will be found in the Commonwealth's own laws—say, the *Customs Act* 1901, the federal *Crimes Act* 1914, the *National Health Act* 1953 or the *Migration Act* 1958. The Federal Police also protect Commonwealth and Commonwealth authorities' property, projects and public service buildings and equipment; or they control traffic at Mascot airport, for instance. Some members of the Federal Police act as personal guards, say for the Prime Minister or for visiting dignitaries. The Head Office is at Canberra; but there are District Offices in the capital cities, too.

Notice, once again, that this agency—as any federal instrumentality—operates *in special areas only*. For example, the Federal Police handle customs offences, counterfeiting of money and watch over international dignitaries. Compare Federal Parliament's special powers in s 51(i), (ii), (xii) and (xxix) of the Constitution, the overseas trade and commerce power, the taxation power, the coinage and legal tender power and the external affairs power. State police, on the other hand, operate in general areas of crime.

• *The Federal Government* runs the country, and its Ministers are in charge of the Government Departments. Its policies on trade, the national economy, defence and other Commonwealth interests, easily become law because its Ministers and party members sit in Parliament, and they hold the majority vote at least in the Lower House.

Regulations, for that matter, are often made by the Governor-General or by the Minister himself/herself (in practice, by the departmental aides with the parliamentary draftsman) to help him run his Department and administer the Acts for which he is responsible. In other words, delegated legislation is possible with us, and no doctrine of separation of legislative and executive powers prevents the Executive making these sub-laws.

So Ministers quite often make extensive regulations "prescribing all matters necessary or convenient for carrying out this Act", viz, the Act of Parliament which authorises the making of the regulations. A Minister may make regulations once only to provide back-up machinery and to spell out details, or the Minister may make ever-amending regulations, for example, to add to the list of prohibited imports under the *Customs Act* 1901. All regulations have the force of an ordinary law. Sometimes they even override an ordinary law, if Parliament so decrees by a "Henry VIII clause" in the parent statute.

> "The *Transport Workers Act* (Cth) cannot . . . be regarded as doing less than authorising the Executive to perform a function which, if not subordinate, would be essentially legislative. It gives the Governor-General in Council a complete, although, of course, a subordinate power, over a large and by no means unimportant subject (of stevedoring operations on overseas or interstate ships), in the exercise of which he is free to determine from time to time the ends to be achieved and the policy to be pursued as well as the means to be adopted. Within the limits of the subject matter his will is unregulated and his discretion unguided. Moreover, the power may be exercised in disregard of other existing statutes"— and this power to make such sweeping Regulations was held to be valid (*Dignan's* case 1931).

* *Thus, you can think of the mass of regulations made by the Executive as a body of law outside the formal Acts brought down by Parliament.*

However, in the first place, the courts make sure that any regulation in a given set of regulations is not inconsistent with its parent Act and does not go beyond the purposes and matters in the authorising Act. A bad regulation is said to be "ultra vires" the Act, and is struck down by the courts. In the second place, Parliament itself, our usual law-making body, does keep some kind of a check on these sub-laws. Regulations must be tabled before Parliament which can then disallow the regulations. This "tabling of regulations" in considered in the next Chapter on "the Federal Government and Parliament", No 2, where I will also consider the Senate's special body for scrutinising regulations, the Standing Committee on Regulations and Ordinances.

Various administrative tribunals and other federal bodies are set up by the Government to assist it in the running of the country, as well as the mesh of regulations I have just discussed.

To begin, this federal administrative machinery functions apart from the ordinary courts, and yet it does control the rights of citizens. Still, it is permitted by our Constitution. Take the particular example of the Commissioner of Taxation and a former Income Tax Board of Review, replaced in July 1986 by the Taxation Appeals Division of the Administrative Appeals Tribunal:

"It is not impossible under the Australian Constitution for Parliament to provide that the fixing of (income tax) assessments shall rest with an administrative officer (the Commissioner of Taxation), subject to review . . . by another administrative body (a Board of Review) . . . The Board of Review appears to be in the nature of administrative machinery to which the taxpayer can resort at his option in order to have his contentions reconsidered."

- *THE AUSTRALIAN INDUSTRIAL RELATIONS COM-MISSION* makes federal awards to settle Australian industrial disputes.

These are the only kinds of disputes that the Commonwealth can deal with under its arbitration power in s 51(xxxv) of the Constitution, as I explained in the Chapter on "the powers of Federal Parliament", No 8—namely, a dispute extending beyond the limits of any one State which is an industrial dispute and concerns an industrial matter. Not only that. The Commonwealth can deal with these kinds of disputes only through conciliation or arbitration—as the Commonwealth does through the Australian Industrial Relations Commission. In March 1989 this body replaced the Australian Conciliation and Arbitration Commission (created as far back as 1904 when it was called the Commonwealth Conciliation and Arbitration Commission) and absorbed other federal industrial tribunals that had specialised roles. See the *Industrial Relations Act* 1988 (Cth).

There are other kinds of disputes that the Commonwealth can deal with under its other powers; in fact, these need only be "industrial issues", not disputes, and need not extend beyond the limits of any State. For example, the Commission can hand down awards for watersiders and maritime workers, or for Commonwealth public servants and the Australian Federal Police. Here the Commonwealth uses its trade and commerce power in s 51(i) or its so-called public service powers.

But take the common type of dispute before the Industrial Relations Commission, the one that attracts the arbitration power. When a dispute is threatening in a State and beyond its borders, the Industrial Relations Commissioner specialising in the area becomes aware of it; the Commissioner finds out about it himself/herself or the employers or the union involved inform the Commissioner. At this preliminary stage, there may be grievance discussions and/or a "compulsory conference". The parties, encouraged by the Commissioner, may settle for an "industrial agreement"; the agreement, certified and filed, operates as an award.

In other words, at the beginning every effort is made to "conciliate" between the warring parties.

However, if these conciliatory approaches fail, then the Commissioner "arbitrates", although in a non technical and informal way. The Commissioner examines the union's letter of demand with its "log of claims" which the employers have refused, or examines the employers' claims or counterclaims. Counsel or industrial advocates present arguments. In the end the Commissioner arbitrates by handing down an "award" which the parties must accept. Thus, there is *compulsory arbitration* in Australian labour law at the federal level. Henceforth, this particular union and these particular employers will look to the award for their conditions, rates of pay and rights generally.

The Industrial Commission is rather like a court, deciding a particular case brought before it. From this quasi-judicial function flows its independence of the Federal Government. It is not an economic instrument of the Government, although it readily hears the Government's views, if not as a party, then as an intervener in award proceedings.

Collective bargaining between employers and employees occurs in other countries, for example, United States. There industrial relations are not regulated by some kind of compulsory process, as with us. Still, from time to time there are moves to deregulate industrial relations in Australia. And, in fact, industry agreements are mushrooming outside the centralised wage-fixing system we have grown used to since 1904. These are arrangements between employers and employees or their unions which rely on the ordinary law of contract, rather than coercive awards, for their enforcement. They differ from industry to industry, or within a particular industry. But return to our present regulatory body.

The federal arbitration machinery has three parts: (1) the basic unit, the many Industrial Relations Commissioners, about 50, who must be qualified with skills and experience in industrial relations (so, union officials or employers' advocates can be appointed); (2) the Presidential and Deputy Presidential members, mostly with legal training, as well as skills and experience in industrial relations; and (3) the Industrial Division of the Federal Court of Australia.

The Federal Court ensures that the Commission's awards are complied with by taking prosecution appeals, by penalising for a breach of an award, or by ordering obedience to an award and then punishing for non compliance with its judicial order. (This division between the making of an award by the Commission and the

137

enforcement of the award by a different body, the Court, is explained in the Chapter below on "the federal courts", No 1 "the separation of powers".) The Federal Court hands down authoritative interpretations of awards. It takes appeals from the lower State courts and territorial courts in federal industrial matters, such as prosecutions or proceedings to recover wages or penalties under federal awards. It hears proceedings about the non observance of union (or employers' associations') rules or about the unreasonableness, etc, of the rules; it watches union elections and orders a new election if there is an irregularity; it protects union members, for example, against wrongful expulsion.

- *THE TRADE PRACTICES COMMISSION* administers and enforces the *Trade Practices Act* 1974 (Cth), an Australia-wide law on restrictive trade practices and consumer protection.

Restrictive trade practices include traders' "understandings" to fix prices, misuse of market power (cf monopolisation), exclusive dealing between manufacturers and wholesalers, or between breweries and tied houses, or between building societies, their mortgagors and insurance companies, resale price maintenance agreements between suppliers and their purchasers, mergers between companies that substantially lessen competition, secondary boycotts where, for example, a union and its officials hinder theatrical agencies in their supply of actors to a film-making company (but there is talk of re-siting secondary boycotts in the *Industrial Relations Act* 1988 (Cth) and under the Industrial Relations Commission). Consumer protection covers unfair practices, such as bait advertising (the "come-on" article that isn't really there), or home-selling harassment, or misleading conduct or false representations. Consumer protection also covers the kind of conditions which a trader cannot (because of the Act) exclude from a sale of goods or the supply of services, such as a condition that a dealer has a good title to the car being sold, or that a computer company does repairs with care and skill.

As regards the provisions on consumer protection, a State *Fair Trading Act*, *Consumer Protection Act* or *Sale of Goods Act* still remains in force, unless there is a contradiction between the State Act and the federal Act, and then the federal Act is followed. Thus, usually a consumer can seek protection or get damages either under the federal Act or a State Act. As regards the provisions on restrictive trade practices, any person affected can seek damages under the federal Act or ask for an injunction, and so on.

Restrictive trade practices and evasions of consumer protection are forbidden by the federal Act. Heavy pecuniary penalties can be imposed for contraventions of the provisions on restrictive trade practices, as much as $10m for companies. The Trade Practices Commission initiates the proceedings to recover the penalties or takes other action (for example, it seeks an injunction or a demerger) under the Act before the Federal Court of Australia. The Commission can also authorise a trader to undertake certain restrictive trade practices which would be otherwise forbidden; and it may allow exclusive dealing. The Trade Practices Tribunal has a limited role; it takes appeals from the Commission in authorisation applications and notifications, and it makes declarations on overseas mergers.

Of course, since the *Trade Practices Act* is a *federal* law, it can apply only in areas where the Commonwealth Parliament has power—areas such as transactions by foreign corporations or by local trading or financial corporations (see the corporations power in s 51(xx) of the Constitution), transactions in overseas or interstate trade (see the trade and commerce power in s 51(i) of the Constitution), or transactions in the two inland territories, the Australian Capital Territory and the Northern Territory (see the territories power in s 122 of the Constitution), and so on. Hence the Act would not usually apply to the man in the corner shop or to a firm of solicitors within a State.

- *THE INDUSTRY COMMISSION* was provided for by a 1989 Act, and began functioning in March 1990. It is the vital authority that supervises government aid to industry and, as a consequence, it is also an important weapon for controlling the national economy.

  As well, the Commission examines industry matters generally to find ways for increased efficiency in industry.

The Industry Commission replaces the Industries Assistance Commission (1974-1990), which had replaced the Tariff Board (1921-1974). The old Tariff Board tended to concentrate on government aid to secondary industry by protective import duties, that is, customs duties (or "tariff") raised on imported goods that would otherwise compete successfully with local products. But the Industries Assistance Commission looked at all kinds of industries (not just secondary industry) and at all kinds of government aid (not just tariff). Thus the IAC exposed the manufacturing industries and their protective cosseting. Then it dragged the service industries into the spotlight, such as coastal shipping which was the subject of an unflattering IAC report in 1988.

And now the Industry Commission has taken on the role of the former IAC. Hence the Industry Commission monitors for the government the whole range of its aid to industry. I mean aid to primary, secondary and tertiary (eg, services or retailing) industries, and I also mean aid by way of import duty relief, bounties, protective tariffs and quotas, special tax concessions . . . in fact, any form of government assistance to industry.

So, before the government assists a particular interest in industry, the proposal may be publicly and independently examined by the Commission to judge its merits—the cost of some protection or assistance and the benefit to the economy as a whole. The spotlighting shows publicly, say, the lack of merit in an inefficient industry. It may show publicly the lack of cost-benefit to the overall economy if protection is continued at the same level, or if assistance is granted to a particular interest in industry.

In addition, the Industry Commission is the government's major review and inquiry body into industry issues generally. Thereby the Commission hopes to bring about greater efficiency in Australian industry, especially to meet international competition.

To name some of the references sent to the Commission within the last few years, the Commission has inquired into, or will inquire into, the car industry (its inefficiency, restrictive work practices, and yet its tariff protection), value-adding to forest products, exploitation of new minerals, meat exports, tourism. But other references have been sent, such as the provisioning of public housing and environmental waste management.

Initiatives come in a reference from the Minister responsible for the administration of the Act. And there's the weakness. References may not be forthcoming, or they may be fashionable rather than potentially damaging. Frankly, all this publicity and this overview of the national economy fomented by the Industry Commission may not suit a government interested in vote-catching sectional interests, or simply interested in not looking for more problems.

The Commission remains an advisory body only. Still, the government would have to justify its refusal to follow the Commission's recommendation, if sought, at least to the Opposition in Parliament where the Commission's report is tabled. The Commission conducts a public inquiry, summons witnesses and calls for documents. These matters are backed by penalties.

On top of all this scrutinising of government aid to industry and this reviewing of industry matters at large, the Industry

Commission has also absorbed the Inter-State Commission. The Inter-State Commission had been established under the trade and commerce power in 1913, lasting until 1920: see ss 101-104 of the Constitution. It was resurrected in September 1983 with an advisory role only. Its Act was repealed in March 1990, making way for the Industry Commission.

The power basis of the Industry Commission—remember every federal authority must find a specific power basis in the Constitution—is the overseas trade and commerce power, the taxation power, the bounties power, the corporations power, the States-grant power and so on, in s 51(i), (ii), (iii), (xx), s 96 of the Constitution.

- *THE AUSTRALIAN SECURITIES COMMISSION*, the ASC, replaced the National Companies and Securities Commission in January 1991.

The NCSC had been created in December 1979—taking over from the multistate Interstate Corporate Affairs Commission, run by the eastern States (1974) and Western Australia (1975)—to deal with companies, securities and takeovers on a wider-than-State basis.

In time the ASC was created by the *Australian Securities Commission Act* 1989 (Cth), which subsequently used the wide-ranging territories power. The *Corporations Act* 1989 (Cth) was rebuilt in December 1990, also on the territories power. This Act became the "Corporations Law", as it is called, for the Australian Capital Territory. Then in 1990 the six States and the Northern Territory passed Acts to apply the Corporations Law as a law of each State and the Territory.

The whole scheme for the Australian Securities Commission and the application of the Commonwealth's Corporations Law to the States and the territories came into operation on 1 January 1991.

In this roundabout way (that is, through the Commonwealth's almost unlimited territories power backed by State and territorial adoptions) we have arrived at a national administration and enforcement of company law. The Australian Securities Commission became the single national authority responsible for the decentralised administration (through Regional Commissions) of companies, securities and futures law throughout Australia.

As a result, there is now a single Australia-wide set of rules of conduct for companies, and there is a single body—the ASC—to supervise stock exchanges, monitor the securities and futures industries, investigate company frauds and the rest throughout Australia.

But the actual incorporation of companies will continue to be effected mainly by the States and territories. These companies will be required to register with the ASC, and thus come under its surveillance. For the High Court denied that the Commonwealth itself could incorporate companies under its corporations power (*New South Wales v The Commonwealth* 1990). Incidentally, it was because of this case that the Commonwealth had to shift the basis of the *Corporations Act*, given above, from the corporations power to the wide territories power.

- *THE ADMINISTRATIVE APPEALS TRIBUNAL*—the AAT—came into being in 1976 to be the common tribunal for appeals from all sorts of federal administrative bodies and officers.

The Tribunal has become an influential body as the surveillant of federal administrative machinery. It has its own reports. The Tribunal has a full time staff: a President, several Deputy Presidents and non presidential members. There are also innumerable part-time members. The full time and part time staff number about 110 Australia-wide. There are now something like 250 Commonwealth Acts under which a decision may be taken by a federal body or officer—and then challenged before the AAT. Small wonder the Tribunal may receive over 2000 applications each year.

The most important part of the *Administrative Appeals Tribunal Act* 1975 is the Schedule, for it shows the citizen when he/she can appeal to the Tribunal against the decision of a Minister, a Secretary to a Department, the Comptroller-General of Customs or a Collector of Customs, the Director-General of Health, the Tax Agents' Board, and so on. For instance, a doctor or chemist may appeal against the Minister when the Minister revokes the doctor's or chemist's authority under the *National Health Act* 1953. A patent attorney who has been refused registration by the Commissioner of Patents or a tax agent whose registration has been cancelled by the Tax Agents' Board may appeal to the Tribunal. A person objecting to a Customs Collector's demands or a taxpayer appealing against the Taxation Commissioner's assessment may appeal to the Taxation Appeals Division of the Tribunal. An alien facing deportation, a TV station that has had its licence suspended, a pilot who has had a flying licence taken away, or a person dissatisfied with a decision by the Australian Securities Commission may also appeal to the Tribunal.

The person objecting to the administrator's decision has the right to ask the administrator for the reasons for his decision, in other words, to get in ammunition for an attack on the bureaucracy. In all these cases the citizen is appealing from one administrative body to another administrative body, the "Administrative" Appeals Tribunal. If there is a question of law, however, one can appeal (as it is loosely called) from the Administrative Appeals Tribunal to the Federal Court of Australia, or the Tribunal itself may refer the question to the Federal Court.

(In February 1985 Victoria became the first State to establish an Administrative Appeals Tribunal. It was modelled on the Commonwealth body.)

The federal Ombudsman, created by a 1976 Act, investigates citizens' complaints (in a given year he might receive over 17,000 complaints), or undertakes inquiries for himself, into federal departments, the Australian Federal Police, the Australian Defence Forces and prescribed bodies. He operates Australia-wide through regional offices or representatives in various States and in the Northern Territory.

The Ombudsman reports to the offending department or authority. If he thinks no action is taken or the complaint has not been adequately rectified, he can report to the Prime Minister, as well as to the two Houses of Federal Parliament. Annually, the Ombudsman's report to Parliament exposes the shortcomings of the federal public service.

————————

Also in the 1970s-1980s the Federal Government engaged in two other self-denying exercises. Since October 1980 when the *Administrative Decisions (Judicial Review) Act 1977* came into operation, an aggrieved person can ask the Federal Court of Australia to check Commonwealth administrators on all sorts of grounds; this is explained below. In addition, the *Freedom of Information Act 1982* allows public access to federal departments' and agencies' documents, for example, their working manuals.

Thus, in these latter days the citizen is protected against the bureaucracy—the federal bureaucracy—by four pieces of machinery:

- *the Freedom of Information Act*—it concedes a right to the citizen to broach the secrecy of the workings of public service departments

143

- *the Ombudsman*—he investigates the administration and reports to Parliament

- *the Administrative Appeals Tribunal*—it takes appeals from all kinds of administrative bodies and officers

- *the Federal Court of Australia*—it takes points of law from the Tribunal and from the bodies and officers just mentioned, and it makes judicial orders to keep these bodies and officers in check

---

All of the administrative tribunals, boards and officers mentioned above—and more—help the Federal Government in its detailed running of the country, for instance, the Registrar of Trade Marks, the Commissioner of Patents, the Copyright Tribunal and, of course, the bodies I explained in detail above.

Some of these tribunals or officers are like the ordinary courts since they settle differences and decide a person's rights. For instance, the Taxation Appeals Division of the Administrative Appeals Tribunal settles a taxation difference between the taxpayer and the Taxation Commissioner, the Commissioner of Patents decides whether he will grant a patent to an inventor, the Registrar of Trade Marks hears and determines an application by an aggrieved person to have the respondent's trade mark removed from the register.

Some of these tribunals or officers are like the ordinary courts since they observe the chief principles of natural justice or apply procedural fairness, as it is now known: they must "hear the other side" and they must not be "judges in their own cause", as well as act fairly in procedure. For instance, the Commonwealth may set up an Australian Wheat Board to assess the compensation payable to a private owner from whom the Commonwealth has acquired wheat. But firstly, this compensation Board must give the owner an opportunity to present his case for fair compensation: it must hear the other side. And secondly, the Board must not simply represent the interests of the Commonwealth: it must not be a judge in its own cause.

Some of these tribunals or officers are like the ordinary courts since they have their own internal appeals. For example, a taxpayer can appeal from the Taxation Commissioner to the Taxation Appeals Division of the Administrative Appeals Tribunal, or a union can appeal from an Industrial Relations Commissioner to the Full Bench of the Commission. And now there is the Administrative Appeals Tribunal, a more general appellate body, to take all kinds of appeals from "the administration" in the federal sphere.

- *Thus, you can think of this system of federal tribunals and officers as forming a system outside the regular network of courts, as you can think of regulations as forming a body of law outside the formal Acts of Parliament.*

Still, in certain circumstances a person can go from the administrative system to the court system. He/she can ask the court to check (by prohibition) a tribunal which exceeds its authority. He can ask the court to order (by mandamus) an officer to perform a public legal duty or to exercise a jurisdiction or discretion when the officer wrongly refuses to do so. He can ask the court to review (by certiorari) the decision of a tribunal which he thinks has made a mistake, and the court may go on to quash the decision.

Again, since 1980 an aggrieved person can go from the federal or territorial administrative system to the court system in a more general way. He can go to the General Division of the Federal Court of Australia to check almost any Commonwealth or territorial "decision of an administrative character", applying for a judicial "order of review": see the *Administrative Decisions (Judicial Review) Act* 1977, in force in October 1980. The aggrieved person can ask the Federal Court to check an administrative tribunal, a Minister of the Crown, a public servant or an officer for a variety of reasons. For example, the tribunal, the Minister, the public servant or the officer may have flouted natural justice or procedural rules, exceeded authority or exercised a power unreasonably. In addition, the aggrieved person can request the reasons for the decision taken, and use this material in an attack on the administration.

And sometimes the dissatisfied taxpayer, inventor and the rest can appeal (to use the term loosely) from a board, tribunal or whatever it may be, to an ordinary court—as, for example, a taxpayer can appeal from the Taxation Appeals Division of the Administrative Appeals Tribunal to the Federal Court of Australia on a question of law.

Besides, apart from judicial control, many of these administrative tribunals and officers are subject to some measure of parliamentary control. They must present to Parliament an annual report on their activities. See the next Chapter on "the Federal Government and Parliament", No 3 "annual reports".

The Federal Government and Parliament

In the running of the country the Federal Government and the Federal Parliament are associated in many ways, as we have just seen. For example, the Government assists Parliament by making "sub-laws", or more accurately, regulations to cover details. Parliament assists the Government by setting up administrative tribunals, such as the Taxation Appeals Division of the Administrative Appeals Tribunal which helps in the collection of revenue for the Government. But here I want to turn to the supervision exercised by Federal Parliament over the Federal Executive, its Ministers, departments and authorities—for, with us, Parliament representing the people, is meant to be the supreme and ultimate organ of Government (using the latter term in the wide sense of the "three arms of government").

In other words, the Commonwealth of Australia has, what is called, parliamentary democracy or, with a different emphasis, parliamentary government.

> Parliament "interferes with administrative matters, and the Ministry are in truth placed and kept in office by (Parliament) . . . A modern Cabinet would not hold power for a week if censured by a newly elected (Parliament) . . ."

> "The first of these principles (which have been gradually worked out by the more or less conscious efforts of generations of English statesmen and lawyers) is the sovereignty of Parliament, which means in effect the gradual transfer of power from the Crown to a body which has come more and more to represent the nation", to wit, Parliament.

1. Responsible government

The prerequisite for responsible government is expressly found in the Constitution, s 64, which stipulates that the Ministers of the Government must sit in one or other House of Parliament. And the point of this is that the Government's Ministers are available in the Parliament to give an account of themselves. I explained ministerial accountability in the previous Chapter on "the Federal Government", No 1 "responsible government".

In Parliament the Federal Government's Ministers—their collective running of the country as a whole and their individual control of particular government departments—are continually under fire. Thereby the Government and its administration are exposed through the media for all the electorate to see.

The criticism comes particularly from the members of the Opposition, less so from the Government's own backbenchers. Still, no matter where the criticism comes from, the fact is that the Government's weaknesses are uncovered in Parliament, and then publicised through the press, radio and television. And this salutary effect comes about through the institution of responsible government.

Responsible government in the particular sense of ministerial responsibility to Parliament has just been explained. Responsible government in the general sense of government responsibility to Parliament is about to be explained. So, No 2 below discusses how the Government tables its regulations for Parliament's scrutiny. No 3 below discusses how the Government's agencies present annual reports to Parliament for examination. No 4 below discusses how the Government's handling of, and access to, public money is accountable to Parliament.

Throughout it is government responsibility to the whole Parliament, not just to the House of Representatives, in the same way as the electorate is represented by the whole Parliament. Historically, people wrested power from the Crown, resulting in parliamentary democracy, not Lower House democracy.

I make the point because of an elision from the idea of the "House of Government" to the error that the Government is responsible to the House of Representatives alone.

The House of Government means that the Lower House alone identifies which political party forms the Government of the day, although the Lower House alone does not supply the Government of the day.

Responsible Government means that the Government is answerable to Parliament. And this body, the Parliament, is spelt out in the Constitution as the Senate and the House of Representatives (as well as the Crown): see ss 1, 53, 57 par 3, 58, 64 par 3, and generally Chapter III Parts II-V. For instance, Ministers sit in one or other House—in 1993 ten Ministers sat in the Senate—and can be censured by a vote of no confidence in either House. (Senator Richardson, Transport and Communications

147

Minister, was censured by the Senate for allegedly misleading Parliament, and a little later, giving his own reason, resigned from the Ministry in May 1992.) Again, the Senate can refuse Supply to the Government, as the House of Representatives can pass a no-confidence vote in the Government, and thereby the Government may be brought down by either House.

So, responsible government in the particular sense and in the general sense means that the government of the day is answerable to Parliament—*to both Houses of Parliament*—in such matters as

- ministerial responsibility
- the tabling of government regulations
- annual reports from government agencies
- the government's handling of, and access to, public money.

---

2. Tabling of regulations

It is true that Parliament authorises the Government's Ministers to make wholesale regulations, as we saw in the previous chapter. But, at the same time, Parliament has laid down a rule in its *Acts Interpretation Act* 1901. All of these regulations must first be tabled before each House of Parliament for examination and possible veto. The Senate, in fact, has its own special scrutineer, the Senate Standing Committee on Regulations and Ordinances. If objection is taken to any regulations within 15 sitting days of their tabling, then either the House of Representatives or the Senate can disallow the regulations, and this has the same effect as a repeal of the regulations.

For instance, the regulations may attempt to impose a tax on the people under the guise of increased postal charges, whereas Parliament itself should alone control public finance and give its clear authority for any such fiscal regulations. The regulations may attempt to deal with matters of policy which should come, if at all, from Parliament as a whole. The regulations may seem to interfere with personal freedom in the way a Crimes Act normally does, and regulations do not unless they do it quite explicitly and clearly. Finally, the regulations may attempt to deal with matters or purposes outside the Act under which the regulations were supposed to be made. Then the regulations are quite plainly to be disallowed because they are "ultra vires" their enabling Act.

Disallowance of regulations is particularly possible when the regulations are to be tabled before a "hostile Senate", as there was for instance between 1962 and 1975 and since 1981.

3. Annual reports

Another way in which Parliament reviews Federal Government action, that is, another way in which government responsibility to Parliament arises, is through the requirement that various reports be tabled in Parliament.

Now, many agencies, bodies, officials, and so on, assist in the general running of the country. These report to Parliament on their activities and on the laws under which they operate. Then the report can become the subject of open debate by the members of Parliament. *In this way, authorities which act almost independently of the Government itself are at least brought within the scrutiny of Parliament.* Thus, the Commissioner of Taxation must report on the working of the *Income Tax Assessment Act 1936*. The Trade Practices Commission reports on its operations in the past year. The Auditor-General puts in his critical annual report, and so on.

All these reports from "the administrators" are presented each year to Federal Parliament for its review—or exposure.

---

4. Public money

Public money raised and later used by the Government is particularly watched by Federal Parliament.

> *A fundamental in our parliamentary system of government is Parliament's control of the Government's handling of public money, both its raising by taxation and its subsequent appropriation for expenditure.*
>
> *And in the final analysis, the Government's access to public money depends on Parliament, both Houses of Parliament.*

But before I deal with this government responsibility to Parliament, in this instance in money matters, I want to say a few general words about the Budget.

The Budget: As each new financial or fiscal year comes around—it begins on 1 July and ends on 30 June—the Treasury prepares the Budget. Really the preparation goes through three stages spread over several months. First, the various government departments submit to the Treasury's scrutiny their proposed receipts and expenses for the new year . . . next, the Treasury collates these submissions, tailored where necessary, and arranges a sheaf of financial documents for Cabinet . . . finally, Cabinet settles the Budget itself.

Chiefly, the Budget is the Government's prediction of its revenue and expenditure for the coming year. To be precise, the Budget which the Treasurer will present in time in the "Budget Speech" (see below) falls into two parts. It lists actual receipts and expenditure for the *past* year. And it lists, as well, an estimate of the receipts and expenditure for the *coming* year—what are called "the Estimates".

The "Estimates of Revenue" set out especially taxation, particularly personal income tax and company tax, as well as customs and excise duties which include sales tax. These Estimates also show profits from government-run businesses (but many of these are being corporatised and then privatised). The "Estimates of Expenditure" list especially the huge sums to be set aside for health, education, welfare and social security, grants to the States and defence. These Estimates list, too, the cost of government departments, government-run businesses, territories, and so on.

Federal Cabinet then reviews these Estimates with the Treasury, especially Estimates which involve matters of policy. For instance, Cabinet may decide to lift the subsidies on rural reconstruction or to pay higher pensions and other social service benefits. To off-set this, Cabinet will increase, perhaps, company tax or sales tax on petrol, cigarettes and motor cars. For some people, in fact, for many people the most important item in the new Budget will be this matter of taxation. Do we now have to pay an extra 3c for a litre of petrol or, on the other hand, has the Government increased the family allowance?

For other people matters of policy are important. Is the defence expenditure disproportionate (because of our GDP), the Aboriginal expenditure generous (because of their numbers), the user-pay system for migrants equitable (because they are, after all, the beneficiaries)? Of course, the three interest groups will run counter arguments.

150

And this is the point: many budgetary matters are less money matters than ideological and sociological issues.

Finally, the Federal Treasurer presents the completed Budget. He "brings down" or "introduces" the Budget in the House of Representatives, usually in August. The debate on the Budget in the House of Representatives and then in the Senate can last until September or October.

(*Supply Acts and Appropriation Acts*: Spending between 1 July and September or October is authorised in May-June by two Supply Acts which follow the pattern in No (ii) immediately below. Thus, the Supply Acts are, in effect, interim appropriation laws. There are two other kinds of appropriation laws: (i) The permanent and special Appropriation Acts, say, for judges' salaries and superannuation; they continue in force until repealed. (ii) The two ordinary annual Appropriation Acts, one for capital expenses, States' grants and new policies, works and buildings, and a second bill "for the ordinary annual services of the Government". This second bill is the main bill, called the Appropriation Bill (No 1); the Senate cannot amend it, see s 53 of the Constitution, and the House of Representatives cannot tack on it non appropriation provisions, see s 54.)

Other financial and economic documents are introduced in the House at Budget time also, and other events occur.

A *White Paper* gives figures on the national economy, our revenue and expenses. Taxation and similar bills, such as postal and telephone charges, are brought in. On the other side, the two annual Appropriation Bills I mentioned in the previous paragraph are also introduced to obtain Federal Parliament's authority for the Government's proposed spending.

The Budget Speech, drafted by the Treasurer with the Prime Minister, is delivered on the second reading of the main Appropriation Bill, Appropriation Bill (No 1). In the speech the Treasurer explains in very broad outlines the Government's general financial program and "the Estimates" in the Budget—why the need for new taxes, for instance, or new postal charges; or why the increases in old age pensions or tax rebates for dependants; or why the need to boost primary industry by higher subsidies.

The Budget debate follows the presentation of the Budget, and is the debate on the second reading of the Appropriation Bill (No 1). But you should not think of this debate as an examination of the figures in the Budget, or even of the Budget as a whole, for that matter. The Budget debate has become in practice a general

151

and wide-ranging "grievance" debate about Government administration and policies. Time limits don't bind the Treasurer or the Opposition Leader. The usual rule about non digression does not apply: members can speak on any matter about "public affairs".

The Appropriation Bills (Nos 1 & 2) are then scrutinised by the Committee of the Whole or by Estimates Committees. The committee reports are debated, followed by the third reading and the passing of the Bills by the House of Representatives. Next the Bills go to the Senate.

Now return to Parliament's supervision of the Government's handling of public money, both its raising by taxation and its subsequent appropriation for expenditure. (Of course, Parliament's supervision of the Government also occurs through the Estimates Committees just mentioned—multiple committees in each House—that scrutinise the main Appropriation Bill each year.)

Taxation to get in revenue is not imposed by the Government. No, it is the Parliament or rather, to be accurate, it is the House of Representatives that introduces the taxation legislation. Then the Senate as part of Parliament joins in the passing of the money bill: on the Senate's joint role, see the last paragraph in s 53 of the Constitution, together with ss 1, 57 third paragraph and 58.

But the point is that the Parliament, not the Government, raises public money.

Far back in the seventeenth century the Bill of Rights, which we have adopted as part of our constitutional law according to Isaacs J (*Wooltops* case 1922), declared "That the levying of money for or to the use of the Crown by pretence of prerogative without grant of Parliament . . . is illegal". During the 1914-1918 War the Hughes' Federal Government made an arrangement with a wooltops-selling company. The Government was prepared to consent to the company's business as long as the company "agreed" to share its profits by paying the Government a "licence fee". But in 1922 the High Court struck down the device. Isaacs J read the subterfuge for what it really was: "a recrudescence of the old struggle between the prerogative and the right of parliamentary control." In the words of the Bill of Rights 1689 there was a government-forced payment "without grant of Parliament".

Supply and appropriation are both within the control of Parliament. Begin with an appreciation that s 81 of the Constitution requires all revenue received by the Government to "form one Consolidated Revenue Fund to be appropriated" in the manner dictated by s 83, given below. Public moneys kept in one fund can be more easily locked in until appropriated—by Parliament. So, taxes and takings from government-run businesses, say, postal and telephone services, find their way into this Commonwealth-purposes fund.

(There is also a Loan Fund to receive loan moneys for public works—mainly State public works these days, for the Commonwealth can draw on revenue. And there is a Trust Fund to secrete money for a later day. The *Audit Act* 1901 prescribes two separate accounts in the Treasury for these Funds. It is argued that these Funds attract "money", not "revenue", and so need not comply with the one-Consolidated-*Revenue*-Fund provision in s 81.)

Next the Governor-General procures supply for his Government by recommending the purpose of the prerequired appropriation by message to the House of Representatives, and he must make this recommendation "in the same session" in which the revenue is to be appropriated: see s 56 of the Constitution. Finally, the recommended money must not be appropriated, or drawn from the Treasury, "except under appropriation made by law": see s 83 of the Constitution. This appropriation is an annual event, an annual parliamentary control of the Government: Parliament sits annually, see s 6, and approves of money for the "annual" services of Government, see ss 53 and 54.

In short, Federal Government expenditure must be approved by Federal Parliament, by its "appropriation *made by law*" each year.

So, when a Federal Minister in July 1989 tripled the parliamentarians' postal allowance—although, as it turned out, Parliament had not appropriated the extra money—the High Court ruled against him: "the power of appropriation is reposed solely in Parliament. It is by ss 81 and 83 that our Constitution assures to the people the effective control of the public purse" (*Brown v West* 1990).

I have already described an occasion in October-November 1975 when some may have thought that the Federal Government was trying to find a way around these constitutional provisions: see the closing pages in the Chapter above on "Federal Parliament machinery". Briefly, on 16 October 1975 Parliament through the

153

Senate deferred Supply to force the Government to resign or to face the electorate. After three to four weeks the Government arranged talks with the banks, somehow to secure money or its equivalent to meet the cost of its ordinary annual services. Legal opinions suggested that this device might be an indirect attempt by the Government to secure money or its equivalent without working under the surveillance of Parliament, without an "appropriation made by law", as explicitly required by s 83 of the Constitution. The Governor-General of the time later, in 1978, wrote of "the unlikely possibility of the scheme becoming operative, especially having regard to its defects and inadequacies and very doubtful legality . . . the dubious banking exercise . . . could not be regarded as fulfilment of the (Government's) duty to obtain supply" from Parliament.

The upshot was, the Government did not get Supply from Parliament and, as the former administration, it was forced to face the electorate *because of Parliament's constitutional power over the supply and appropriation of public money.*

Even when the Federal Government, its departments and bodies have received money from the Treasury by the consent of Parliament that is not the end of Parliament's control of public money.

Parliament has three ways by which it checks the Government's use of money:

- The Auditor-General.
- The Joint Committee of Public Accounts.
- The Parliamentary Standing Committee on Public Works.

The Auditor-General and both the Committees are formally set up by a special Act of Parliament in each case, unlike some of the informal Parliamentary Committees. And so, we go to their respective Acts to find their purposes, their functions and their powers.

The Auditor-General with assistants is Parliament's own independent, roving overseer of public money. He is not controlled by the Treasurer or any other Minister. His position is rather like that of a High Court Justice. That is, he is appointed by the Governor-General; until he reaches retirement at 65 he is irremovable during good behaviour; and if he is to be removed, it must be on an address from the Houses of Parliament. He appears in one of Parliament's first Acts, the *Audit Act* 1901.

The Auditor-General keeps a critical eye on the receipts and expenditure of public money and on the stores in Government departments or authorities. He can demand access to all kinds of documents, accounts, records and vouchers relating to receipts and expenditure. And he can compel persons to come before him to be examined in these matters—particularly Commonwealth accounting officers, that is, persons who receive money and stores on behalf of the Government.

Now, in the first place, every few months the Treasurer prepares an itemised list of moneys required out of the Treasury. He also adds the purposes for which the moneys are needed. And the Treasurer notifies the Auditor-General accordingly. Next the Auditor-General examines the list with its purposes. He will then attach his certificate if he thinks it is justified.

This Auditor-General's certificate states that the purposes for which the moneys are to be applied are legitimate purposes. Furthermore, no money can be paid out of the Treasury without this certificate, as well as the Governor-General's warrant to the Treasurer which is issued only after the Auditor-General's certificate has been given.

Thus, the Auditor-General is the key figure in the release of public money for government spending—and hence the imperative requirement of his independence of government.

But, quite apart from uncovering irregularities and surcharging the responsible officers, the Auditor-General watches out for overspending because of careless estimates, or just plain uneconomic expenditure . . . and that kind of thing. And so, each year—or more often if he thinks fit—the Auditor-General reports any irregularities together with his suggestion to each House of Parliament. Parliament can then check a defaulting department or authority by tightening the laws which govern the body's activities. Or, Parliament can call for a closer investigation by its own Public Accounts Committee, or by the Treasury and the Public Service Board.

For example, stung by continual Opposition badgering, the Government asked Parliament's overseer of public money, the Auditor-General, to investigate the Aboriginal Affairs Department and the Aboriginal Development Commission. In March 1989 the

Auditor-General's report to Parliament alleged uneconomic spending by the Commission, unusual accounting procedures, and money used for purposes not clearly within the enabling Act.

The Joint Committee of Public Accounts, as we have just seen, is Parliament's own guardian of public money. The present Committee was set up by a special Act, the *Public Accounts Committee Act* 1951 (superseding the first Act of 1913). It is a Joint Committee, and so it consists of members both from the Senate, three, and from the House of Representatives, seven, appointed as each new Parliament sits. (As a by-product, the Committee is a useful training ground for prospective Ministers.) More to the point, in practice members of the Committee are drawn from the Opposition party, as well as from the Government party. The Committee acts on its own behalf, that is, it is free to determine its own reference, or it acts on the report of the Auditor-General or at the request of either House of Parliament.

Its function is to look closely at "the accounts of the receipts and expenditure of the Commonwealth", "the financial affairs" of authorities under the Act and the Auditor-General's reports (to quote the Act's provisions).

It is the most invasive of Parliament's committees, for it oversees the handling of billions of dollars and the dealings of thousands of Commonwealth public servants or even outsiders, say over-servicing doctors or fraudulent social service recipients.

Usually the Committee holds its meetings in public. It summons witnesses. It asks for documents. And it may issue a warrant against a reluctant witness. In time the Committee draws up a report and makes suggestions for Parliament to act on. All of this means, in effect, that the Government's Minister who is in charge of the running of some department or body may be examined in money matters by Parliament which has been warned by its Public Accounts Committee.

In other words, once again the Federal Government's handling of public money is under Parliament's surveillance.

The Committee on Public Works, or to give its full title, the Parliamentary Standing Committee on Public Works, is yet another aid by Parliament to watch public funds. It also has its own special statute, the *Public Works Committee Act* 1969 (replacing the first Act of 1913). This is a joint Committee with three members from the Senate and six from the House of Representatives, both Government and Opposition members, appointed as each new

Parliament sits. This Committee, too, conducts a public inquiry, summons witnesses, calls for documents, takes evidence, and issues warrants.

The Committee's function is to consider and report to both Houses of Parliament on any proposed public work that is referred to it by either House. Works of the Commonwealth, its authorities and instrumentalities come under scrutiny.

A public work that exceeds $6m must be referred to the Committee. But a work that is declared "urgent" by the House of Representatives or that is declared "for defence purposes" by the Governor-General (to use the terms in the Act) is exempt from this scrutiny. The Committee reports on the necessity of the work, its likely production of revenue, its public value, its suitability for the stated purpose, and so on. Then the House of Representatives decides whether "it is expedient to carry out the work" (to quote the Act again).

To sum up: A sovereign Parliament, on behalf of the people, its electors, controls the Federal Government in many ways—

- through responsible government
- the tabling of regulations
- annual reports
- the supervision of public money.

The political party system: (Incidentally, political parties appear nowhere in the Constitution, except in the uncharacteristic provision in s 15 about casual vacancies in the Senate.) Now, it would be unrealistic of me simply to speak of Parliament's supervision and control of the Government through responsible government, the tabling of regulations, and the rest. This is the ideal form of parliamentary democracy in which the independent Parliament of the people truly watches and checks the Government.

But in practice, because of our political party system, Parliament's control of the Government is at times not too impartial and effective.

157

Take first the Government political party. This is the party which can command a majority vote in the House of Representatives. It consists of the Ministers especially, up to 30 of these. These hardcore members of the party will surely vote for any bill, resolution or motion which favours the Government. The Government party also consist of its backbenchers. These members, too, are likely to vote with their party. They probably do not care to displease their party chiefs, from whom they may expect promotion one day to Ministerial rank. At any rate, for reasons of loyalty or discipline or for some other reason, the members of the Government party in the House of Representatives will vote as party members, not as individual members.

These party members, voting as a united whole, command the majority vote in the House. Consequently, Government bills, resolutions and motions will pass through the House of Representatives as a matter of course. Then, when we say the House of Representatives controls the Government, we really mean the Government members—or a junta of senior Ministers—control the Government!

Still, things are not quite as bad as that, fortunately for the ideal of parliamentary democracy, that is, the governing by Parliament as the representative of the people.

In the first place, there can be "rebel members" in the Government party, principally among the backbenchers. These can vote against an unpopular Government program. True, such mavericks are thin on the ground, and are likely to have short political lives. Nevertheless, rebel members do appear from time to time and, if anywhere, in the Senate.

Next, while the Government must, of course, command a majority vote in the Lower House—otherwise it would not be in Government—the Government may not have a similar majority in the Upper House, as happened between 1962-1975 and again in July 1981 on. In such a situation every Government bill or resolution which must be approved by Parliament as a whole will face a "hostile Senate", as it is called.

And finally, there is the Opposition party which can join forces with the Government's rebel members to block Government measures.

Her Majesty's Opposition is the political party (or parties in a coalition) which has the second largest membership in the Lower House and is, therefore, not the governing party. The Opposition party has its own distinctive platform which differs from that presented by the Government party and currently accepted by the electors. At all times the Opposition members can expose the Government's maladministration and sinister purposes for all the electorate to see, especially during open debate in Parliament, during question time and in joint committees.

When you think of it, this is a bizarre idea, bizarre to our friends on the other side of the curtain. *We elect a group to run the country and actually pay another group to get rid of the first group*—Her Majesty's Loyal Opposition, as it is quaintly described.

The Opposition has its own Leader, Deputy Leader and Whip in each House. In addition, it allots "portfolios" to its "shadow Ministry" and "Cabinet". A "Shadow Minister" is the Opposition's expert and spokesman on the matters with which one of the Government Ministers is concerned. In other words, certain Opposition members, sitting in the front benches on their side of the House, shadow their Government counterparts sitting in the front benches on the other side. For instance, one Opposition member, skilled in foreign affairs, will watch the Government's Minister for Foreign Affairs. And this particular Opposition member is likely to become the new Foreign Affairs Minister when the Opposition takes over the Government of the Commonwealth. Thus, the Opposition party ever lies in wait to govern the country—if the electors choose.

And so, in the last analysis, if not Parliament, then at least the Opposition controls the Government—firstly, by its continued criticism; secondly, by its attractiveness to the electorate.

In recent times, however, the effectiveness of the Opposition in Parliament has been weakened. Question time, usually an embarrassment to Ministers, is abused by Dorothy Dixers contrived by government members to let in propagandist ministerial statements. Fewer sitting days further erode question time. Grievance debates are also decreasing. Urgency debates on matters of public importance can be proposed by the Opposition—but they may not be allowed. Government business days pre-empt general business days more and more.

Nevertheless, the Opposition is still there and heard, even if muted. And a free press, radio and television amplify this voice of dissent in Parliament against the Government.

The federal courts

1. General matters

In Australia there are three separate systems or networks of courts to administer justice.

> There is **the federal system of courts** with its three-fold organs. I will discuss this here when I look at the High Court, any other federal court, and the State courts acting in federal matters.

> There is **the State system of courts** operating in each of the six States. It deals with general matters and with State law. In a later Chapter on "the States", No 6 "courts", I will discuss these courts acting as State courts taking matters on the general law and on State law.

> There is **the territorial system of courts**. The larger territories have their own Supreme Courts, Magistrates' Courts and Courts of Petty Sessions. Like the State courts, the territorial courts have a general jurisdiction—over territorial matters and territorial law. I discussed these courts in the Chapter on "the powers of Federal Parliament", No 9.

Because of the cross-vesting of jurisdiction between these systems and within these systems—it began in 1988 and will be explained later—the three systems do not seem to stand apart now as much as they used to. There is instead considerable overlapping of jurisdictions. But first, I will discuss the federal courts with their special jurisdictions, their traditional jurisdictions, then I will point out the unfortunate jurisdictional conflicts or split proceedings that result, and finally I will discuss the attempted way out, the cross-vesting scheme itself.

I will now turn to what I just described as the federal system of courts with its three-fold organs. When Chapter III of the Constitution speaks of "the (Federal) Judicature" it speaks of three kinds of courts.

- The High Court of Australia.

160

- Other federal courts. There are now only two: the Federal Court of Australia and the Family Court of Australia.

- State courts which the Commonwealth may use for its own federal matters.

Strictly speaking, only the first two are federal courts. But since the Commonwealth can use the State courts for its own federal purposes, these courts may be considered under this aspect as part of the federal court system, too. And so, for convenience I will refer to the whole three sets simply as "the federal court system".

Special jurisdictions only can be exercised in the federal court system (leaving aside the possibility of cross-vested jurisdiction), whereas the State courts when they are simply acting as State courts in State matters exercise general jurisdictions. You recall that Federal Parliament can make laws only on special Commonwealth matters. State Parliaments on the other hand have much wider and more general powers. The same contrast can be made in regard to jurisdictions, federal in contrast to State.

Put aside for a minute the High Court when it takes appeals from State Supreme Courts in a variety of matters, but otherwise include the High Court along with the other courts in the federal court system as a court with jurisdiction in certain matters only. Then read the following passage.

> The High Court, as much as any other federal court, "has not a general jurisdiction over the liberty of the subject . . . it is not a common law court but a statutory court. To the Constitution and the laws made under the Constitution it owes its existence and all its powers, and whatever jurisdiction is not found there either expressly or by necessary implication does not exist. 'The Constitution does not in general terms, as in the case of the State Constitutions with reference to Supreme Courts, endow the High Court at a stroke with all the powers of the Court of King's Bench.' "

The nine special cases which courts in the federal court system can hear are the following only.

(i) Cases dealing with an international treaty.

(ii) Cases dealing with a consul.

(iii) Cases where the Commonwealth itself is a party, or one of its representatives is a party such as a federal Minister or the Commonwealth Trading Bank of Australia.

(iv) Cases between, say, South Australia and Victoria, or between a South Australian and a Victorian, or between South Australia and a Victorian.

161

(v) Cases where a person complains about a Commonwealth officer, say, a federal Industrial Relations Commissioner who refuses to settle an industrial dispute or who, on the other hand, attempts to settle a dispute that does not extend beyond the limits of a State.

(vi) Constitutional cases in which the court decides the meaning of some section in the Commonwealth Constitution, for instance, the meaning of a trading corporation in s 51(xx) of the Constitution.

(vii) Cases arising under Commonwealth law, such as the *Income Tax Assessment Act* 1936, the *Trade Marks Act* 1955, the *Trade Practices Act* 1974, the *Family Law Act* 1975.

(viii) Cases on shipping and admiralty.

(ix) Cases on the same subject matter claimed under the laws of different States.

These nine special cases of federal jurisdiction are set out in the Constitution: in ss 75 and 76 for the High Court; in s 77, which incorporates the matters in ss 75 and 76, for any other federal court and for the State courts when these exercise federal jurisdiction on behalf of the Commonwealth.

The judicial power of the Commonwealth, given by s 71 of the Constitution to the courts in s 71, is a special kind of power, too. It is the only kind of power, along with incidental powers, that the courts in the federal court system can exercise when they act within their special jurisdictions, that is, when they hear any of the special cases just listed (or when the High Court takes appeals). Moreover, this kind of power, the judicial power of the Commonwealth, cannot be exercised by tribunals or officers that are outside s 71 of the Constitution. The s 71 courts are the High Court, the Federal Court of Australia, the Family Court of Australia and the State courts when acting for the Commonwealth.

When a federal court, as well as a State court acting as a federal judicial agent, hears one of those special cases mentioned, the court *must decide the case so as to bind the parties, settling the legal position; and the court must determine the pre-existing rights of the parties, not only for the future, but also as regards the past*.

Of course, the parties may still be able to appeal to a higher court. But that is another matter. For the time being and at the present level the parties' rights and claims have been settled. A court in the federal court system cannot give a kind of advisory opinion which does not affect anyone in particular. It cannot make

162

a recommendation on which a Minister may or may not act. And it cannot merely conduct an inquiry, the kind of thing a Royal Commission does to assist the Government. The reason is, advisory opinions, recommendations and inquiries do not settle people's rights and claims—and yet, this is the sort of process that is usually associated with courts. Finally, a court in the federal court system does not do the kind of thing the Industrial Relations Commission does. The Commission makes an industrial award that binds the parties for the future, whereas a federal court declares the law here and now, and (in theory) as it has always been.

As for federal tribunals or federal officers that are outside s 71 of the Constitution and their attempted exercise of this special kind of power, the judicial power of the Commonwealth, see the next sub-heading.

The separation of powers: I said that, when courts are acting as courts in the federal court system, they can exercise only the judicial power of the Commonwealth. Similarly, State courts used by the Commonwealth in federal jurisdiction can exercise only the judicial power of the Commonwealth. By the same token, federal tribunals which are not courts—for example, the Administrative Appeals Tribunal, the Industrial Relations Commission or the Trade Practices Commission—can not exercise the judicial power of the Commonwealth.

The separation of powers doctrine demands that judicial powers be kept separate from non judicial powers. The High Court has read s 71 of the Constitution as identifying certain bodies as courts to exercise the judicial power of the Commonwealth—and those bodies alone. The ideal is to keep the courts independent in a separate world, away from government and legislative control or influence (Boilermakers case 1956-1957). And the ultimate aim is to safeguard the life, liberty and property of the subject (Deane J Re Tracey; ex p Ryan 1989).

An example of the doctrine—not that every example including this example has much to do with the ideal and aim I just mentioned—occurred in 1955. Then we had the old Commonwealth Court of Conciliation and Arbitration. This Court mainly helped the Federal Government by making awards to settle industrial disputes. However, such award-making is more like law-making for the future than the mere declaring of existing law, the mere settling of pre-existing rights, which the courts are said to do. In other words, the Arbitration Court's award-making was a non-judicial act. But as well as making awards, the Arbitration Court used to give binding interpretations of industrial awards, to impose fines, to commit for contempt of its orders, and to make other coercive orders. These acts are judicial acts.

And so, in the *Boilermakers* case (1956-1957) the High Court and, on appeal, the Privy Council declared that the Arbitration Court could not be given these two sets of powers—the non judicial powers and the judicial powers.

As a result, Commonwealth Parliament thereupon separated the powers by giving them to two separate bodies. First, the Commonwealth Conciliation and Arbitration Commission now made the awards. Secondly, the Commonwealth Industrial Court, a new body, was henceforth to give binding interpretations of the Commission's awards, to impose fines, to commit for contempt of the Court's order to obey the Commission's awards, and to make other coercive orders. And that's the explanation of the present anomaly. One body, the Australian Industrial Relations Commission (as it is now called), makes the award. A different body (that replaced the old Industrial Court), the Industrial Division of the Federal Court of Australia—that has not made the award and that probably sees the award for the first time—later interprets and enforces the award.

Lately, however, the High Court is not applying *Boilermakers* doctrine on the separation of judicial and non judicial powers with as sharp a distinction as it did before.

On one hand, the (non judicial) Trade Marks Registrar was allowed to settle a controversy between a registered owner-company and its opponent and then expunge the owner's name from the Register, thereby determining its pre-existing statutory rights—the kind of act that had seemed to be appropriate to a court (*Quinn's* case 1977). On the other hand, the (judicial) High Court was governed by a wide discretion based on what was "just and equitable" when it upheld certain agreements—the kind of act that had seemed to be appropriate to an administrative body (*Talga v MBC* 1976). Then, while the separation of judicial and non judicial powers still exists under the Commonwealth Constitution, the doctrine means less now since these powers are not as clearly distinguished from one another as they used to be.

A fixed tenure is given by the Constitution to the Justices of the High Court of Australia and of the other federal courts.

To be exact, s 72 of the Constitution itself makes the Justices of the High Court and of any other federal court irremovable unless there is an address from both Houses of Parliament, and even then only on the ground of proved misbehaviour or incapacity. The provision has never been invoked fully. In May 1986 a Parliamentary Commission of Inquiry into the Conduct of a Judge (Murphy J of the High Court) was set up by Act of Parliament. The Judge became gravely ill, and the Commission did not complete its investigation into the allegations made. The Commission was wound up by Parliament in September 1986 when the Act was repealed.

Before 1977 Justices often remained on the High Court into their seventies; in those days the Justices were appointed for life. Rich J 1913-1950, Starke J 1920-1950 and McTiernan J 1930-1976 were still on the bench in their eighties. Since the referendum in July 1977 on the "Retirement of Judges" altered s 72 of the Constitution, an appointment to the High Court is made until the Justice reaches 70 years of age.

The judges on the other federal courts, that is the Federal Court of Australia and the Family Court of Australia, must also (since July 1977) retire at 70 unless Parliament has fixed a lower age, as it has for Family Court appointees between 1977 and 1991 (these retire at 65); appointees after 1991 retire at 70.

But the tenure of the Judges on the State courts, which are also used by the Commonwealth for its purposes, depends upon State law, not the Commonwealth Constitution.

The separation of powers doctrine, separating the judicial power in s 71 from federal executive or legislative power, and the fixed tenure granted to the High Court and federal courts by s 72, making their members well-nigh irremovable, guarantee an independence to these courts, especially from interference by the Federal Executive.

---

2. The High Court of Australia

The High Court stands at the apex of all Australian courts, namely, the High Court itself when composed of a single Justice, any other federal court (at present the Federal Court of Australia and the Family Court of Australia), the State courts and the territorial courts. "Here (in the High Court of Australia) rests the ultimate responsibility of declaring the law of the nation" (Brennan J *Mabo's* case 1992).

The High Court has a dual role. It is a federal court. It is a national court.

The High Court is a federal Court because it decides *federal* conflicts of power between the Commonwealth and the States and between the States themselves, and because it interprets the *federal* Constitution. The High Court tells an Australian citizen which law should be obeyed in a given case—the Commonwealth's or the State's. It determines how far Commonwealth powers can go, say, the arbitration power, the corporations power or the marriage power. It makes sure that the Commonwealth and the States obey the prohibitions and guarantees in the Constitution, such as the prohibition against State excise duties, or the guarantee of freedom of interstate trade against Commonwealth or State interference.

The High Court is a national Court as well. You can think of the High Court as a supra-State Court sitting at the head of the six State Supreme Courts (and at the head of other courts, namely, the federal courts and the territorial courts). In regard to the State Supreme Court the High Court is a general court of appeal. It is not a mere special federal court, although, of course, it takes federal matters coming up from the State Supreme Courts. The High Court discusses general law coming on appeal from the general State Supreme Courts, law on all sorts of topics—a *Landlord and Tenant Act* or a *Dog Act*, company law or criminal law, property or sale of goods. As a matter of fact, this kind of general law takes up a large part of the High Court's time.

High Court Justices: The High Court began in October 1903 with a Chief Justice and two other Justices, puisne Justices as they are called, for s 71 of the Constitution stipulates a minimum only—three. Between 1931 and 1946 there were six members on the Court. Since 1913, putting aside the 1931-1946 period, there have been seven members almost continually.

> *What kind of men go on to the High Court with its enormous influence on the sprawl of Commonwealth powers, with its enormous influence on the shaping or distorting of the federation, with its enormous influence on the general law of the land?*

In the past 86 years—my closing date is February 1989 when the latest appointment occurred—the 38 members of the High Court, with one exception (Powers in 1913 had been a Commonwealth

Crown Solicitor), have come from the bar, although not necessarily immediately from the bar, principally the New South Wales bar (20) and the Victorian bar (11). Mostly the members have been "silks" or Queen's Counsel, relinquishing lucrative practices. Eighteen have come to the High Court with earlier experience on a federal court or a State court, that is, nearly half the Justices that have sat on the Court have already been "tried" on other courts. The small States—Tasmania, South Australia and Western Australia—gained their first "representative" since the Court sat in 1903 when the Western Australian Solicitor-General, Wilson, was appointed to the Court in May 1979. Tasmania and South Australia have never been "represented" on the Court. A Victorian Solicitor-General, Dawson, was appointed in 1982, and a New South Wales Solicitor-General, Gaudron (the first woman appointee), in February 1987.

A dozen have been active politicians, Liberal, Labor or their counterparts; eight of these were federal politicians before their appointment. The first three members of the bench, appointed on 5 October 1903, had all been politicians. Griffith CJ had been Queensland's Premier on two occasions, and its Chief Justice as well. Barton and O'Connor JJ had been in New South Wales and federal politics. Barton was in fact Australia's first Prime Minister in 1901-1903, and O'Connor had been a New South Wales senator. The next two appointees in 1906, Isaacs and Higgins JJ, came from Victorian and federal politics to the High Court bench. Evatt and McTiernan JJ were Labor politicians appointed by a Labor government in 1930. Latham CJ was a UAP politician appointed by a UAP government a little later, in 1935. Then, in 1964, Barwick CJ was a Liberal politician appointed by a Liberal Government. In February 1975 Murphy J, a Labor politician, was appointed by a Labor Government; he was the last former politician to be appointed. You might recall that, since the High Court has functioned, we have had mostly conservative governments at Canberra, and they make the High Court appointments: 26 in 38 appointments.

Powers, 1913, was a former Commonwealth Crown Solicitor, Mason, 1972, a former Commonwealth Solicitor-General. Three Chief Justices were former Commonwealth Attorneys-General: Barwick, 1964, Latham, 1935, and Isaacs, 1930. Two puisne Justices, Murphy, 1975, and Higgins, 1906, were also former Commonwealth Attorneys-General. Thus, in all these cases of former Commonwealth Attorneys-General, one may say that "their" legislation came up for review by them from time to time.

Back in February 1975 New South Wales set up a Legislative Assembly Select Committee to recommend constitutional amendments "which will ensure that . . . (High Court) appointments are made in a more equitable and acceptable manner"—from the State's point of view. Another New South Wales Committee recommended in 1979 an Advisory Commission of the seven Attorneys-General. The 1979 Act mentioned in the next but one paragraph is the Commonwealth's response. In July 1985 Queensland argued for a kind of State veto on High Court appointments. Barwick as Chief Justice advocated in July 1977 an independent Judicial Commission as the appointing or recommending body.

Chief Justices, apart from the three just mentioned, include Griffith, 1903, Knox, 1919, Gavan Duffy, 1931, Dixon, 1952, Gibbs, 1981, Mason, 1987. So there have been nine Chief Justices since Federation. Barwick CJ, 1964-1981, served the longest of these. McTiernan J, 1930-1976, had the longest term of all High Court Justices.

Usually a High Court Justice is recommended by the federal Attorney-General. Since the *High Court of Australia Act* 1979, this Attorney-General "shall . . . consult" (but it is merely "consult") the State Attorneys-General before an appointment is made, and it seems he consults the Chief Justice as well. Cabinet then accepts or rejects the nominee. Finally—and formally—the Governor-General-in-Council appoints the Justice.

> *So, in an appointment to this enormously influential body, the High Court of Australia, the States play no critical role. The Commonwealth Government alone—not even the Commonwealth Parliament—appoints to this vital arbiter between the States and the Commonwealth Government.*

> *Moreover, the first notice we ever have of an appointment to this enormously influential body, the High Court of Australia, is a newspaper report.*

Contrast the exposure of Presidential nominations to the United States Supreme Court, where the Senate publicly monitors—and at times refuses its consent to—the President's nominee. True, that exposure has been political and personal. But this is not a commentary on the system of public scrutiny before appointment. Rather, it is a commentary on the wisdom of laying down a Bill of Rights, which invites prying into a nominee-judge's predilections.

Composition of the Bench: The High Court may sit as a Full Court with "any two or more Justices" (the *Judiciary Act*), or it may sit with a single Justice. When the High Court takes an appeal from another court—commonly a State Supreme Court, but also the Federal Court of Australia or the Family Court of Australia—a Full Court of five to seven Justices sits (it is more likely to be seven nowadays), or three if it is an appeal from a single Supreme Court Justice. The same number of five to seven (again usually seven) sits in a constitutional case; such a case may get into the High Court on appeal, or on removal midstream from another court, or on an application for a writ against a Commonwealth officer, or otherwise in its original jurisdiction. Special leave applications are heard by three Justices. All of this is what happens in practice.

If the case affects Commonwealth constitutional powers, at least three Justices must concur in the decision; so, at least five Justices sit; this is what is required by the *Judiciary Act*, and is not merely practice.

Apart from the more important cases, such as constitutional cases, whenever the High Court takes a case in its original jurisdiction, one Justice sits.

In a split decision the majority prevails. In an equally divided opinion the Chief Justice (or senior Justice) prevails—unless the Court is taking an appeal from a High Court Justice, the Federal or Family Court or a State or Territory Supreme Court; then the decision given by the lower tribunal stands (the *Judiciary Act*).

The Principal Seat and Registry of the High Court was Melbourne 1903-1973, Sydney 1973-1980. In May 1980 a High Court building was opened in Canberra, and on 1 September the seat of the High Court was fixed there, at the Seat of Government.

Thereafter the High Court almost ceased to be a "peripatetic court", sitting in every capital city. It now has for the most part a fixed venue at Canberra, as Washington is for the United States Supreme Court, Ottawa for the Canadian Supreme Court. But the High Court is still peripatetic, sitting in capital cities, other than Sydney and Melbourne (which are close to Canberra), if there is sufficient business. In fact, in its first three years at Canberra, 1980-1982, the High Court also sat in Brisbane, Adelaide, Perth and Hobart. In 1984 the High Court again took up regular sittings in Sydney and Melbourne, and occasional sittings in Brisbane and Adelaide, in order to screen applications for special leave. In other words, the Court is to some extent reverting to its peripatetic role. Registries in the various capital cities receive documents.

In 1979 the High Court secured its charter—the *High Court of Australia Act*—which granted the Court a unique control of its own affairs, its staff, budget and building.

The course of a normal hearing before the High Court runs as follows: At the outset counsel supplies the Court with a list of authorities and legislation intended to be used, and since 1982 the Court has also required counsel before the Full Court to hand up a brief outline of submissions. During "argument" counsel submits the plaintiff's case from the bar table, facing the Justices on the bench. Defendant's counsel then argues the defendant's case. Plaintiff's counsel replies. Throughout the argument the Justices ask questions, criticise the points made, often summarise counsel's arguments along the way. There is no time limit to this argument. It may take only one day or less because the issue is slight or because the Court does not consider it worthwhile to call on the other side. It may take 20 days. But it is more likely to run for two or three days. The Court may then at once deliver an oral "Judgment"—in the form of a court order to the parties—together with its reasons. But this is uncommon. Or, the Court may announce its decision and promise its fully drafted reasons at a later date.

However, more often the Court "reserves its judgment". That is, in due course, maybe four or five months afterwards—these days the complaint is made that sometimes it is as long as 12 months afterwards—the Court "hands down judgment". Each Justice states the decision reached and then literally hands a written judgment across the bench to a judge's associate. The Justices do not now read their judgments aloud as once they did. Each Justice may write a separate judgment with the aid of a lawyer-associate in some cases. Or the Justices together may write a single joint judgment. Several joint judgments and dissenting judgments also occur.

But mostly our High Court Justices are individualists. While they often read draft judgments of their colleagues, they do not hold a weekly conference as the United States Supreme Court Judges do, to reach a consensus on a majority decision. When Chief Justice Barwick had hoped for prejudgment discussions in the new court building at Canberra with its conducive facilities the Justices persisted in going it alone. For my part, I find separate judgments help me to understand the issues and to see, through the piercing eyes of the dissenters, what the majority Justices are really writing and what are the consequences of their decision.

The judgments of the High Court are printed, checked by the Justices and then published in an authorised (because judge-revised) series called the Commonwealth Law Reports, "CLR"—ready to be used as precedents in subsequent cases before the High Court and before all other Australian courts.

In other words, a High Court decision binds every other court in Australia, and even the High Court itself will follow its earlier decision (but it is not bound to).

It is not uncommon to find a judgment moving across 40 pages of the CLR or an important constitutional law matter spread over a couple of hundred pages. The longest case, the *Banking* case (1948), ran into 400 pages, swollen by another 145 pages from the Privy Council on appeal; the *Communist Party* case (1951) went to 285 pages, the *Tasmanian Dam* case (1983) 326 pages, the *War Crimes Act* case (1991) 222 pages and *Mabo's* case (1992) 217 pages. But it isn't so much the raw figures that are significant as the enormous variety of subjects, not just handled, but *mastered* by the Justices of the High Court. The intricacies of constitutional law, the niceties of jurisdictional law—tax law and accountancy—patent law and technical formulas—company law and balance sheets—criminal law, equity, property, contracts, torts, State legislation and regulations.

. . .

> **(a) Litigants can go into the High Court on appeal** from some other court, and in this case the High Court exercises its appellate jurisdiction, almost always given to it by s 73 of the Constitution.

The Court does not hear the case all over again, taking account of fresh evidence and new legislation. Instead, the High Court simply re-considers the facts and the legislation as these were found by the court appealed from. Indeed, in practice, mostly the High Court only reconsiders the law as propounded by the lower court. It may let in new submissions not made in the court below.

Parties who are dissatisfied with the decision of one of the Justices of the High Court can ask the Full Court of the High Court, made up of several Justices, to review the decision. A party can appeal from the Federal Court of Australia (and is increasingly doing so) or from the Family Court of Australia to the High Court. A party can also appeal to the High Court from a State Supreme Court *on all kinds of matters*. In other words, when an appellant goes from a State Supreme Court to the High Court, the appellant does not have to show that there was some constitutional element or some federal element in the case before the State Supreme Court below, as an appellant does on an appeal to the United States Supreme Court. Or, a party can appeal from some other State court, such as a Court of Petty Sessions, but only when the Commonwealth is using the State court as part of the federal court system, or to put it another way, only when the State court is exercising federal jurisdiction.

A party can appeal to the High Court from the Northern Territory Supreme Court. Other territorial appeals go to the Federal Court of Australia, and then to the High Court. In these cases the High Court exercises its appellate jurisdiction, not under s 73, but under a federal Act authorised by s 122 of the Constitution. Moreover, in these cases the High Court exercises a general appellate jurisdiction, just as it does in appeals from State Supreme Courts.

But a party cannot always go freely from one of the courts I mentioned above to the High Court. A party appeals from the Federal Court of Australia, a State Supreme Court, or any State court if this court exercised federal jurisdiction, or the Northern Territory Supreme Court, only if the High Court grants "special leave" to appeal. The same rule applies to the Family Court of Australia, except that this Court can grant a certificate (about an important question of law or public interest) allowing an appeal as of right to the High Court; in fact, the Family Court has rarely granted a certificate. An appeal as of right to the Full High Court from a single Justice of the High Court itself is available in most cases.

"Special leave to appeal" means that the High Court considers that the question involved has a general application and, therefore, is important or that the case involves a serious miscarriage of justice, or there are differences of opinion below, or the interests of the administration of justice demand an appeal. Of the 150-160 or so applications for special leave only about 40 are granted each year. The leave application and, if granted, the substantive case itself are heard together in criminal matters, but heard separately in civil matters.

In some rare cases Parliament has made an exception to the High Court's appellate jurisdiction. Parliament is given this power in s 73 of the Constitution ("with such exception . . . as the Parliament prescribes"). For example, appeals to the High Court may be blocked from the Industrial Division of the Federal Court of Australia or from State Courts of Petty Sessions, in either case in certain federal industrial matters.

(b) Litigants can go into the High Court and ask it to exercise its original jurisdiction, that is, jurisdiction where the parties enter a court for the first time when they go into the High Court. The jurisdiction is found in s 75 of the Constitution or can be authorised by Federal Parliament under s 76 and, for territorial matters, in these sections or in s 122. (The cross-vesting scheme which attempts to loosen up the jurisdiction of federal courts does not apply to the High Court.)

In this original jurisdiction the High Court can take certain matters only. These matters were listed above when I spoke of the "special jurisdictions" of the courts in the federal system. I will repeat here the cases that could arise in the High Court. But only Nos (iii) and (iv) are likely to occur in practice, and Nos (i) and (ii) less so.

(i) One of the parties appearing before the High Court is the Commonwealth, or, someone on behalf of the Commonwealth, for example, a federal Minister or a Repatriation Commission or the Commonwealth Trading Bank of Australia. See s 75(iii) of the Constitution.

(ii) Two States appear in the High Court, one as plaintiff, the other as defendant. Or, residents from two different States appear, no matter how trifling is their case or what kind of a case it is. A Queenslander holidaying in New South Wales might have a slight car accident with a New South Welshman. The Queenslander can then take action in the High Court. See s 75(iv) of the Constitution.

(iii) A person has a complaint against a Commonwealth officer. For example, a complainant wants the Taxation Commissioner or an Industrial Relations Commissioner to perform a public legal duty or to exercise a jurisdiction or discretion when the Commissioner has refused to do so. The High Court may then grant mandamus, ordering the Commissioner to perform the duty or to exercise the jurisdiction or discretion. Alternatively, either of these Commissioners (or Commonwealth officers) or a judge of the Family Court of Australia or the Federal Court of Australia (who is also a Commonwealth officer) may go outside limits prescribed by a federal Act or by the Constitution. The High Court may then grant prohibition, preventing the officer from exceeding the authority or jurisdiction. See s 75(v) of the Constitution.

(iv) A constitutional question arises. For instance, South Australia charges a road haulier in a State court with a traffic offence. But the haulier says that he was on an interstate journey at the time, and so he cannot be interfered with because s 92 of the Constitution guarantees freedom for interstate traders. If the cause is removed into the High Court, this Court will then decide whether the haulier has correctly interpreted the Constitution s 92. See s 76(i) of the Constitution. Incidentally, constitutional cases are very often removed into the High Court to be completed there, especially from State courts, and from the Federal Court or Family Court as well.

Of course, constitutional cases can be taken immediately to the High Court, and frequently are.

(v) Some matter arises under a Commonwealth law. An indictable offence (a serious crime) against a Commonwealth law may be tried in the High Court. See s 76(ii) of the Constitution.

But in the last two cases, Nos (iv) and (v), the Commonwealth Constitution itself does not give the High Court the power to hear the cases. Federal Parliament does. It is Parliament's *Judiciary Act 1903*, passed under s 76 of the Constitution, that gives the High Court jurisdiction. In other words, some original jurisdiction is given to the High Court only by a supplementary Act of Parliament; and Parliament can later amend or repeal its Act. But the High Court's other original jurisdiction—that flowing from the Constitution itself, s 75, and instanced in Nos (i), (ii) and (iii) above—cannot be taken away by an ordinary Act of Parliament. Hence Parliament cannot stop the High Court taking jurisdiction over the Commonwealth or its representative or stop the High Court granting mandamus or prohibition against a Commonwealth officer, say, an Industrial Relations Commissioner or a Judge of the Family Court or the Federal Court.

The five cases listed do not have to go to the High Court. They may go to other courts. For example, almost all the cases that arise under Commonwealth Acts, No (v) above, go first to the lower federal courts or to State courts, usually State Supreme Courts.

But among the cases I listed there are instances where the case must go to the High Court, such as where the parties are the Commonwealth and a State or their representatives, and where the parties are two or more States or their representatives. Where an applicant asks for mandamus, prohibition or an injunction against an officer of the Commonwealth, the applicant can, since 1983, go into the Federal Court of Australia; but Industrial Relations Commissioners, Family Court Judges and Coal Industry Tribunal members still come within the High Court's exclusive jurisdiction.

Matters arising directly under a treaty are also within the High Court's exclusive jurisdiction. It is the *Judiciary Act* that deals with the various cases in this paragraph.

remittal proceedings: Since 1983 nearly all the matters in the High Court's exclusive jurisdiction, just given, may be remitted— even on the High Court's own motion, whether the parties like it or not—to the Federal Court or to a State or territorial court. Since 1977 nearly all the matters in the High Court's ordinary original jurisdiction may be remitted, again on the High Court's own motion if necessary, to any federal, State or territorial court, having jurisdiction over the subject matter and the parties.

The result is that the High Court's original jurisdiction has decreased to make way for appellate work and constitutional cases.

3. The Federal Court of Australia, the Family Court of Australia

There are now only two federal courts below the High Court which have been set up permanently by Commonwealth Parliament acting under s 71 and s 77(i) of the Constitution—*the Federal Court of Australia (1977) and the Family Court of Australia (1976)*.

There was at one time a Federal Court of Claims, created by the *Banking Act* 1947. It was to have exclusive jurisdiction over compensation claims by dispossessed banks against the Commonwealth Bank of Australia. However, the Court of Claims was found invalid by the High Court in the *Banking* case (1948) before it got under way. There were also, until recently, two other specialised federal courts; the Bankruptcy Court and the Industrial Court.

The Federal Court of Bankruptcy was created in 1930 by the *Bankruptcy Act* 1928, largely because New South Wales and Victoria protested against the amount of bankruptcy proceedings they had to handle. The Bankruptcy Court was, of course, concerned with bankrupts throughout Australia.

The Australian Industrial Court was so named in 1973. It simply continued in the role of the Commonwealth Industrial Court which had been established in 1956 by the *Conciliation and Arbitration Act* 1956. But since as far back as 1904 a predecessor, the Commonwealth Court of Conciliation and Arbitration, had been established. The Commonwealth Industrial Court arose as a result of the High Court's decision in the *Boilermakers* case

(1956-1957) which I explained in No 1 above, when I spoke of "the separation of powers". The Commonwealth Industrial Court was rather an appendage to the federal industrial machinery, for it backed up the awards made by the Commonwealth Conciliation and Arbitration Commission by interpreting and enforcing them. The Australian Industrial Court had also been given a hotchpotch of other duties. For instance, it could take an appeal from a decision of the Australian Public Service Arbitrator, or it could hear actions and take proceedings under the earlier trade practices legislation.

In 1977 the Federal Court of Australia took over the many functions of the Australian Industrial Court, as well as the specialised function of the Federal Court of Bankruptcy.

The Federal Court of Australia: This is one of the two present federal courts below the High Court.

It was created by the *Federal Court of Australia Act* 1976 (Cth) and began functioning in February 1977. Its Judges sit in the six capital cities, especially in Sydney (the principal registry) and Melbourne, and they sit in Canberra and Darwin. At first there was a Chief Judge with 18 Judges. Now there are about 35 Judges, including the Chief Justice of the Court. All but two of the 19 "foundation" Judges already sat on the old Bankruptcy Court or Industrial Court (or the Australian Capital Territory or Northern Territory Supreme Court).

- That is, the Federal Court of Australia was meant to supplant the former Bankruptcy Court and Industrial Court . . . to become a general federal court below the High Court . . . to relieve the High Court of some of its original jurisdiction arising under federal statutes.

All of this and what follows constitute the Federal Court's own limited jurisdiction. That is, since the 1988 cross-vesting scheme, the Federal Court may exercise a much wider jurisdiction that breaks down the barriers of its own limited jurisdiction; for instance, this wider jurisdiction includes the general jurisdiction now vested in the Federal Court by the six State Parliaments. Yet it is useful to have some idea of the Federal Court's own jurisdiction. It will help you to understand the point of the cross-vesting arrangement. As well, where a proceeding is taken in a State or territorial Supreme Court and, before cross-vesting, the Supreme Court was incapable of taking such a proceeding but the Federal Court was capable, then the Supreme Court may transfer the proceeding to the Federal Court as the more appropriate court.

Besides, there are gaps in the cross-vesting scheme—say criminal matters—and then we need to know the Federal Court's own limited jurisdiction.

divisions: In the Federal Court there are two Divisions, an Industrial Division and a General Division.

The Industrial Division was explained in the Chapter on "the Federal Government", No 2 "Australian Industrial Relations Commission". Briefly, the Industrial Division backs up the Commission and generally exerts judicial control in federal industrial matters. The General Division covers the rest of the cases taken by the Federal Court; many of these cases follow.

cases taken by the Federal Court: Matters arising under federal statutes, whether begun in the Federal Court or on appeal there, are the most common in the Federal Court's own limited jurisdiction. This kind of case does not begin and end as a case under a federal statute. Because of "accrued jurisdiction", such a case may include a claim based on State law or the general law, if the State or general law claim is inseverable from the federal statute claim. In this way the Federal Court acquires jurisdiction over a lot of State or general claims that might have otherwise gone to the State Supreme Courts. I will explain this later: see "jurisdictional conflicts or split proceedings" below.

The Federal Court is particularly occupied with administrative law, that is, particularly occupied with watching the federal bureaucracy by taking points of law (on a reference or by way of an "appeal") from the Administrative Appeals Tribunal, the Copyright Tribunal and other tribunals, and by issuing a judicial order of review against a federal administrative tribunal or official under the *Administrative Decisions (Judicial Review) Act* 1977 (Cth), as explained in the closing pages of the Chapter on "the Federal Government" above. The Federal Court is also particularly occupied with industrial relations law, federal taxation cases, and with restrictive trade practices legislation. The latter legislation now includes popular consumer protection measures and has opened up novel claims and remedies which lawyers are utilising more and more for their clients. The Federal Court takes bankruptcy matters and industrial property matters, viz, copyrights, patents, designs and trade marks.

All these cases raise matters arising under federal statutes, the first kind of cases that the Commonwealth gave to its new Court. Later the Commonwealth gave the Federal Court other kinds of cases.

177

Thus, in 1983-1984 the Commonwealth Parliament gave the Federal Court a supervisory jurisdiction. Here the Federal Court acts as a watchdog over officers of the Commonwealth, broadly federal officials. But Industrial Relations Commissioners, Family Court Judges and Coal Industry Tribunal members are excepted. Since 1984 the Federal Court may have several kinds of cases (which begin in the High Court) remitted to it by the High Court: for example, a case where the Commonwealth or its representative is a party or a case between two States.

appeals: The Federal Court hears appeals from three avenues. (i) Internal appeals, that is, appeals from a single Judge of the Court itself. (ii) Appeals from territorial Supreme Courts (save for the Northern Territory Supreme Court which is, once again, appealable with special leave to the High Court), thereby cutting down the High Court's former appellate load; in these appeals the Federal Court has a general appellate jurisdiction, criminal as well as civil, just like a State Supreme Court. (iii) Appeals from State courts exercising federal jurisdiction in certain cases (such as income tax appeals), but not from the Full Court of a State Supreme Court.

Thus, in the first half dozen years of its existence the Federal Court of Australia grew enormously in size and influence, from about 440 matters commenced in 1977 (apart from bankruptcy) to about twice as many matters commenced in 1982—and its growth has not abated. For instance, since 1984 the Federal Court has had its own set of voluminous law reports. Again the Federal Court began in 1977 with 19 Judges. There are now about 35 Judges. There are also something like 100 Acts which deal with the jurisdiction of the Federal Court of Australia.

The Family Court of Australia: This is the second of the present federal courts below the High Court.

It was created by the *Family Law Act* 1975 (Cth) and began operating in January 1976. It can sit in every State and in the territories. There are about 53 federal Judges (assisted by State Judges in Western Australia, as mentioned below), making it the largest superior court in Australia.

While the Family Court does, indeed, have its own limited jurisdiction, it is also party to the cross-vesting scheme, just as the Federal Court is. Hence my earlier remarks about the Federal Court, its own limited jurisdiction, its much wider jurisdiction because of cross-vesting and, nevertheless, the need to be still aware of the Court's own limited jurisdiction . . . these remarks are apposite here, too.

178

The strange thing about the Commonwealth's Family Court venture is that the Commonwealth Parliament has no simple and direct power "with respect to family law". However, Parliament has two powers which it can make use of: a power with respect to "marriage", and a power with respect to "divorce and matrimonial causes". See s 51(xxi) and s 51(xxii) of the Constitution.

(Parliament can also make use of its not-so-qualified territories power in s 122 but, of course, for family law matters in the territories only.)

"marriage" matters: Under its marriage power Parliament passed the *Marriage Act* 1961. This Act deals with impediments to a valid marriage (which may lead to nullity proceedings in the Family Court) and the form of marriage. But the Act also validly deals with the crime of bigamy, and with the legitimation of a child by a subsequent marriage, as well as the legitimacy of a child in a putative marriage, for these three matters are associated with the act of marrying (*Marriage Act* case 1962).

Furthermore, under its marriage power (its territories power and its divorce power) Parliament passed the *Family Law Act* 1975. Here Parliament, through the Family Court of Australia and to a lesser extent State Magistrates' courts, makes provision for *matters associated with the institution of marriage.*

So the Family Court can make orders for the maintenance of a wife or husband and the maintenance and custody of children, or orders settling what is to be done with the family home. In either case—and this is the point—the Family Court can validly make these orders without going to the length of dissolving or annulling the parties' marriage (*Russell v Russell* 1976). Usually these orders will directly affect those within the marriage circle: for instance, the Family Court makes a custody order for the mother against the father in respect of the child of their marriage. However, third parties may also be affected (*Dowal v Murray* 1978). For instance, the Family Court can make an order for the wife and children against the husband and father requiring the exclusive possession of the matrimonial home for the wife and children, even if this means that the husband's parents must also vacate the home.

Notice that the Family Court of Australia—and this is its great weakness—is restricted to "marriage" (leaving divorce aside for a while).

The Family Court cannot in its own limited jurisdiction wind up a company or appoint a receiver of a partnership's assets just because the sole shareholders or partners happen to be husband and wife. It cannot deal with an infant's contract or a child delinquent just because a child is involved. It cannot deal with a de facto "marriage". It cannot deal with an ex-nuptial child of one of the parties to a marriage, even if the child was born during the marriage and has become an ordinary member of the household. Such a child is not a child of both parties to the marriage, by birth, adoption or legitimation. Companies, partnerships, infants' contracts, child delinquency, ex-nuptial children, neglected children, State wards . . . none of these matters comes within the Family Court's own limited jurisdiction.

"divorce and matrimonial causes": The Family Court of Australia also takes proceedings for divorce or annulment of a marriage, and here the Court has a wider control over property. When it deals with the economic consequences that arise out of the break up of a marriage because of divorce or annulment, the Family Court can make orders in respect of the separate property of either party, as well as their joint or "marriage" property.

Under the *Family Law Act* the Family Court takes the following three classes of cases: (i) Matrimonial causes, that is, divorce proceedings and nullity suits, maintenance of a wife or a husband, settlement of property as between a husband and wife, access to and custody of children of a marriage. In practice the Family Court does not really spend a great deal of its time on divorce proceedings and nullity suits: these are readily disposed of. The Court spends an enormous amount of time on property declarations and alterations, a fair amount of time on access and custody applications. (ii) Matters under the federal *Marriage Act*. (iii) Matters associated with the two matters I have just enumerated.

The Family Court of Western Australia: Western Australia has agreed with the Federal Government to run its own "Family Court of Western Australia". It is a special court at Supreme Court level, taking federal *and State* jurisdictions. And this is its virtue. There is no danger of the split proceedings which I will now examine.

Jurisdictional conflicts or split proceedings: Before leaving the Commonwealth's "own" courts, I should advert to a disadvantage—indeed, a pitfall—arising from these federal courts, as long as each is acting within the confines of its own limited jurisdiction. Precisely because they are federal creations, the Federal Court and the Family Court have specialised jurisdictions.

Assume a part-federal-part-State case arises in a particular set of circumstances. Should this mixed case be taken to one of the federal courts or to one of the State courts?

For example, one party has a federal trade practices matter and a related contract matter: does the plaintiff go to the Federal Court of Australia or to the State court? A second party wants custody of a child of his marriage with the respondent and a child of his household: does he go to the Family Court of Australia or to his State Supreme Court to get a custody order for both children? A third party in the Federal Court of Australia on appeal has come up from a State Supreme Court which took a case on a trade marks claim with a passing-off claim: the first claim is a federal matter, the second a State matter. Does the appellant argue both claims in the Federal Court? Alternatively, does each of these three parties split the case, taking the federal element to a federal court, the State element to a State court?

Thus arises the drawback of the Commonwealth with its limited jurisdictional powers venturing into the judicial system—namely, split proceedings or overlapping jurisdictions.

The High Court resolved the problem, but only partly (*Fencott v Muller* 1983, *Phillip Morris* 1981). If the State element (for example, the contract) is "inseverable" from the federal element (for example, the trade practice) or, to put it another way, if the State and federal elements are supported by "a common substratum of facts", then the federal court can take the whole matter, exercising its "accrued jurisdiction" over the State element. But not otherwise, for then the State element must go to a State court, the federal element to a federal court, unless a State court happens to have been given jurisdiction over the federal element.

The last remark reveals that much of this jurisdictional conflict was self-inflicted.

The Commonwealth created the Family Court in 1975, the Federal Court in 1976, each with its many exclusive jurisdictions. Unlike the United States, the Commonwealth could have invested the jurisdictions in the State courts. See the Family Court of Western Australia above and especially the material that follows in No 4 below. Or the Commonwealth could have left things as they were in the pre-1975-1976 days.

Cross-vesting of jurisdiction: Because of the jurisdictional conflicts or split proceedings just explained, a 1984 committee of the Australian Constitutional Convention proposed a scheme to cross-vest jurisdiction between federal and State courts. This vesting of State jurisdiction in the two lower federal courts (the main objective really) and the vesting of a wider federal jurisdiction in the State courts (the trade off) was supported by a transfer-of-proceeding provision as between these courts, that is, a proceeding in one court was to be transferred to the appropriate court, State or federal.

"Jurisdiction" or "proceeding" here refers to the kind of case a particular court can take, and "the two lower federal courts" are the Federal Court and the Family Court of Australia (each lower than the High Court). The cross-vesting legislation came into force in the Commonwealth, the six States and the Northern Territory, and territories generally, in July 1988. See, for instance, the *Jurisdiction of Courts (Cross-vesting) Act* 1987 (Cth) or the New South Wales of Victorian Act with the same title.

Thus, the two elements in this Australia-wide arrangement became in broad outline:

- *A cross-vesting of jurisdiction* between the two lower federal courts and between the State and territorial Supreme Courts, and a cross-vesting between the federal courts themselves and between the Supreme Courts themselves.

- *A transfer of a proceeding* from one of these courts to a more appropriate court within the scheme, or a transfer that is otherwise in the interests of justice.

The details are legion. I will list half a dozen. The courts involved are the two lower federal courts—the Federal Court of Australia and the Family Court of Australia—the Family Court of Western Australia, as well as the State and territorial Supreme Courts. There is vesting from the State sphere to the federal and territorial sphere, and vice versa. There is also vesting within each sphere, that is, there is cross-vesting between the two lower federal courts, between the six State Supreme Courts, and between the territorial Supreme Courts. The vesting is in civil matters, not criminal.

These matters, however, come from different sources, federal, territorial, or this or that State source. Therefore, there are still various laws coming from different sources to be applied, even if jurisdiction now seems to be common to the different courts because of the scheme.

Some matters are outside the scheme altogether, such as federal industrial relations and secondary boycotts. Other matters are called "special federal matters", for instance, federal administrative law matters and most restrictive trade practices matters. A State or territorial Supreme Court must transfer a special federal matter to the Federal Court, or in certain cases to the Family Court or the Northern Territory Supreme Court, unless the Supreme Court exercises its option to keep the matter in the Supreme Court.

Each court in the scheme retains its own traditional jurisdiction in the sense that, if a proceeding is taken into court A when there is a more appropriate court elsewhere, then court A may transfer the pending proceeding to the more appropriate court. A transfer may also be made in the interests of justice.

To give one example: the Federal Court of Australia can now take a claim for damages for misleading conduct under the federal *Trade Practices Act* with a claim for deceit under the general law, both claims supported by a common substratum of facts, and—and this is the point—an additional, separate claim (not arising under that set of facts) for a State statutory charge or for a breach of contract between the parties. Another example: the Family Court of Australia can now grant a maintenance application by a mother against the father for the children of their marriage and, in addition—again this is the point—for an ex-nuptial child of the mother that was a member of their household.

The upshot is: Broadly, the Federal Court of Australia and the Family Court of Australia (the High Court stands outside the scheme), each retains its own limited jurisdiction, its specialised jurisdiction in certain matters only, as I explained when dealing with each court. But since the cross-vesting scheme of 1988, the jurisdiction of the Federal Court and the Family Court has become enlarged by the addition of a general jurisdiction in State matters which State Parliaments have vested in these two federal courts; the Federal Court and the Family Court have also received another general jurisdiction in territorial matters which Commonwealth Parliament has vested in these courts.

As a result, for the most part a litigant can now go safely through the door of the Federal Court or the Family Court (or a State or territorial Supreme Court) without being ejected because of a conflict of jurisdiction between this court and some other court. At worst, the whole proceeding, and not a split proceeding, may be transferred to another court.

4. State courts used by the Commonwealth

The State courts, referred to in s 77(iii) of the Constitution and used by the Commonwealth as its judicial agents, retain their own judges and officers. They keep their own organisations. Their running remains a State matter. The Commonwealth cannot interfere with all that. So the Commonwealth was not permitted by the High Court in 1929 (*Le Mesurier v Connor*) to inject into the personnel of the Western Australian Supreme Court a Commonwealth-seconded officer as a Registrar in Bankruptcy. Neither was the Commonwealth permitted in 1976 (*Russell v Russell*) to require State courts, in federal matrimonial proceedings, to act as closed courts as a general rule.

But the Commonwealth is allowed by s 77(iii) of the Constitution to give some matters to a State court, that is, to invest a State court with federal jurisdiction. And the State court then has authority to hear these matters and dispose of them for the Commonwealth, say, matters between residents of different States, or matters involving the interpretation of a section in the Constitution, or matters under a federal statute.

In the United States there is a whole separate system of general *federal* courts, namely, the circuit courts of appeals and the federal district courts. These courts are used by Congress as its judicial agents. (Quite independently of this federal system there is a State system of courts, too, for State law in the main.) In Australia, however, there is no separate system of general federal courts. Instead, the existing State courts have been used by Commonwealth Parliament for its own purposes, ever since the *Judiciary Act* 1903. Thus, the State courts throughout Australia now serve two distinct purposes:

- If a person is prosecuted under a State Crimes Act the State court acts under the authority of the State. It exercises State jurisdiction.

- If another person is prosecuted, but this time under the Federal Crimes Act, the *same* State court now acts under the authority of the Commonwealth.

Federal jurisdiction is the name given to this kind of authority which Commonwealth Parliament grants to State courts. It is an authority to judge, given by the Federal Parliament to State courts in certain Commonwealth matters.

These special matters I listed at the beginning of this Chapter when I spoke of "special jurisdictions". For example, a New South Wales creditor may take an action to recover a debt from a Victorian in a New South Wales Local Court. This Court will then be exercising federal jurisdiction. Or, suppose a Tasmanian police officer charges a road haulier driving through Tasmania with a traffic offence. When the road haulier appears before a Tasmanian Court of Petty Sessions, the haulier says he cannot be charged because he was on an interstate journey. That is, he claims to be free from interference because of the guarantee for interstate traders in s 92 of the Constitution. The road haulier's defence raises federal jurisdiction.

And when a State court is exercising federal jurisdiction, the consequences are: (i) An appeal from the lowest State court can be taken directly to the High Court although, it is true, only by special leave. (ii) The cause in the State court may be removed, without waiting for a decision, into the High Court. (iii) The State court can exercise judicial powers only.

The Judiciary Act 1903 is the Commonwealth law that grants federal jurisdiction to the New South Wales Local Court and to the Tasmanian Court of Petty Sessions, just instanced. The *Judiciary Act* lays down certain conditions for State courts acting for the Commonwealth but, generally, the Act simply accepts existing State jurisdictions and procedures. Thus, a party with a civil action—say, the New South Wales creditor—must take his matter to a State Local Court because it is a civil action between private parties and because the debt is not large. But a prosecution—say, the charge against the road haulier in Tasmania—is taken to a Court of Petty Sessions because it is a criminal matter and because it is a minor offence.

The *Judiciary Act* also tells parties when they go on appeal from a State court to the High Court. The New South Wales creditor or the road haulier in Tasmania can both go directly from the State court mentioned to the High Court itself (if the High Court gives them special leave to appeal). They do not have to go first to the State Supreme Court in New South Wales or in Tasmania.

As well as the *Judiciary Act*, there are many other federal Acts which deal with State courts and the Commonwealth's use of these courts.

For example, the federal *Family Law Act* 1975 gives jurisdiction to a State Supreme Court in the full range of matrimonial causes if the State government agrees, as Western Australia (alone) has agreed. The Act also gives minor matrimonial causes to State Magistrates' Courts, such as custody, access and maintenance applications, but not divorce or nullity suits. The *Trade Practices Act* 1974 gives jurisdiction to State courts in certain consumer protection matters under this Act; and State Supreme Courts take cases on copyrights, patents, designs and trade marks, all dealt with in federal Acts.

And now, since the federal *Jurisdiction of Courts (Cross-vesting) Act* 1987, State Supreme Courts have picked up a wider federal jurisdiction. See the explanation in "cross-vesting of jurisdiction" immediately before this present heading, No 4.

The "Special Federal Court", incidentally, which sits in Sydney, is not really a federal court at all. It is simply a State Local Court composed of a magistrate, but the court exercises only federal jurisdiction. This State magistrate takes such federal matters as import or drug prosecutions under the Commonwealth's *Customs Act* 1901, or the magistrate takes minor tax prosecutions under the various federal taxation laws.

In all these cases—under the *Judiciary Act*, the *Family Law Act*, the *Customs Act* and the rest—the Commonwealth is making use of the State courts as its judicial agents, although they remain State courts. And the Commonwealth is authorised to do so by the express provision in the Constitution, s 77(iii).

> "The Parliament may create Federal Courts, and over them and their organisation it has ample power. But the Courts of a State are the judicial organs of another Government. They are created by State law; their existence depends upon State law."

> "The phrase 'Federal jurisdiction' . . . means jurisdiction derived from the Federal Commonwealth . . . it denotes the power to act as the judicial agent of the Commonwealth."

Thus the Commonwealth makes great use of the State courts as its agents, especially in recent years (say, 1973 on) for matters arising under the Commonwealth Acts.

The courts are still State courts and they act as ordinary State courts, but they deal with Commonwealth matters, and they exercise federal jurisdiction.

The Privy Council is not of course a federal court, but I am dealing with it here for convenience. Australian litigants used to appeal from the High Court and from State courts, especially State Supreme Courts, to the Privy Council in London. Since 1968 things have radically changed.

(i) *As regards the High Court and the Privy Council*: There is now only one matter that can go from the High Court to the Privy Council, and even this is in the realm of theory. An "inter se question"—a question dealing with the powers of the Commonwealth vis à vis the States or with the powers of the States as between themselves—can still be taken to the Privy Council, if the High Court gives its certificate under s 74 of the Constitution. In October 1912 the High Court gave its one and only certificate: the Royal Commissions case (*Colonial Sugar Refining Co v Attorney-General*). Since an inter se question is peculiarly within the expertise of the High Court, the Court is not likely to allow the question to go abroad again.

As for the rest, the *Privy Council (Limitation of Appeals) Act* 1968 stopped appeals in federal matters, and the *Privy Council (Appeals from the High Court) Act* 1975 stopped appeals in other matters. So these Commonwealth Acts in combination have now ended the one or two appeals that used to be taken to the Privy Council from the High Court each year.

(ii) *As regards the State Supreme Courts and the Privy Council*: Appeals on purely State matters, for example, on State legislation, criminal law, property or contracts, were still being taken to the Privy Council in 1985-1986 under the *Judicial Committee Acts* 1833 and 1844 (Imp) and Orders-in-Council. The *Australia Acts* 1986 (Cth & UK) repealed those Acts and Orders in regard to Australian courts, and expressly abolished appeals to the Privy Council.

The overall result: no appeals are now taken from Australian courts to the Privy Council.

The States

If you look at the Commonwealth Constitution and the States you will not find much written on the States. *State institutions—their Parliaments, Governments and Courts—are pretty well not described at all by the Commonwealth Constitution. Neither are State powers.*

In the first place, s 106 of the Commonwealth Constitution insists that the Constitutions of the former six Colonies shall continue even after Federation, subject only to the Commonwealth Constitution. And, in the second place, s 107 of the Commonwealth Constitution insists that the parliamentary powers of the former six Colonies shall continue along the following lines: unless the Constitution has made a power an exclusive Commonwealth power or unless the Constitution has taken away a power from the States, the State Parliaments shall continue to have all the powers they already had as Colonial Parliaments before Federation.

> "The powers of the States were left unaffected by the Constitution except in so far as the contrary was expressly provided; subject to that each State remained sovereign within its own sphere. The powers of the State within those limits are as plenary as are the powers of the Commonwealth."

> "By s 107 (of the Constitution) every State power is saved unless it is exclusively vested in the Commonwealth or withdrawn from the Parliament of the State."

- Thus, we look to the States' own Constitutions to see what powers the States have.
- We look to the Commonwealth Constitution only to see what State powers have been cut down.

---

1. Constitutional history

The merest school child knows that Captain James Cook landed on the east coast of Australia in 1770; that Britain, having lost its American colonies, now looked to this outpost, New South Wales (as Cook called the whole of eastern Australia), for placing its convicts; and that Governor Arthur Phillip came to these new parts in 1788 to run a penal settlement. On 26 January, "Australia Day", 1788 Governor Phillip raised the Union Flag (the St George cross with St Andrew's cross) at Sydney Cove and took possession of eastern Australia on behalf of His Majesty the King, George III.

I say Governor Phillip "took possession . . . on behalf of His Majesty" because in those days the continent was regarded in international law as "terra nullius", literally the land of no one, as though the land was largely uninhabited, and therefore could be freely claimed by Phillip for the King's beneficial ownership. The continent might have been regarded instead as inhabited land, and therefore could be claimed only by conquest or cession. The High Court has now decided that the notion of terra nullius was built on false premises and that, in 1788, the indigenous people held what we might call land titles in their several communities, according to their law or custom (*Mabo's* case 1992). (Consequently, the Meriam people, including Mabo, were entitled to the possession etc of the Murray Islands off Queensland, since their native law or custom gave them that title, and Queensland had not extinguished it.)

From 1788 to pre-Federation days, cairns marking colonial constitutional progress are placed at—

- 1788-1823 — the Governors rule in New South Wales.

- 1823-1825 — New South Wales gains a Legislative Council (1823), and later an Executive Council (1825); both institutions are established to advise the Governors.

- 1842-1850s— some elected members get into the Legislative Councils of New South Wales (Australian Constitutions Act No 1, 1842), Van Diemen's Land, South Australia, Western Australia and Victoria (Australian Constitutions Act No 2, 1850).

- 1855-1890 — Constitutions and self-government are granted to New South Wales, Victoria, Tasmania, South Australia (1855-1856), Queensland (1859) and Western Australia (1890).

Between 1788 to 1823 the Governors of New South Wales ran a tight ship, seen for the most part as a convict ship.

For those 35 years the Governors ruled the Colony like local monarchs—Phillip, Hunter, King, Bligh and, from 1810-1821, Lachlan Macquarie. Relying as much on royal prerogative as on Imperial law, the Governor legislated, adjudicated, governed. You should appreciate there was no local legislature or, until 1814, no Supreme Court, no Executive Council—none of these restraining institutions. In detail, the Governor issued proclamations and "government orders", imposed taxation without representation or parliamentary consent, established and interfered with law courts, civil as well as criminal, took appeals from the Judge-Advocate and the Supreme Court, appointed civil servants, handed out land grants, maintained the New South Wales Corps (1790-1809) or an armed force, not just for defence but also for law and order.

In 1823 the penal settlement became a civil colony when an Imperial Act, known as the New South Wales Act (4 Geo IV, ch 96), established a *Legislative* Council to advise the Governor, but not to overrule him, in making laws. The Legislative Council, however, consisted of nominees of the Crown, at first five, later seven; the Crown acted through a Secretary of State in England or a Governor in the colony. As well as this legislative advancement there was an administrative advancement. In 1825 Governor Darling had an *Executive* Council inflicted on him, under instructions from the Imperial authorities. The new body comprised four Councillors: the Lieutenant-Governor, the Chief Justice, the Archdeacon and the Colonial Secretary. These advised the Governor, not that he had to follow their advice.

Representative government—both in the legislature and in the Executive—came later.

The 1823 Imperial Act, the New South Wales Act, is the genesis of two grants that still distinguish the States from the Commonwealth.

• On law-making, the 1823 Act conferred power on the Governor, advised by the Legislature Council, "to make laws . . . for the peace, welfare, and good government" of New South Wales and Van Diemen's Land, but not laws repugnant to English laws. This wide power has come down to the six States, but now State laws repugnant to English laws are possible, although only since the Australia Acts of 1986. See "4. the powers and limits of State Parliament" below.

• On judicial power, the 1823 Act authorised the constitution of two new Supreme Courts. A Charter of Justice, known as "the Third Charter of Justice", relied on the authority, and set up separate Supreme Courts in New South Wales and Van Diemen's Land. These Supreme Courts were to have general jurisdiction over "all pleas . . . and jurisdiction in all cases whatsoever . . . (just as in Her) Majesty's Courts . . . at Westminster", London. This wide power, too, has come down to the six States, and was later amplified. See "6. courts" below.

New South Wales thereafter mothered three colonies: Tasmania, Victoria and Queensland. That is, a slice of territory was cut off New South Wales in 1825 to become Van Diemen's Land. (It was officially named Tasmania from January 1856.) Next, another slice of territory, to be called "Victoria", was separated from the mother colony by an 1850 Imperial Act proclaimed in force in 1851, the Australian Constitutions Act No 2. Lastly, the third slice of territory, to be called "Queensland", parted from New South Wales under letters patent of 1859.

The remaining two Colonies were founded independently. Western Australia started out in 1826, but was not formally claimed by Britain until its 1829 Act provided "for the Government of Her Majesty's settlement of Western Australia". South Australia was colonised by an 1834 Imperial Act, the Colonisation Act: and a settlement was there in 1836 when it was known as the "Province of South Australia".

> These six Colonies became the six "Original States" in the Commonwealth when it was established on 1 January 1901. See covering clause VI of the Constitution. No States have been added since, although since July 1978 Northern Territory is on the way to statehood.

An 1828 Imperial Act, the Australian Courts Act (9 Geo IV, ch 83), supplied the colonial courts with an instant and adaptable law library. The Act provided that "all laws and statutes", then in force in England, should be applied in the courts of New South Wales and Van Diemen's Land, "so far as the same can be applied within the said Colonies". Such "received" laws could be amended locally; see, for instance, the Imperial Acts Application Act of Queensland (1984) or of New South Wales (1969) which repealed these kinds of English laws. (Other English laws "extending to the colony", that is, made applicable to the Colonies/States, could not be repealed until after the Australia Acts of 1986, see below.)

In addition, the 1828 Imperial Act allowed a larger Legislative Council. But this incipient law-making body was still composed of Crown nominees, not members elected by the people. Representative government had not yet arrived.

The next staging post in the constitutional progress of the Colonies was the expansion of the 1823 Legislative Council in New South Wales. An Imperial Act of 1842, "An Act for the Government of New South Wales and Van Diemen's Land" (the Australian Constitutions Act No 1, 5 & 6 Vic ch 76), permitted 24 *elected* representatives in the Council which was now enlarged to 36 members.

At this point you can identify certain basic constitutional doctrines expressly found in the 1842 Act. "No taxation without representation" . . . that is, the newly constituted people's institution was to make laws, including the taxation laws. "The financial initiative of the Crown" . . . that is, the Governor must first recommend to the legislature the specific purpose to which public money was to be appropriated. "Parliament controls the expenditure of public money" . . . that is, an appropriation of (most) revenue must be made by the legislature, and in no other manner.

But there was still only one House and it was one-third nominated. In addition, the Governor was in effect the Premier, in effect the head of Government and resident head of State rolled in one; and a Minister's tenure depended solely on Crown pleasure, not on the confidence of the Legislative Council.

Nevertheless, for the first time in Australia a mild form of representative government, if not responsible government, went into action. The 1842 Act was proclaimed in force in the following year, and Australians voted at their first general elections in June-July 1843.

As the other colonies were hived off New South Wales or founded independently, they too at first received *nominated* Legislative Councils, their embryonic law-making bodies: Van Diemen's Land in 1825, Western Australia in 1830, South Australia in 1842 and Victoria in 1851. The Moreton Bay district (Queensland) was yoked to New South Wales until 1859. Then, like New South Wales under the 1842 Act (the Australian Constitutions Act No 1, given above), Van Diemen's Land, South Australia, Western Australia and Victoria progressed, not all at the same time, to a two-thirds *elective* Legislative Council under "An Act for the better Government of Her Majesty's Australian Colonies" 1850 (the Australian Constitutions Act No 2, 13 & 14 Vic ch 59). The Moreton Bay district (Queensland) was still the exception: from 1843 to 1859 it elected representatives to the New South Wales Legislative Council.

You can see a pattern in the constitutional evolution of the Australian Colonies in the nineteenth century that reflects the people's constitutional struggle in England in the seventeenth century—the people gradually wresting from the Crown the power to make law and the power to raise taxes and expend public money.

Thus, in the beginning, the Governor of a Colony was assisted by a Legislative Council. This began as a nominated body, nominated by the overseas Secretary of State or by the local Governor. Often the nominees were officials, at times subordinates of the Crown. Then the nominated members were outweighed by 2:1 by elected members. Not that these were elected on a wide democratic basis; for instance, voters did not include emancipists or people who did not have a stipulated property qualification. In time the Council became wholly elective. It was this body that assisted the Governor: first by advice or even persuasion, later by directive.

It was this body, the Legislative Council, that progressively took over from the Governor—that is, took away from the Crown, as occurred in England in the seventeenth century—the power to make law and the power to raise taxes and control expenditure.

Whence our constitutional monarchy. Certainly an hereditary *monarchy* represented by the Governor (or the Governor-General) appears, or is assumed, in the six State Constitutions (as well as in the Commonwealth Constitution), principally in the provisions on the Executive, less so in the provisions on Parliament. But ours is a *constitutional* monarchy—that is, a system of government in which the Crown is not the head of government running the country, only the head of State, a system of government in which the Crown does not exercise absolute power, only limited power under the Constitution. For instance, and especially, the Crown is advised by its Ministers who are answerable, through Parliament, to the people.

As the government institutions evolved, the Colonies grew towards independence, and they were encouraged by the Australian Constitutions Act No 2, mentioned above. This 1850 Imperial Act authorised the Legislative Councils to make their own constitutions, New South Wales at once, the other Colonies in time or when they had Legislative Councils.

Hence the Legislative Councils in New South Wales, Victoria, South Australia and Van Diemen's Land in the mid 1850s and in Western Australia in the late 1880s drafted Constitutions. These were sent off to the Colonial Office in England for approval, and then to the Queen for her assent: see the *Tasmanian Constitution Act* 1855 (Tas) and the *South Australian Constitution Act (No 2)* 1855-1856 (SA). Because New South Wales and Victoria exceeded their authority in the 1850 Act, their Constitutions were exonerated by a later Imperial Act: see the *New South Wales Constitution Act* 1855 (Imp) or the *Victorian Constitution Act* 1855 (Imp), both enacted on the same day, and containing the local Constitution as a schedule to the Imperial Act. The Western Australian Constitution of 1889 was also encased in an Imperial Act: see the *Western Australia Constitution Act* 1890 (UK). Queensland was to receive its Constitution in an Order-in-Council of 1859.

So, the State Constitutions were essentially home grown, even if monitored by the Imperial authorities and, in four instances, contained in Imperial Acts or Instruments. Later the Commonwealth Constitution would also be drafted in Australia, and found in a schedule to an Imperial Act.

Responsible and self government was effected by the Acts and Order just listed: for Tasmania, New South Wales and Victoria in 1855, South Australia 1855-1856, Queensland 1859, Western Australia 1890. Responsible and self government actually arrived with a Premier as follows: for Victoria in November 1855, New South Wales June 1856, South Australia October 1856, Tasmania November 1856, Queensland December 1859 and Western Australia December 1890.

In each instance the Colonies sought and received three components of independence:

- a bicameral legislature
- an elective legislature, at least in the Lower House
- responsible government or, at any rate, the beginnings of a cabinet system: the Governor's commissioned advisers were also Ministers of State and these sat in the legislature where they could be made answerable to Parliament.

Parliament was opened or first sat—that is, as a bicameral body—in New South Wales in May 1856 (the earlier Legislative Council held its first session in August 1824, the first in Australia); in Victoria, November 1856; in Tasmania, December 1856; in South Australia, April 1857; in Queensland, May 1860; and in Western Australia, December 1890.

At Federation on 1 January 1901 the former Colonies became States, keeping their Constitutions, laws, powers, Houses of Parliament, courts and governments. However, some of their laws might be pre-empted in time by the new Commonwealth's laws, some of their powers were lost to the new Commonwealth Government and, generally, the States became subject to the provisions in the Commonwealth Constitution. See "4. the powers and limits of State Parliament" below.

The coming of the Federation, and so a continuation of the constitutional history just given, appears in the Chapter on "how the Constitution was made".

2. Constitutional documents and their alteration

The constitutional documents of a State consist of, not just a State Constitution, but also such laws as the Australia Acts, a Supreme Court Act and perhaps a Charter of Justice, an Electoral Act, an Officials in Parliament Act and so on, as well as the Commonwealth Constitution, and recent Letters Patent. Documents such as these are the source material for a State's institutions of government, a State's powers, functions and officers. Conventions, not found in documents, play a part too, say the parliamentary control of public money or responsible government.

The Constitutions of the States are now found in some main document which has been subsequently added to. Here I will list only the basic Act or Acts without mentioning later amendments some of which go into the 1990s. Thus, there is the *Constitution Act* 1902 (NSW) . . . the *Constitution Act* 1975 (Vic) . . . the *Constitution Act* 1934 (Tas) together with the *Australian Constitutions Act (No 2)* 1850 (Imp); the latter Act gives Tasmania its general law-making power . . . the *Constitution Act* 1934 (SA) . . . the *Constitution Act* 1867 (Qld) . . . the local *Constitution Act* 1889 (brought into force by the Imperial *Constitution Act* 1890) and the *Constitution Acts Amendment Act* 1899 (WA).

The Australia Acts 1986 (Cth & UK)—the Commonwealth Act appears at the back of the book—severed the Imperial connection with the States. These Acts accomplished for the States what the *Statute of Westminster* 1931 (Imp) did for the Commonwealth, and more. (On the Statute and the Commonwealth, see the Chapter on "the powers of Federal Parliament", No 1.)

In 1985 each of the six States passed an Australia Acts (Request) Act addressed to the Commonwealth and United Kingdom Parliaments. The "request" sought from each Parliament an Australia Act, broadly to grant greater autonomy to the States. The two Parliaments then passed their respective Australia Act (Cth & UK) simultaneously, and both laws came in force on 3 March 1986. Why the need for the two near-matching Acts? There was doubt about the use of the Commonwealth power (s 51(xxxviii) of the Constitution) and, on the other hand, the assured use of the United Kingdom power to break United Kingdom ties with the States.

The resultant law, like a "rigid" constitution, cannot be simply amended or repealed by the Commonwealth or the States; and it cannot be overridden by a repugnant Commonwealth law. Any amendment or repeal must, according to the Australia Acts themselves, be done by a Commonwealth Act that has been requested, or concurred in, by "the Parliaments of all the States". However, the Australia Acts leave the door open for the Commonwealth Parliament to initiate a s 128 referendum to gain a federal power to amend or repeal the Acts; then the State Parliaments need not be consulted, and only four States need agree to pass the referendum.

The effect of the Commonwealth-United Kingdom exercise was to liberate the States from their (to me, largely theoretical) subjection to United Kingdom power. So, the following ties were undone.

• *The legislative link was broken*. No United Kingdom Act henceforth extends to a State (or to the Commonwealth or a territory, for that matter). That takes care of United Kingdom Acts "passed after the commencement of this (Australia) Act". As for Acts passed before "this Act", a State is given power to override such Acts: see below. A State has "full power" to make laws for the peace, order and good government of the State that have—and this is the point—an extra-territorial operation. Further, a State is now given "all legislative powers" that the United Kingdom Parliament might have exercised before 1986 for the peace, order and good government of that State, but the State does not gain thereby an external affairs power. The *Colonial Laws Validity Act* 1865 (Imp), which used to invalidate a State law repugnant to Imperial laws "extending to the Colony", was repealed; and, for the future, a State law may override Imperial laws extending to a State.

But a State cannot use any of those three powers (on extra-territorial matters, United Kingdom matters and repugnant matters) so as to affect the Commonwealth Constitution, the Australia Acts or the Statute of Westminster.

The Australia Acts had more to do with United Kingdom-State relations than with Commonwealth-State relations. Hence, the Acts take care to warn that the Commonwealth Constitution is not affected by any new State powers gained under the Acts. So the division of powers between the Commonwealth and the States remains, as do constitutional prohibitions. Likewise, State manner-and-form provisions (examples are given below) are bolstered by the Australia Acts; similar provisions, Imperial as well as State, used to be made effective by the Colonial Laws Validity Act, now repealed by the Australia Acts.

• *The executive link was broken.* All powers and functions formerly exercised by the Queen in regard to a State (for example, common law Royal prerogative powers) are exercised only by the Governor of a State, except the power to appoint or dismiss a Governor, unless the Queen is personally present in the State (when she may, for example, open Parliament or assent to a bill). Furthermore, the Governor's powers used to be limited by the State Constitution, the Governor's Commission and Instructions; now those powers are equated to the Crown's plenary powers in regard to the State. The Governor, in other words, has become more like a plenipotent viceroy than a subordinate delegate of the Crown. In a State matter (such as the power to appoint or dismiss a State Governor) the Queen is advised directly by a State Premier, not by a United Kingdom Minister, the Secretary of State for Foreign and Commonwealth Affairs, as was the case.

A bill assented to by the Governor cannot be disallowed by the Queen. The Governor can no longer be required by any law or instrument to withhold assent to any bill, or reserve certain bills for the Queen's pleasure; the latter was prescribed by the *Australian States Constitution Act* 1907 (UK).

In short, the United Kingdom Government "shall have no responsibility for the government of any State" or, to put it another way, the United Kingdom Government has surrendered its former powers over any State.

• *The judicial link was broken.* All appeals to the Privy Council are abolished from any Australian court. The High Court is excepted, but it has its own provisions ending appeals to the Privy Council, save appeals on inter se questions.

But you must not think of the Australia Acts as something negative, merely breaking State links with the United Kingdom. The Acts were a positive exercise. Think, for instance, of the conceded plenitude of State law-making, as ample as that of the United Kingdom Parliament, going as far as the power to override United Kingdom Acts extending to the State. Think, too, of the Governor's elevation in State affairs, and the Premier's direct contact with the Queen in State matters.

Thus, the Australia Acts are charters of State autonomy, as well as part of its constitutional law.

Alterations of the Constitutions: The Commonwealth Constitution has a special provision dealing with alterations to this Constitution: s 128. But the States, when amending their Constitutions, rely on a general provision, the ordinary law-making power to make laws for the peace, welfare and good government of the State (*Clayton v Heffron* 1960). This "ordinary law-making power" is explained in "4. the powers and limits of State Parliament" below.

Generally the State Constitutions can be amended easily: they are flexible Constitutions. For instance, Queensland's Constitution Act was once impliedly—one suspects unwittingly—amended by an ordinary Act, the *Industrial Arbitration Act* 1916 (allowing a seven year term appointment of judges) that was found to be inconsistent with the earlier *Constitution Act* 1867 (prescribing a life appointment of judges). The Privy Council upheld the amendment, explaining that the Queensland Constitution was an "uncontrolled" Constitution (*McCawley v R* 1920).

But in certain parts of its Constitution a State Constitution becomes a "controlled" Constitution. You recall that the whole of the Commonwealth Constitution is a controlled Constitution since s 128 of this Constitution prescribes a general "manner-and-form provision" (explained below) for altering any section of the Constitution: there's to be no amendment unless there is an absolute majority vote in Parliament followed by a referendum. Similarly, but for designated sections only which are regarded as critical sections in a Constitution, the States enact from time to time a special manner-and-form provision. Thereby certain parts of the State Constitution become a controlled Constitution. (Thereby too—indeed, this is the point—those controlled parts now become protected against ill-considered amendment.)

In 1992 a Victorian Act, in effect, directed the Supreme Court to accept certain documents as binding between Collingwood Council and a football club; the documents were then being reviewed by the Court for enforceability. Now, firstly, this interference with the Court's jurisdiction was contrary to the Victorian Constitution but, as a general rule, the Parliament could amend the Constitution simply by an ordinary Act. However, secondly, the Constitution prescribed a special manner-and-form provision (about certain parliamentary majorities) for amendments in this area, and the Parliament had not followed the procedure. The upshot: the Act was invalid (*Collingwood City v Victoria* 1993).

A manner-and-form provision may stipulate the prerequisite of the electors' approval in a referendum and/or an absolute majority or a two-thirds majority vote in the legislature, or some such restrictive condition, before a particular constitutional provision can be altered. The manner-and-form provision itself is usually safeguarded by an "entrenched clause", that is, a clause which imposes the restrictive condition on any alteration of the manner-and-form provision.

On top of this, there is now a fundamental law that backs up certain manner-and-form provisions, although not all manner-and-form provisions.

The fundamental law used to be the *Colonial Laws Validity Act* 1865 (Imp), but this has now been repealed by the *Australia Acts* 1986 (Cth & UK), explained above. The 1986 Acts, however, went on to dictate that henceforth a State law on "the constitution, powers or procedure of the Parliament" must follow any existing State manner-and-form provision—such as a State law on altering the term of Parliament, abolishing an Upper House, expanding or limiting Parliament's law-making powers or requiring a special kind of quorum or majority in Parliament's proceedings. There is, it seems, another fundamental law, this time backing up manner-and-form provisions found in a State Constitution that deal with an alteration to "the Constitution of the State": see s 106 of the Commonwealth Constitution which guarantees the continuance of a State Constitution until it is altered, but "in accordance with the Constitution of the State" (*Wilsmore v Western Australia* 1981).

In April 1979 New South Wales inserted in its Constitution five entrenched manner-and-form provisions on compulsory voting and method of voting, Legislative Assembly electorates and elections; and in December 1991 it enacted a special manner-and-form law, this time on a fixed term for the 1991-1995 Assembly, except in certain circumstances. Hardly a democratic exercise, for what was easily cemented in by the ordinary legislators can be taken out only by the cumbrous machinery of a referendum. (Contrast the Australian Capital Territory where the entrenching law must be first submitted to the electors.) Be that as it may, the New South Wales Parliament first got the electors' approval in a referendum before it altered the method of election to the Upper House (in June 1978)—its abolition also requires a referendum—and before it extended the term of the Lower House to four years (in September 1981) and reduced the term and numbers of the Upper House (in May 1991).

South Australia, too, has a referendum provision, for example to alter the powers of its Upper House. In addition, both of its Houses are protected against abolition unless the electors want it. In Queensland it is the reverse. The Upper House there cannot be restored unless the electors want it back. Queensland also requires the electors' approval if the term of its Parliament is to extend beyond three years and, in fact, a referendum in March 1991 was held (the electors said "No" to a four year term). Queensland requires the electors' approval if the office of the Governor is to be altered or abolished. Victoria cannot alter the constitution of its Parliament, or of either House, unless the amending bill is passed by an absolute majority in each House. Western Australia has a similar provision, but it demands in addition a referendum of electors who must agree with the legislative absolute majority. Likewise, an alteration or abolition of the office of Governor must be preceded by the same kind of majority and a referendum. Tasmania has only one manner-and-form clause (which is not itself entrenched): it requires a two-thirds vote in the House of Assembly before its four year term can be amended.

So while the State Constitutions can mostly be altered by ordinary Acts, each of the States has restrictions—or safeguards—on certain constitutional provisions. These commonly deal with the abolition of the legislative Houses, one or both, and any amendment to the term of the Lower House. The restrictions may take the form of a prior consent by the electors in a referendum and/or an absolute or two-thirds majority vote in the legislature.

3. State Parliament machinery

As in the Commonwealth Constitution, there are provisions in a State Constitution on the machinery of Parliament. These provisions look to such matters as the composition of the legislative

Houses, parliamentary offices, elections, money bills, Parliament's control of public money, deadlocks between the Houses.

Two Houses—the Crown, through the Governor, is the third element in the legislature—are found in five States. The exception is Queensland.

There the Upper House, the Legislative Council, was abolished by a Labor Government in March 1922. The Lieutenant-Governor, a former Labor Minister, swamped the Council with a suicide squad of Labor nominees. A few years previously a substantial majority of electors in a referendum had voted against its abolition. The New South Wales Labor Government has made two attempts to abolish the Upper House. First, in 1926 the Lang Ministry had the Governor appoint a band of Labor nominees in the Council. But these reneged when the Abolition Bill appeared. Second, in 1961 the Labor Party again failed, this time in its referendum to abolish the Council. The Western Australian Labor Government, too, failed to dislodge its Legislative Council in 1972.

(The New Zealand National Party, the conservative party, abolished the Legislative Council there in 1950. As well as Queensland in Australia, the Northern Territory and the Australian Capital Territory have one House only.)

And yet, you can see the same principle of institutional checks and balances in a paid Opposition, a federal system and a bicameral legislature.

You are likely to witness checks and balances between the institutions of the two Houses if, for example, the electoral basis for the Houses differs or the tenure differs (Legislative Councillors have a longer tenure than Assembly members in New South Wales, Victoria, South Australia and Tasmania). Whether you consider this bicameral tension a good thing will depend on your priority— Government or Parliament. And remember Parliament is supposed to represent the people, not the Government; and Parliament has a wider basis in the people than the Government.

The Upper House in the five States that have two Houses is called the Legislative Council.

The Lower House is the more numerous and more important House—it controls finance and it supplies the Premier, probably the Deputy Premier and certainly the Treasurer, as well as most of the Ministers. The Lower House is called the Legislative Assembly in New South Wales, Victoria and Western Australia. In South Australia and Tasmania it is called the House of Assembly. In Queensland the one House is a Legislative Assembly.

The number of parliamentarians varies over the years, upwards usually. In 1990-1991 New South Wales actually reduced its parliamentarians by 13. The State-by-State numbers are roughly (they change from time to time): New South Wales Legislative Councillors 42, Legislative Assembly members 99—Victoria, 44 and 88—Tasmania, 19 and 35—South Australia, 22 and 47—Western Australia, 34 and 57—Queensland has 89 Assembly members. The Commonwealth Parliament has 76 senators and 147 House of Representatives members.

So, the States between them have about 580 parliamentarians. This, together with the federal and territorial parliamentarians, gives Australia something like 845 parliamentarians.

There are certain offices in the State Parliament, just as in the Federal Parliament: a Speaker in the Assembly and a President in the Council, each of whom upholds the standing orders and gives rulings; a New South Wales Act in December 1992 "recognised as . . . independent and impartial" the Speaker and the President, and required a secret ballot for the election of the Speaker with the further requirement of (usually) a two-thirds vote. There is also in the State Parliament a Leader of the House (the Premier or Deputy Premier) who organises the order of business in the House; a Chairman of Committees for each House. I explained these parliamentary terms in the Chapter on "Federal Parliament machinery".

Elections: All Houses, both Upper and Lower, in each State are directly elected by the people of the State. A New South Wales referendum, as late as June 1978, introduced popular elections for the Legislative Council instead of the previous joint-sitting vote by the Assembly and Council.

Victoria, Tasmania, Western Australia and South Australia once required special qualifications—such as property, war service, professional (eg doctor or lawyer) or academic (eg graduate)—for electors who could vote for the Upper House. But now each of these four States (South Australia only since 1973) elects to the Upper House on the basis of universal adult suffrage. The qualifications of State electors are the same, whether voting for Upper House or Lower House members. These qualifications are much the same as those of federal electors which I listed when discussing federal elections, namely, enrolment, residence, civic adulthood (18 years) and Australian citizenship. Voting is compulsory.

202

The Lower House general elections are held no later than every four years in five States. The States are New South Wales, Victoria, South Australia, Western Australia and Tasmania; Tasmania reduced the term from five years by a 1972 Act. (The Northern Territory Legislative Assembly also has a maximum four year term.) Queensland, for its one House, has a maximum three year term (the Federal Parliament also has a maximum three year term, while the Australian Capital Territory Assembly has, as a rule, a fixed three year term); between 1859-1890 Queensland had a five year term, but an 1890 Act cut the term down to three years; then in March 1991 a Queensland referendum said "No" to a four year term.

Because the terms are maximum, not fixed, a Premier is able to call snap elections when it suits the party.

But a New South Wales Act of December 1991 took a bold step. First, it fixed the term (of four years) for the next general elections for the current Legislative Assembly, 1991-1995, not to be broken unless there is a no-confidence vote or a refusal of Supply and, even then, in either case there must be no viable alternative government. Second, the 1991 Act foreshadowed a 1995 referendum to cement these provisions permanently into the Constitution. Tasmania in December 1992 took the first of these steps. Tasmania fixed a four year term for the current House of Assembly, 1992-1996, with an exception arising from a no-confidence vote where there is also no alternative government available, or arising from a refusal of Supply. In each instance of New South Wales and Tasmania it was a conservative Government that acted.

Victoria and South Australia had already gone some way towards similar electoral responsibility. In each of these States the normal term is four years but, once three years have elapsed, the Premier can ask the Governor for premature general elections for the Assembly. Even this three year period can be cut short, as follows: (i) a vote of no-confidence is taken in the Assembly; or (ii) a bill of special importance is declared by the Assembly and refused by the Council; or (iii) (in Victoria) an appropriation bill dealing "only" with the ordinary annual services of the Government is delayed beyond a month by the Council; or (iv) (in South Australia) a bill is refused by the Council, the Assembly is dissolved and again the bill is refused by the Council, then both Houses are dissolved. (The Australian Capital Territory is the only other legislature in Australia with a fixed term, qualified as in Victoria or South Australia.)

The Legislative Council in each of the five States that supports a Council has a continuous life. It is not dissolved as the Assembly is; its composition is merely altered from time to time under a rotation system to be explained next. There is an exception: in South Australia the Legislative Council may be dissolved, along with the Assembly, to break a deadlock, see "deadlock provisions" below.

Under a rotation system only part of the Legislative Council faces periodic elections (which are held at the same time, except in Tasmania, as the Lower House general elections). In New South Wales, Victoria and South Australia half the Legislative Council, turn and turn about, goes to the electorate. In Tasmania at its annual periodic elections and in Western Australia the number of councillors that stand varies.

Legislative Councillors stay in office longer than four years because of the rotation system. In New South Wales (since May 1991) and in Victoria a councillor's term is for two terms of the Lower House, that is, a councillor's term is eight years. In South Australia the general rule is that a councillor has a minimum term of six years. In Tasmania a councillor's term is six years. In Western Australia a councillor has a minimum term of four years. Queensland no longer has a Legislative Council.

Electoral disputes, or questions about vacancies in either House, or questions about the qualification of a councillor or a member . . . any one of these three matters is settled rather as it is settled at the federal level—viz, either by the appropriate House or by a Court of Disputed Returns. But, of course, in the State it is the Supreme Court that acts (if it is the body to act), usually sitting as a Court of Disputed Returns; and it alone decides the matter of electoral disputes, not Parliament.

Money bills, that is, bills appropriating revenue and bills imposing taxation, must originate in the Lower House in each of the five States that have two Houses. The Upper House may not amend a money bill, although it may suggest an amendment to the Lower House. But the Upper House may reject a money bill, with the consequence of a deadlock on the money bill; deadlock provisions are discussed below, where some qualifications are introduced, for example, in regard to New South Wales and Victorian money bills.

There is to be no "tacking" of non money provisions on to (certain kinds of) money provisions by the Lower House, as it attempts to side-step the Upper House; for the Upper House is not restricted in amending non money provisions as it is in regard to money provisions. In Western Australia the Lower House cannot tack foreign matter on to an appropriation bill for the ordinary annual services of the Government, or tack foreign matter on to a bill imposing taxation. But in New South Wales, Victoria or Tasmania tacking on to an appropriation bill for the ordinary annual services of the Government is alone expressly banned; (Tasmania also has a provision about one subject of taxation). In South Australia an appropriation bill for a previously authorised purpose must not contain an appropriation provision outside that specific purpose.

An appropriation bill must be preceded by the Governor's message to the Lower House, recommending the purpose of the appropriation; in New South Wales (since 1987) a Minister may introduce an appropriation bill without the Governor's message. It is in this way that the Governor procures Supply for the Government, and "the financial initiative of the Crown" is ensured or, in practical terms, the Government of the day runs the expenditure program.

These several provisions on the relations between the two Houses in money matters are reflected, of course, in the Commonwealth Constitution (see ss 53, 54, 55 and 56) since they are fundamentals in constitutional law.

The "fundamentals" are: the predominance of the Lower House in money bills—and yet, the abiding role of the Upper House even in money bills, for it too represents the electorate—the financial initiative of the Government of the day in money matters.

Parliament controls public money: At least in some States, namely, in the three eastern States and in Western Australia, all revenue goes into a Consolidated Revenue Fund. Then money goes out of this fund only by an appropriation law, in other words, by an Act of Parliament. It is Parliament that authorises an appropriation and the purpose of the appropriation. *The Government does not simply help itself to public funds without parliamentary scrutiny.* In the same way at the federal level it is the Commonwealth Parliament alone that authorises, "by law", the drawing of money from the Commonwealth Treasury: see s 83 of the Constitution. In South Australia and Tasmania, Parliament also controls public money, not by express constitutional provisions, but by historical practice, that is, by convention.

In fact, if Parliament believes that the Government should face the electorate, *Parliament can refuse Supply to the Government—*

at any rate, an Upper House can refuse Supply, even if it is only in four States. See "deadlock provisions" immediately below. I single out a ("hostile") Upper House because in the practical politics of party discipline you will scarcely find a Lower House blocking Supply.

Thus, between monitoring appropriation of public money and even refusing appropriation, Parliament keeps an eye on the Government on behalf of the electors.

Deadlock provisions to decide a disagreement between the two Houses are found in some of the State Constitutions.

In New South Wales take first a certain kind of money bill, namely, "any bill appropriating revenue or money for the ordinary annual services of the Government"; that is, in this instance, not a bill imposing taxation. If the Legislative Council rejects this kind of money bill, or fails to pass it (and this includes delaying it for a month) or returns it with unacceptable amendments, the Legislative Assembly, acting alone, may forward the bill to the Governor for assent. The upshot is that the Legislative Council may delay Supply for a month; then Supply will go through anyway, and without the Assembly being dissolved.

Other deadlocked bills are unlocked as follows. The Legislative Assembly passes a bill and the Legislative Council blocks the bill for the first time (say by delaying it for two months in this instance)—there is a three month delay—the Assembly again passes the bill—the Council blocks the bill for a second time—a conference between managers appointed by each House (but this is not obligatory) and then a joint sitting of the Houses attempt to break the deadlock—the Assembly resolves that the bill be put to the electors in a referendum (after a two month delay for certain bills)—if the electors approve, the bill is submitted to the Governor for assent. So, in this kind of deadlock you can say that the electors with the Legislative Assembly "pass" the bill.

In Victoria a certain kind of money bill again, namely, "a bill dealing only with the appropriation of the Consolidated Fund for the ordinary annual services of the Government", can be rejected by the Legislative Council, or the Council can fail to pass the bill within a month. If either event occurs, the Legislative Assembly may be dissolved at once and go, with half of the Council, to the electorate; (contrast New South Wales where a deadlocked money bill simply by-passes the Council). In the case of other bills, a bill is passed by the Assembly and is rejected by the Council. The

Assembly must then declare the bill "a bill of special importance", and pass the bill. Again the Council rejects the bill. The Governor may dissolve the Assembly. Thereafter there are general elections for the Assembly and half of the Council.

In the other States no special favourable treatment is given to money bills, as in New South Wales and Victoria. Instead all bills can become deadlocked in the same way.

In South Australia a bill is passed by the House of Assembly and rejected by the Legislative Council. Then there must be intervening general elections for the Assembly. The new Assembly again passes the bill which the Council rejects for a second time. Thereupon the Governor may dissolve both Houses (compare the double dissolution to resolve a federal deadlock in s 57 of the Commonwealth Constitution), or there is an election of two additional councillors (the State votes as one electorate). Another method is the "bill of special importance" process (compare Victoria above): that is, the Assembly sends up such a certified bill, and the Council rejects it; then the Governor may dissolve the Assembly.

In Western Australia and Tasmania there are no special deadlock provisions as in the other States. A compromise would just have to be reached, in each case by a conference between managers from both Houses; otherwise the bill would never become law.

Queensland with one House of Parliament since 1922 calls for no deadlock provisions.

So, New South Wales is the only bicameral State where the Upper House's refusal of Supply will not bring the Government out to meet the people, either because the constitutional provisions (as in Victoria and South Australia) call for a dissolution of the Lower House, or because the practical realities (as in Western Australia and Tasmania) would dictate such a dissolution to get the country running. You may reflect on whether it was wise of New South Wales to throw out this mechanism in 1933—a mechanism whereby Parliament, through the Legislative Council, can force the Government to answer to the electorate midterm; the electorate can then decide whether Parliament acted according to its wishes. The Tasmanian Upper House in 1948, for example, and Victorian Upper Houses in 1947-1952 used the machinery to get the Government of the day to the people. In some of these cases the people did, in fact, agree with Parliament's action.

4. The powers and limits of State Parliament

The law-making power of a State Parliament is extraordinarily wide. Commonly its law slips through the simple test of a law "for the peace, welfare and good government" of the State. And yet there are limits. For one thing, the law must be connected with the State, or concern the State. And there are other limits that arise from the Commonwealth Constitution.

The powers of State Parliament, and the limits to those powers, can be given in six propositions.

(i) A State Parliament can make laws on all kinds of matters, whereas Federal Parliament can make laws only on the special Commonwealth matters which I set out in the Chapter on "the powers of Federal Parliament". Hence a State Parliament can make laws on general matters, such as public health, education, local government, property, contracts, wills, crime and police, general administration of justice, traffic regulation, town and country planning, companies, State marketing, prices and rent control.

The source of this wide power is typified in s 5 of the *Constitution Act* 1902 (NSW). It provides simply that the New South Wales Parliament shall

> "have power to make laws for the peace, welfare and good government of New South Wales in all cases whatsoever"—subject always to the provisions in the Commonwealth Constitution, of course.

The Victorian Constitution says that its Parliament can "make laws in and for Victoria in all cases whatsoever". The Queensland Constitution says that the Queensland Parliament can "make laws for the peace, welfare and good government of the colony in all cases whatsoever". South Australia can make laws for the "peace, welfare and good government" of South Australia. Tasmania has the same formula, for "the peace, welfare and good government" of Tasmania. The Western Australian Constitution uses a slightly different phrase, to make laws for "the peace, order and good government" of Western Australia; nothing turns on the difference.

The law must be for **"the peace, welfare, and good government"** of the State which makes the law, of course.

This does not mean that the law must bring or promote peace, welfare and good government in the State (*Union Steamship Company* 1988). It may mean that a State law must observe certain fundamental rights, such as the right to a parliamentary democracy and an independent judiciary, as the New South Wales Chief Justice once suggested (*Building Construction Employees & BLF v Industrial Relations Minister* 1986). Later the High Court seemed to query this obligation, but did not explore the issue (*Union Steamship* above).

We can be sure of this much. The requirement of "peace, welfare" etc in a State law means that the law must have a sufficient "nexus" with the enacting State or, to put it the other way, that the enacting State must be concerned with the matter in the law (*Union Steamship* above).

For example, South Australia is concerned with the matter in its law which manages lobster fishing up to 200 nautical miles offshore to conserve this limited resource for lobster traders living in South Australia (*Port Macdonnell Fishermen's* case 1989). If the matter has some kind of connection, say with Victoria as much as with South Australia, then probably the State showing more links with the matter will prevail (*Port Macdonnell* just given). The three cases below that illustrate extra-territoriality illustrate also the required State interest or concern in the person, conduct or thing affected by the State's law.

A law may operate extra-territorially, to use the technical term, that is, a law may affect persons, conduct or things even outside the State.

And now the *Australia Acts* 1986 (Cth & UK) confirm that a State has "full power to make laws for the peace, order and good government of that State that have extra-territorial operation". How far the State law may operate extra-territorially depends on whether the law continues to be a law for the peace, welfare and good government of the State, that is, whether the law continues to have a sufficient connection with the enacting State. For the purpose of the 1986 Acts was not to allow the State to make a law although it has no connection with the State: *Union Steamship* and *Port Macdonnell* above were cases decided after those Acts of 1986, and they still required a "nexus" with the enacting State.

For instance, the New South Wales Parliament might exact a tonne-kilometre charge from the owners of vehicles which travel on New South Wales roads. Even if an owner lives in South Australia and permits somebody else to drive the vehicle in New South Wales, the owner must still pay the road charge. After all, the New South Wales law is concerned only with the presence of the vehicle *in New South Wales* and with the use of roads *in New South Wales* by that vehicle (*O'Sullivan v Dejneko* 1964). New South Wales might demand stamp duty on share transfers even though the parties, the transfer and the shares are all outside New South Wales, just as long as the company itself is in New South Wales. In this case again there is something in New South Wales which has been *created by New South Wales and relies on New South Wales for its existence*—the company (*Myer Emporium v Stamp Duties Commissioner* 1967). And, of course, New South Wales can prosecute a cotton farmer whose spraying in Queensland allegedly kills fish in a river that flows into New South Wales (*Brownlie v State Pollution Control Commission* 1992).

But a New South Wales law on the hijacking of planes flying towards New South Wales, or a New South Wales law taxing a shareholder's dividends from a business in New South Wales although the shareholder and the company are in Victoria, might not have a sufficient connection with New South Wales. And so the law on hijacking or the law on taxation of dividends might not be valid.

(ii) A State Parliament can make laws even on many of the special matters which the Commonwealth Constitution lists for Federal Parliament.

Therefore, State Parliament as much as Federal Parliament can make laws on interstate trade, banking, insurance, marriage and divorce, industrial disputes, etc. However, if Commonwealth Parliament also passes a law on interstate trade, etc, and the State law is inconsistent under s 109 of the Commonwealth Constitution with the Commonwealth law, then the State law does not operate —as has happened in the fields of banking, life assurance, marriage and divorce and to some extent industrial disputes.

(iii) But a State Parliament cannot make laws on matters which the Commonwealth Constitution says are exclusive to Commonwealth Parliament: see s 107 of the Constitution.

For instance, the New South Wales Parliament cannot make laws for the Australian Capital Territory: see s 52(i) of the Constitution. No State Parliament can make laws for "places acquired by the Commonwealth for public purposes", such as Tullamarine or Mascot Airport: see the same section. (However, Federal Parliament has adopted for its Commonwealth places the State laws that surround those places: see the Chapter on "the powers of Federal Parliament", No 9.) No State Parliament can make laws for the administration of Australia Post or the Australian and Overseas Telecommunications Corporation: see s 52(ii) with s 69. No State Parliament can impose customs or excise duties (including sales tax) or grant certain kinds of bounties: see s 90 which is explained in the Chapter on "prohibitions and guarantees". And then there are some subjects that no State Parliament could deal with anyway, such as Commonwealth credit, naturalisation, aliens and Commonwealth constitutional amendments: see s 51(iv), s 51(xix) and s 128.

(iv) A State Parliament cannot make laws on matters which the Commonwealth Constitution has taken away from the States: see s 107 of the Constitution. So, a State cannot raise an army or coin money: see ss 114 and 115 of the Constitution.

(v) A State Parliament cannot make laws which offend some prohibition in the Commonwealth Constitution, such as s 92. For instance, Victoria cannot discriminate against Queensland-Victoria tobacco sales in order to protect sales within Victoria. Another prohibition, s 117, prevents one State discriminating against the residents of a sister State. Both s 92 and s 117 are discussed in the Chapter on "prohibitions and guarantees". Because of a third prohibition, s 114, no State can tax, or through its municipal council levy rates on, property belonging to the Commonwealth or its agency, say the Commonwealth Bank of Australia.

In 1992 the High Court discovered two freedoms implied in any Constitution that accepts representative and responsible government—a freedom of political discourse and a freedom of criticism of government institutions. Hence there is a prohibition against any State law that interferes with either of these constitutional freedoms. Again see the Chapter on "prohibitions and guarantees".

(vi) The *Australia Acts* 1986 (Cth & UK)—they were explained more fully in No 2 above—enhance the powers of a State Parliament, as follows.

A State Parliament can now make the kind of law the United Kingdom Parliament used to make for the peace, order and good government of that State. Moreover, a State Parliament can make a law repugnant to a United Kingdom Act, and so override the latter Act. A State Parliament's power to give its law an extra-territorial operation is confirmed. The Australia Acts also liberate State legislative processes: a bill assented to by the Governor cannot be disallowed by the Queen; certain bills no longer have to be reserved for the Queen's pleasure.

5. Governments

The State Governments are much the same kind of Governments as the Commonwealth Government is—except for the fact that, on the one hand, State Governments have general powers and, on the other hand, State Governments control only the area within the State.

The Governor, like the Governor-General for the Commonwealth, represents the Queen, in this instance the head of State for the State. He (or she, as Mitchell in South Australia in 1991, and Forde in Queensland in 1992) is "Her Majesty's representative in each State", as the 1986 Australia Acts affirm. The Governor-General, by the way, has no power over the State Governors. State Governors are appointed and act quite independently of the Governor-General. In this sense the name, Governor-General, is misleading.

The Governor is appointed by the Queen by Royal Commission during Her "pleasure"—in practice, usually for five years, but the term is often extended (witness the term of Sir John Northcott 1946-1957 or Sir Roden Cutler 1966-1980, both in New South Wales). The appointment (or dismissal), however, is made on the advice of the relevant State Premier. You should know that the Queen is now advised in a State matter directly by the State Premier, not by the United Kingdom Secretary of State for Foreign and Commonwealth Affairs, as was the case previously: see the *Australia Acts* 1986 (Cth & UK), discussed fully in No 2 above. The Governor is likely to be Australian these days; New South Wales, for instance, has had Australian Governors since 1946.

The source of the powers, functions and office of the Governor used to be found in early Letters Patent and Royal Instructions, as well as local State Constitutions. Then came the "upheaval" of the 1986 Australia Acts. Hence now we look for the Governor's powers, etc, in the 1986 Australia Acts, 1986 Letters Patent (for some States), local Constitutions and constitutional statutes, such as the *Constitution (Amendment Act)* 1987 (NSW), the *Constitution (Governor's Powers) Act* 1992 (Vic) or the *Constitution (Office of Governor) Act* 1987 (Qld).

All powers and functions formerly exercised by the Queen in respect of a State are exercisable now only by the Governor, except the power to appoint or dismiss a Governor; this change, too, was effected by the Australia Acts. When the Queen is personally present in the State, she is not precluded from exercising her powers and functions in respect of the State; for example, she may summon Parliament or assent to a bill.

The Governor, just as the Commonwealth counterpart, the Governor-General, appoints and dismisses Ministers of the Crown, as well as Judges (who can be removed only on an address from Parliament, see "6. courts" below), procures supply for the Government (see "money bills" above), summons, prorogues and dissolves the Lower House of Parliament (except in South Australia where the Governor may also dissolve both Houses in a deadlock), and assents to bills. The assent can no longer be disallowed by the Queen, and the Governor can no longer be required to withhold assent or reserve certain bills for the Queen's pleasure: again see the Australia Acts, discussed above. South Australia permits its Governor, when presented with a bill, to suggest an amendment to either House of Parliament.

The Governor can remit sentences, penalties, or fines. He can grant pardon by exercising the Royal Prerogative of mercy. In capital cases he must first take the advice of the Executive Council. In other cases he takes the advice of the Minister of Justice.

A Governor also formally makes regulations under a parent statute, and issues proclamations in the Government Gazette, for example, to proclaim an Act in force.

The "Executive Council", advising the Governor, consists of all the Ministers: when sworn in as Ministers, the Ministers are also sworn in as Executive Councillors, that is, Ministers are ex officio members of the Executive Council.

At the regular weekly meeting of the Executive Council only two Councillors attend. The Governor presides, or the Lieutenant-Governor or the Vice President (a Minister specially appointed) or the senior Councillor. This body, representing the Government of the day, clothes with formal authority decisions that are, in fact, usually made elsewhere, say by Cabinet (as in South Australia), or by a responsible Minister or Cabinet (as in Victoria or Tasmania at times: it depends on the current Government). The formal act will have been initiated by an Executive Council Minute, which is a terse recommendation prepared by the Minister in charge of the Department that administers the matter in the Minute.

Almost invariably the Governor acts on the advice of the Executive Councillors, that is, the Ministers.

There are a couple of instances where the Governor does not. For example, the Governor may choose not to assent to a bill that contains an inaccuracy or seems inconsistent with the law. Historically, too, there have been exceptional cases when a Governor has not followed the advice of the Ministers, defeated in

213

the Assembly, who wanted a dissolution. Instead, the Governor has commissioned the Opposition to form a government, when satisfied that it will have the confidence of Parliament and will secure Supply to the Crown—as in Victoria in 1872, 1950, 1952, in Tasmania in 1879, 1914 and, through the Administrator, in 1923. And then there was the case in 1932 of Sir Philip Game and Lang which I discussed in the Chapter on "the Federal Government", No 1 above. The New South Wales Supreme Court (*Greiner v ICAC* 1992) acknowledged the Governor's personal discretion to dismiss a Premier or Minister, as the New South Wales Legislature (*Constitution (Fixed Term Parliaments) Etc Act* 1991) acknowledged the possibility of the same discretion to dissolve the Legislative Assembly.

But these are rare and extreme circumstances. So, as I said, "almost invariably" the Governor acts on the advice of the current Ministers.

Premier, Ministry, Cabinet, Responsible Government: Each State has its own counterpart to the Commonwealth's Prime Minister, namely, a Premier who is the head of Government in the State. Since the *Australia Acts* 1986 (Cth & UK), given at the beginning of this Chapter, the Premier no longer works through a United Kingdom intermediary, but has direct contact with the Queen in State matters, say in regard to the appointment of a new Governor.

Each State has its own Government with its Ministry or Cabinet. The Premier convenes Cabinet, arranges the agenda and is the Chairman of a Cabinet meeting. In a State all Ministers are Cabinet members. This is not the case with the Commonwealth Government where only the senior Ministers are Cabinet members. But remember that the number of Commonwealth Ministers can be as high as 30, and these can well be broken down to a small effective body, a Cabinet. Most State Ministries, however, are already small bodies. Their numbers range from 9 or 10 in Tasmania, 13 in South Australia, 17 in Western Australia, up to 18 in Victoria or Queensland, and up to 20 in New South Wales.

Each State has responsible Government. Thus, the Governor will almost invariably act on the advice of the Ministers: see "the Executive Council" above. These Ministers, in turn, sit in Parliament and are answerable or responsible to Parliament, individually and as a collective body.

Well, this is the convention, although it is not technically provided for by the law in some States. The Victorian Constitution requires Ministers to sit in Parliament and implies that there will be a certain number of Ministers, not only in the Legislative Assembly, but also in the Legislative Council. The South Australian and Tasmanian Constitutions require Ministers to sit in Parliament. Compare with these three State Constitutions s 64 of the Commonwealth Constitution which stipulates that federal Ministers must sit either in the Senate or in the House of Representatives. On the other hand, the Constitutions of New South Wales, Queensland and Western Australia do not explicitly insist that Ministers must sit in Parliament. But there are implications; for example, Western Australia declares that at least one Minister shall be a member of the Legislative Council. Anyway, the various Colonies certainly took on board responsible government in the 1850s and, for Western Australia, in 1890, as we have already seen in "1. constitutional history" above, and this principle of the Westminster system would persist even if a State has no specific constitutional provision.

Each State has an Executive which keeps law and order within the State, which runs the State Departments, which makes regulations and sets up administrative tribunals to assist the Government in the running of the State.

6. Courts

State courts are far more numerous than federal courts, and they exercise wider, more general jurisdictions. So, State courts operate at many levels, from superior courts, through intermediate courts, down to inferior courts and on to smaller special tribunals. State courts operate in many areas, such as general criminal and civil matters, industrial and workers' compensation claims, land and valuation, environment and mining cases, consumer protection and tenancy matters.

State courts, in short, are the staple courts of the land, not the federal courts.

- *State courts fall into three classes: superior courts, intermediate courts and inferior courts. There are also special courts and tribunals.*

The superior courts are the State Supreme Courts—"Supreme" because this court is the highest court and the court of final appeal within the State. All matters, regardless of the amount involved, can be taken by these courts, unless it is shown otherwise—at least, this is the legal distinction between a superior court and another court. In fact, however, the State Supreme Courts try what are called indictable offences or serious crimes and take important cases, "important" because of the issues, money or property involved. By contrast, in the intermediate or inferior courts you must be able to show whether a particular matter or a particular amount is within the court's jurisdiction.

It is for this reason that the prerogative writs lie against intermediate or inferior courts, but not against Supreme Courts. For example, an applicant can get a writ of prohibition to stop an inferior court going outside its jurisdiction because it *is* limited. Again it is the Supreme Court that grants the prerogative writ. It is the Supreme Court that has certain important inherent powers (powers that do not depend on a statute for their existence), such as an inherent power to punish for contempt, for these kinds of inherent powers belong to "a superior court of record".

There is another distinction between Supreme Courts and lower courts. The Supreme Courts have a general jurisdiction "in equity". So, a Supreme Court can issue an injunction against a respondent (eg to stop a nuisance), or grant specific performance (eg to compel a party to complete a contract), or make a declaration (eg to explain the parties' rights under the law), or enforce a trust. By contrast, while the intermediate courts, and even some inferior courts, have an equitable jurisdiction, this jurisdiction is strapped with conditions (eg it may only bolster money or property claims, or it may not involve cases above a particular amount). Thus, the New South Wales District Court has an equity jurisdiction comparable to the Supreme Court there, but within monetary limits or in regard to certain matters only; it is similar in Queensland and South Australia.

The Supreme Court in New South Wales with a Chief Justice and about 44 Justices ("puisne Justices") is the third largest court in New South Wales, next to the District Court (about 58 Judges) and the Local Courts (about 126 magistrates). This Supreme Court appears under several titles, but it is throughout the one Supreme Court. In original jurisdiction, it is the Supreme Court or the Central Criminal Court. On appeal, it is the Court of Appeal (which also takes some matters in original proceedings, such as the supervision of certain tribunals) or the Court of Criminal Appeal. In other States, save Queensland (but it now boasts a Court of Appeal), the Full Court of the Supreme Court sits as a Court of Criminal Appeal also. But the other States, apart from Queensland

216

since 1991, have no distinct—and to some extent autonomous—court like the New South Wales Court of Appeal (since 1965) with its President and its Judges of Appeal; those "other States" may have an Appeal Division of the Supreme Court, as in Victoria.

Speaking of Divisions, you will hear of Divisions in original jurisdiction also. To take New South Wales, there is the Commercial Division (dealing with business transactions), the Probate Division (dealing with wills), the Equity Division (dealing with trusts and trustees, for instance), and so on. Each Division will have its regular specialist judge/s, such as the Chief Judge in Equity in New South Wales.

Administrative officials, in contrast to judicial officers, the judges, run the various Supreme Courts—such as masters, prothonotaries, registrars. It is the master who will "tax costs", that is, review contested costs in a court case. The master, as well, may have judicial duties; for instance, the Master of the New South Wales Supreme Court decided whether the federal Health Minister could claim Crown privilege for documents that the plaintiff in the case wished to inspect (*The Commonwealth v HCF* 1982)

Intermediate courts below Supreme Court level are found in all States, except Tasmania. In Queensland, New South Wales, South Australia and Western Australia there are District Courts; in Victoria there are County Courts. These various courts take criminal as well as civil matters.

Inferior courts below the intermediate courts deal with minor civil matters and minor offences—Local Courts in New South Wales, Courts of Petty Sessions in Western Australia (the latter also has Local Courts to take minor civil matters), Magistrates Courts in Queensland, South Australia and Victoria. In Tasmania the Magistrates Court may act as a Court of Petty Sessions for criminal matters and as a Court of Requests for civil matters or (since 1989) a Small Claims Division.

A Local Court, a Court of Petty Sessions or a Magistrates Court, incidentally, takes committal proceedings, that is, the Court conducts a preliminary examination to see if there is a prima facie case of an "indictable" (a serious) crime. If so, the accused is "committed" for trial before an intermediate or a superior court, depending on the gravity of the crime. Then the Attorney-General, usually advised by the Solicitor-General, may—he is free not to—file an indictment against the defendant; or the Attorney-General may lay a charge, based on the committal proceedings, for a different crime.

The various general courts that I have listed differ in the kind of matter they can take (whether civil or criminal), the amount of money involved or the seriousness of the offence before the court. The court costs and the parties' costs, including counsel's costs, also differ.

The States have special courts and tribunals, besides the general courts given. For instance, there is the Land and Environment Court (established in 1979) or the (workers') Compensation Court (1984), both in New South Wales, the Local Government Court in Queensland (1966), the Industrial Court in South Australia (1912), or there are the many State industrial authorities which I discussed in the Chapter on "the powers of Federal Parliament", No 8 above.

Small Claims Tribunals appeared in the mid-1970s in Queensland, Victoria and Western Australia; Consumer Claims Tribunals appeared at the same time in New South Wales. A Tribunal deals with consumers' complaints against traders in what are called consumer transactions. A Tribunal deals with a complaint in an informal and inexpensive way; so, no costs are awarded and legal representatives do not normally attend. The referee, usually a lawyer, tries to get the customer and the trader to settle their difference at a round-table discussion. If not, the referee, that is, the Tribunal, makes an order or dismisses the complaint. The other two States simply use their regular courts for small claims: the Magistrates Court in South Australia, the Small Claims Division of the Magistrates Court in Tasmania.

Alternative Dispute Resolution, or Dispute Resolution, has also appeared the last 10-15 years. This is a mediation process outside the ordinary court framework (until lately anyway). A mediator discusses the problem with each party in turn, trying to persuade the parties to settle their difference. True, the process is not carried out in the open and will not necessarily resolve the dispute, but the cost, delay and trauma of a court appearance are avoided.

- *State courts, especially State Supreme Courts, have wider and more general jurisdictions than the federal courts have.*

The federal courts have special jurisdictions only, as was explained in the Chapter on "the federal courts", No 1 "special jurisdictions". The federal courts take special cases in the sense that there is a particular party before the court, such as the Commonwealth or a Commonwealth officer, or there is a particular matter before the court, such as a constitutional matter or a matter under a federal law, say the federal Bankruptcy Act,

the Family Law Act or the Trade Practices Act. (In these remarks
I am referring to the federal courts, each with its own limited
jurisdiction, unaided by the 1988 cross-vesting scheme. Anyway,
for all the cross-vesting, each federal court retains its distinct
jurisdiction as its predominant way of operating. By no means has
a given federal court become a general court, certainly not in
practice.)

In contrast to the special jurisdictions of the federal courts, take
as a typical example of the general jurisdictions of the State courts
the wide jurisdiction given to the New South Wales Supreme Court.

> The Supreme Court was established and given altogether
> general jurisdiction under "the Third Charter of Justice"
> authorised by an 1823 Imperial Act, known as the New
> South Wales Act—namely, jurisdiction over "all pleas, civil
> and criminal or mixed, and jurisdiction in all cases what-
> soever as fully and amply . . . as (Her) Majesty's Courts . . .
> at Westminster", London. In time other jurisdiction was
> added: jurisdiction in equity, lunacy, divorce and
> matrimonial causes, wills and bankruptcy.

The current Supreme Court Act of New South Wales continues
the Court "as formerly established", adding that it "shall have all
jurisdiction which may be necessary for the administration of
justice in New South Wales". The Victorian Supreme Court has
jurisdiction "in all cases whatsoever and shall be the superior Court
of Victoria with unlimited jurisdiction". And so it is with the other
State Supreme Courts. For example, the 1823 Imperial Act
mentioned applied equally to the Supreme Court of Van Diemen's
Land; and now the Supreme Court of Tasmania, formerly Van
Diemen's Land, draws equally wide jurisdiction from an Imperial
Act of 1828 with a Charter of Justice, replacing the 1823 source.

(On top of their own traditional general jurisdiction, the State
Supreme Courts now receive jurisdiction in territorial and many
federal matters under the 1988 cross-vesting scheme: see the
Chapter on "the federal courts", No 3 "cross-vesting of
jurisdiction".)

In the same way the States have intermediate or inferior courts
also with their general jurisdictions, more or less.

A person can use these State courts no matter who is on the
other side. It might be the next-door neighbour, it might be the
State Government. A plaintiff does not have to show that the party
on the other side is a consul, the Commonwealth Government or
its officer, or a person who lives in some other State—as the

plaintiff would when using the federal courts. And a person can use these State courts for any kind of matter at all. It might be a dispute about a contract, a will, a Dog Act; it might involve a traffic offence, a landlord and tenant matter, and the rest. A plaintiff does not have to show that the case concerns only a treaty or the Commonwealth Constitution or a federal law—as the plaintiff would when using the federal courts.

It can be seen from what I just said that the State courts can, of course, take federal matters, as well as their much more common State matters. So, a Local Court, a Court of Petty Sessions or a Magistrates Court can decide a constitutional case. Some of these courts can also grant a custody application under the *Family Law Act* 1975, take a prosecution under the *Industrial Relations Act* 1988 or hear a consumer protection claim under the *Trade Practices Act* 1974; each of these Acts is a federal law. A Supreme Court, too, can take matters under some federal statutes. A Supreme Court can—and not infrequently does—take constitutional cases. For instance, the Queensland Supreme Court has decided a case on the inconsistency between a State and federal law under s 109 of the Constitution (*McWaters v Day* 1989). State courts and federal matters are also explained in the Chapter on "the federal courts", No 4 "State courts used by the Commonwealth".

But in some instances the Federal Parliament has reserved exclusive jurisdiction for "its" courts, thus cutting down the wide jurisdictions of the State courts. For example, a State v State case or a Commonwealth v State case (or vice versa) must go to the High Court, since the *Judiciary Act* 1903 has made jurisdiction in these cases exclusive to the High Court. Secondary boycotts under the *Trade Practices Act* 1974 must be decided by the Federal Court, as do most of the matters under the *Industrial Relations Act* 1988; (secondary boycott provisions may be re-sited in the *Industrial Relations Act* 1988 (Cth) and placed under the Industrial Relations Commission). These are two cases where the 1988 cross-vesting scheme does not apply; hence the cases stay in the Federal Court.

As well as having wider jurisdictions than the federal courts, the State courts have wider powers in the sense that they are not restricted to the power which the High Court has called judicial power. More generally, no doctrine of separation of powers binds the States or, if there is such a doctrine, the States can alter it.

For instance, State compensation courts can act both as courts deciding cases and as administrative agencies calculating compensation. Other State courts can grant a liquor licence, or engage in the kind of award-making which would be forbidden to the

Industrial Division of the Federal Court of Australia. The New South Wales, Queensland or Victorian Constitution does not separate judicial and legislative powers, so that the legislature in any of these States is able to "meddle with" the judicial process (see respectively *Building Construction Employees & BLF v Industrial Relations Minister* 1986, *Mabo v Queensland* 1988 and *Collingwood City v Victoria* 1993). The South Australian Constitution does not separate judicial powers and electoral powers (*Gilbertson v South Australia* 1978).

- *The State Supreme Courts, just as the High Court, have an original and an appellate jurisdiction.*

A State Supreme Court, like the High Court, has original jurisdiction, that is, jurisdiction where the parties are in a court for the first time.

In addition, also like the High Court, a State Supreme Court has what is called a "supervisory" jurisdiction—it is still original jurisdiction—where the Supreme Court watches to see if some lower court or tribunal in the State deals with matters that are beyond its jurisdiction or outside its authority, or to see if the lower court or tribunal, on the other hand, refuses to deal with matters that are within its jurisdiction or its authority. For example, a District Court may have gone above its jurisdictional amount, or a Mining Warden may have refused to grant an occupation licence to a person who is entitled to it. In either case the Supreme Court, normally the Full Court, will exercise its supervisory jurisdiction to see that the District Court or the Mining Warden acts according to law. The Supreme Court may then go on to prohibit the District Court or to mandamus the Mining Warden.

Again like the High Court, a Full Court of a State Supreme Court or a distinct Court of Appeal (as in New South Wales or Queensland alone) takes appeals from the lower State courts, if only on points of law.

The tenure of Justices: In all States the Supreme Court Justices have a security of tenure and an independence of the Executive.

The Justices find this protection, or provision anyway, in the Constitution (as in New South Wales but only since 1992, or in Victoria or South Australia), or in a Supreme Court Act (as in Tasmania in the *Supreme Court (Judges' Independence) Act* 1857 (Tas)), or in both (as in Queensland or Western Australia)—not that a Constitution is any more sacred than a Supreme Court Act. Unless there is a special manner-and-form provision on the Justices (as in Victoria since 1991), the State Constitution can be amended as easily as a Supreme Court Act; in fact, the Queensland Constitution was amended in this very area by an inadvertent law elsewhere (*McCawley v R* 1920). New South Wales, however, proposed in 1992 a referendum to be held in 1995 to "entrench" the Justices' independence in its Constitution, the kind of protection that Victoria provided in 1991.

Supreme Court Justices hold office "during good behaviour"; the Tasmanian Act does not mention "good behaviour". But in New South Wales (since December 1992) the Justices rely "on the ground of proved misbehaviour or incapacity". By law, then, the Justices of the various State Supreme Courts can be removed only by the Governor or the Queen (now in effect the Governor) on an address by both Houses of Parliament, or by the one House in Queensland, even if it is (except for New South Wales Justices) for any cause thought sufficient. Tasmania, as I said, does not mention even "good behaviour". That is, apart for New South Wales, the grounds for removal are not spelt out as they are for federal Justices in s 72 of the Constitution. The State procedure has been used once only: in Queensland Vasta J's commission was withdrawn in June 1989. (In the 1840s-1860s Supreme Court Justices Willis, Montagu and Boothby were "amoved" by the Governor in Council, acting alone, in New South Wales, Tasmania and South Australia, respectively.)

The protected tenure of the Supreme Court Justices does not mean, however, that all these Justices have life tenure. In fact, in all States the Supreme Court Justices retire at 70 years of age.

7. Local government

Local Government covers the subordinate "government authorities" operating in each State (and the Northern Territory).

But I must confess that local government, which existed well before the Commonwealth Constitution was enacted, is nowhere found in this document. A referendum proposal in September 1988 to enshrine local government recognition in the Constitution was rebuffed heavily by a national vote of 2:1 against. Rather, the Constitution deals mostly with the Commonwealth, somewhat with the States, a little with the territories. Between the late 1970s and 1989 all State Constitutions gave formal recognition to the institution of local government. In 1988 Victoria went beyond bare recognition on to provisions on democratic elections, parliamentary areas of law-making in local government and dismissal only by statute.

Local government is made up of municipal councils or shire councils, district or city councils. A shire council extends over a wider area with sparser population than a municipal council; and so a shire council is usually found in a rural area, a municipal council in an urban area.

There are four terms used in local government which I will give in their order of concentration: a city, a town, a municipality and a shire (or district council). For example, a city has a greater population and is more densely populated than a town; it has a distinct identity; and it gets in more revenue—mostly from rates— than a town. Other terms are: a lord mayor of a city council, say, Sydney, Newcastle or Brisbane; a mayor of a municipal council or a president of a shire; councillors or aldermen or women.

The council body itself, that is, the corporation, consists of a mayor or a shire president and aldermen. There are 850-900 councils with 8,500-9000 elected councillors throughout Australia. There is the permanent staff, especially the town clerk or the shire clerk; there are also the engineer, the clerks, the inspectors and the outdoor workers—in all, say 150,000 workers.

The council gets revenue mainly from rates, or it gets revenue from service charges, loans, State grants and, through the respective State, Commonwealth financial assistance grants.

The Council's function is to provide health and sanitary services within the municipality or shire, to maintain streets and footpaths, parks and reserves, to supervise building regulations and town and country planning. And these days the council goes into other things, too—such as the supply of electricity, services for the aged or preschoolers, libraries and recreation and sporting centres.

- At one end, the council is answerable to its ratepayers who vote in—and, when dissatisfied, vote out—the members of their council.

- At the other end, the council is under the supervision of the Local Government Department. The council's charter is the Local Government Act: there is one such Act in each State. The council is thus wholly created by, and dependent on, the State in which it is.

So, it is really inaccurate to speak of three tiers of government: a Commonwealth, a State and a local government.

Certainly, the council is not an autonomous body in relation to the State as the State is an autonomous body in relation to the Commonwealth. As a matter of fact, occasionally a council may be dismissed by the Local Government Minister who then puts in a public servant, an administrator, to straighten things out. It has happened more than 20 times since the 1920s in New South Wales.

However, you can speak of three tiers of government if you wish, but only in the following loose sense. Right at the outset, I spoke of the two governments in the *Federation* of Australia, the Commonwealth and the State. And you can now say that, as well as the two sets of laws, elections and taxes for the Commonwealth and the State, there is a third set of by-laws (or ordinances), elections and rates—that for local government.

———————————

To sum up, the States have their own Constitutions which can, as a general rule, be more easily amended than can the Commonwealth Constitution.

And the States—their Parliaments, Governments and Courts—can deal with much more general matters than the Commonwealth can.

Prohibitions and guarantees

The prohibitions under the Commonwealth Constitution which I have in mind are the following. There are others, but I have taken the four main ones only.

> 1. The Commonwealth and the States are forbidden to interfere with traders or others who have business between the States or who travel between States.

> 2. The States are forbidden to tax goods which are imported into, or exported out of, Australia; or to tax goods which are already in Australia.

> 3. Federal Parliament is forbidden to make a law about the acquisition of property without providing just terms.

> 4. Federal Parliament is also forbidden to set up any religion or to interfere with any religion.

From another point of view you can call these prohibitions guarantees. For example, an interstate trader speaks of the freedom which the Constitution guarantees him, or Christians speak of their religious guarantees under the Constitution.

———————

Incidentally, in spite of popular notions and even at times counsel's notions, there is no general guarantee in the Constitution which prevents the Commonwealth or the States from discriminating against particular individuals or classes of persons. We have no "due-process-of-law" clause or "equal-protection-of-the-laws" clause in our Constitution, as the United States has in the Bill of Rights and 14th amendment attached to its Constitution.

Speaking more generally, the Australian Constitution—and, for that matter, each of the State Constitutions—just does not have a Bill of Rights.

Senator Murphy promoted a Bill of Rights in 1973-1974; it lapsed. Another Labor Senator, Evans, also argued forcefully for a Bill of Rights in 1985-1986. This Bill got through the House of Representatives. But it languished in a filibustering "hostile Senate", and was dropped by the Government in August 1986.

With us, basic rights are for the most part simply and negatively assumed. To put it broadly, we have freedom of speech, provided we don't transgress the law of sedition or defamation. We have freedom of assembly and freedom of movement, provided we don't trespass, or commit a breach of the peace, or come up against a restraint spelt out in express law. And so on.

Still, the Commonwealth Constitution has the following rights specifically laid down by the Constitution.

The Commonwealth is not to discriminate between States or parts of States in taxation laws; see Constitution s 51(ii), and compare s 99. So, taxpayers in New South Wales cannot be taxed more heavily than those in Tasmania, and taxes related to zones are suspect. But the provisions do not prevent the Commonwealth taxing pornographers only, or taxing hire-purchase companies at a higher rate than life assurance companies. Again, there is a no-expropriation-without-just-terms clause in s 51(xxxi) of the Constitution; it is discussed below. There is a very limited trial-by-jury clause in s 80, "limited" because the guarantee applies to trials on indictment only and these serious trials can be made triable in a different way, that is summarily; then s 80 does not apply. Interstate traders and travellers are guaranteed freedom to trade and travel between States: see s 92 of the Constitution. Certain religious freedoms are assured by s 116 of the Constitution. Both of these rights are also discussed below.

Because of s 117 of the Constitution a State is not to discriminate against residents from another State just because they come from a rival State. So, Tasmania cannot inflict disadvantages on Victorians which the Victorians would not suffer if they were in fact Tasmanians. For example, if a Queensland law imposed restrictions on a barrister coming from New South Wales (or from any other State), such as residence in Queensland and carrying on a principal practice there—restrictions that would not apply if the barrister actually lived in Queensland—the Queensland law would be invalid (*Street v Queensland Bar Assn* 1989).

Apart from the few rights laid down specifically, two rights are found impliedly in the Constitution.

First, there is a constitutional right of freedom of political discourse, or a freedom of communication in political and public affairs. The freedom is found in our system of representative and responsible government, that is, a system that requires a government, answerable to the people, to keep the people informed and to respond to their wishes. So, the High Court struck down the

Commonwealth's partial banning of political advertising on radio and television during election and referendum time (*Australian Capital Television v The Commonwealth*, the *Political Advertising Ban* case 1992).

The other constitutional right is a freedom of criticism of government and government institutions, and its basis is much the same as the first freedom. Of course, the criticism must be fair and must not offend the laws of defamation or sedition, for example. The Commonwealth was not able to penalise, without allowing any kind of defence, the use of words bringing its Industrial Relations Commission into disrepute (*Nationwide News v Wills* 1992).

These two newly discovered freedoms—or, from the government's viewpoint, prohibitions—apply at all levels of government: Commonwealth, State, territorial and local.

As for State or territorial prohibitions and guarantees, Tasmania alone of the States has guarantees and these are: religious freedom and no religious test for office.

The Australian Capital Territory and Northern Territory have two guarantees, both borrowed from the Commonwealth Constitution, viz, s 51(xxxi) and s 92. That is, in each Territory an acquisition of property shall be on just terms, and trade, commerce and intercourse into and out of the Territory shall be free.

1. Trade, commerce and intercourse among the States shall be absolutely free

This sweeping declaration in s 92 of the Constitution says that interstate traders, or anyone else who engages in business between the States, or who simply travels between the States, shall be "absolutely free". Taking the prohibition at face value, then, neither the Commonwealth nor a State can interfere with a trader or traveller going interstate.

Interstate travelling or trade: Take the easier case first, the case of a traveller going interstate. Even during World War II the Commonwealth could not rely on its defence power to stop Dulcie Johnson travelling from Sydney to Western Australia just to see her fiancé there (*Gratwick v Johnson* 1945). This guarantee of personal freedom to pass to and fro among the States without interference is still the law (*Cole v Whitfield*, the *Crayfish* case 1988).

227

That 1988 decision and the cases that follow it are powerful reminders of the High Court's governance of the Constitution, reminders of the High Court's creativity in constitutional law.

The 1988 decision propounded a new test for the second kind of case, the case of interstate trade or commerce. If a trader claims that a Commonwealth or State law interferes with interstate trade, the law must have two ingredients. It must discriminate against interstate trade as compared with local trade, and it must protect local trade, that is, protect local industry against competition from industry in another State.

> "Section 92 precluded the imposition of protectionist burdens . . . whether fiscal or non fiscal, which discriminated against interstate trade and commerce". To give a different emphasis, s 92 frees this trade and commerce "from discriminatory burdens having a protectionist purpose or effect".

Tasmania's Fisheries Act in the *Crayfish* case prescribed a minimum legal size for crayfish (to allow time for reproduction), whether the crayfish were caught in another State, such as South Australia here, or in Tasmania. Because Tasmania's law was not discriminatory against interstate trade and not protective of Tasmania's crayfish trade, it was allowed to pass.

But, four or five weeks later, Victoria's *Business Franchise (Tobacco) Act* 1974 did not fare as well. A Victorian retailer who purchased tobacco wholesale from another State, Queensland in this instance, had to pay Victorian duty on the tobacco. Had the retailer bought from a Victorian wholesaler, the retailer would not have paid the duty; under the Act the wholesaler would have already paid it. The High Court struck down the Victorian Act, reasoning that, from the retailer's viewpoint, it was discriminatory against interstate purchases of tobacco, and it was protectionist, protecting Victorian purchases against competition from interstate purchases (*Bath v Alston Holdings* 1988).

Eighteen months later South Australia's Beverage Container Act also offended "the new s 92". The Act discriminated against interstate breweries using non-refillable containers and, as well, protected against that interstate competition South Australian breweries, using mostly refillable containers. But the High Court did show a State (or the Commonwealth) how it could escape. The challenged law must pursue the objective of the State's well-being (say litter control or energy conservation), and provide measures appropriate and adapted to the objective; on top of this, any burden on interstate trade is merely incidental and is not disproportionate to the objective. South Australia's measures were found to be ill-adapted to its stated objective of litter control and energy conservation (*Castlemaine Tooheys v South Australia* 1989).

To complete this sketch of the new s 92, consider *Barley Marketing Board v Norman* (1990). The Normans in New South Wales agreed to sell their barley to a maltster in Victoria. But the New South Wales Marketing of Primary Products Act deemed a barley contract void unless it was with the Barley Marketing Board of New South Wales—any contract, even one between a New South Wales grower and a Victorian maltster. The Normans failed in their case since the Act did not discriminate against interstate trade and favour intrastate trade. Yes, the Act *stopped* the Normans' trade with Victoria, but now there was a new s 92 test.

There were earlier cases that would still be decided the same way, using the latest discrimination-plus-protectionism test.

For instance, back in 1909 a Western Australian wine shop proprietor, Robbins, was selling wine produced in the State, and for this he paid a two-pounds licence fee. Robbins also sold wine produced in Victoria, but for this he should have paid a 50-pounds licence fee. The High Court branded the Western Australian law that imposed the licence fees a discrimination that disadvantaged goods from the other States (*Fox v Robbins*).

Much later, the New South Wales Dairy Industry Authority registered milk vendors to sell milk, but only if the milk sold had been supplied by a pasteuriser, registered under the Authority's Act. The effect of this (and probably the scheme) was to protect New South Wales milk producers and pasteurisers against competition from Victorian producers and pasteurisers, such as North Eastern Dairy. The High Court exposed this practical effect of the New South Wales law—its discriminatory protectionism—and struck the law down (*North Eastern Dairy* 1975).

Intrastate trade: When I dealt with the Commonwealth's trade and commerce power in the Chapter on "the powers of Federal Parliament", I pointed out that this power can sometimes allow the Commonwealth to control intrastate trade, as well as overseas or interstate trade. But under s 92 of the Constitution intrastate trade is not so easily protected from interference.

Once a manufacturer, Marrickville Margarine, made margarine in New South Wales. When the margarine was made up, a substantial proportion of the total output went to other States. Now, the New South Wales Government set up a licensing and quota system for the manufacturing of margarine, no matter where

229

the margarine was to be sold. A licensee was restricted to a certain annual output, not that a manufacturer was sure of getting a licence. Marrickville Margarine did not hold a licence, and was prosecuted. The company claimed, of course, that the New South Wales licensing-quota system interfered with its interstate sales of margarine.

The High Court held (*Grannall's* case 1954) that the New South Wales licensing-quota system affected, strictly, the manufacturer's intention to bring into existence margarine, by manufacturing it, and that this act took place before there was any interstate movement—and that, therefore, Marrickville Margarine could not call on s 92. Nowadays the New South Wales law would not be invalid anyway, since it was not discriminatory and protectionist.

But sometimes a person who trades wholly within a State may come within the guarantee held out by s 92.

The example of the Western Australian wine shop proprietor given above is a case in point. You remember he was selling wines in Western Australia, and he had to pay a licence fee to sell his wines. But when he sold wines which had come from Victoria he had to pay a heavier fee than when he sold Western Australian wines. The High Court protested that the licence was bad because it discriminated against Victorian wines. And yet the fee affected the sale of a glass of wine in Western Australia, an activity that was wholly within the State. Still, the fee did single out and penalise wines from other States, unlike the New South Wales margarine quota. For I already pointed out that the New South Wales quota applied equally to traders who had nothing whatever to do with interstate transactions.

There are different cases where the trade or commerce was also wholly within a State, and yet s 92 was activated. In these cases, however, the intrastate trade or commerce was so closely associated with the interstate movement that it would have been unrealistic to hive off the intrastate portion—for, example, the sale in the State of destination by an importer of goods from another State.

Incidentals of interstate trade: An interstate trader cannot call on s 92 for protection from every and any kind of Commonwealth or State interference.

Sometimes the interference affects what the High Court brushes aside as mere incidentals or concomitants of interstate trade, things which are not interstate trade itself but only connected with interstate trade. For example, a Victorian road haulier travelling on

New South Wales highways could be asked by New South Wales to fill in a return which shows his use of roads in New South Wales. (New South Wales might use the return, for instance, to monitor the congestion on New South Wales highways.) Western Australia might have a land tax to be paid by anyone who owns land in Western Australia. An interstate airline service could be required to pay the land tax on its passenger terminal in Perth. And it would not matter if the terminal was used solely for interstate passengers. Neither would it matter, probably, in any of these cases if the law was discriminatory and protectionist, as is now required to attract s 92.

Law and order: At the beginning I said that Commonwealth Parliament and State Parliaments must not interfere with interstate traders or travellers at all—if s 92 is to be taken at face value. Section 92 says that interstate trade and travelling shall be "absolutely free". Does this mean that a person has an absolute right to travel between the States, unmolested by Commonwealth or State law?

Certainly, a traveller's personal freedom to pass to and fro among the States without interference was acknowledged in the *Crayfish* case above. But the High Court added, this does not mean that a fugitive offender, for example, cannot be arrested as he flees to a second State. And the Court reminded us of the continuing dilemma in applying s 92: anarchy or licence must not be confused with liberty, and it is liberty that concerns s 92.

- *Thus, s 92 guarantees freedom to interstate trade and travelling, but it is freedom within a community of law and order.*

2. A State cannot tax goods which are imported into, or exported out of, Australia; or tax goods which are already in Australia

A tax which is imposed on goods imported into Australia, or exported out of Australia, is called a customs duty. A tax which is imposed on goods already in Australia is called an excise duty. None of the States can impose these kinds of taxes. Only the Commonwealth can. The prohibition against the State in this area is expressly laid down in s 90 of the Constitution. The States can still impose taxes which are not connected with goods, say,

231

entertainment tax, pay-roll tax, stamp duties on documents, certain licence fees for carrying on a business ("business franchise" fees), land tax and if the States want to, personal or company income tax. The States can also demand charges for services rendered.

Customs duties: Since Federation in 1901 this kind of tax can no longer be imposed by any of the six States or the territories. The Federal Government is thus able by its customs tariff to protect local industry throughout the whole of Australia—without interference from the States with their different trade policies.

Excise duties are also taxes on goods, again to be imposed by the Commonwealth alone.

Suppose a jeweller is about to sell an article for $3 to a customer. But the jeweller is required to pay a sales tax of 33 1/3 per cent to the federal Taxation Commissioner on the sale of each of these articles. So he just adds $1 on to the price, and then he asks the customer for $4. In time, the jeweller will pay $1 to the Taxation Commissioner. This sales tax is an excise duty.

- *It is indirect*—in the sense that the sales tax can be passed on to the customer. The jeweller is technically the taxpayer. But the customer is the one who actually pays the tax to all intents and purposes.

- *It is a tax*—that is, the sales tax is a compulsory exaction of money by a public authority for a public purpose.

- *It is a tax on goods*—in the sense that it looks as if the goods pay the sales tax rather than the jeweller. The tax is just tacked on to each article which goes along with its tax to the consumer. Usually, too, an excise duty increases with the number or value of goods handled.

  Duties of excise are "duties charged upon goods produced or manufactured in Australia itself or upon a sale of such commodities".

  " 'The substantial effect is to impose a levy in respect of the commodity.' "

  " 'A duty (of excise is) charged on home goods.' "

There are other examples of duties of excise apart from the sales tax example given above. Once New South Wales attempted to tax newspaper publishers 1/2d. for every newspaper sold. This was held to be an excise duty, and so New South Wales had to end its tax (*John Fairfax v NSW* 1927). Once Victoria attempted to tax milk distributors 1/8d. per gallon of milk distributed. This was also an excise duty, and so Victoria had to stop its tax, too (*Parton v Milk Board* 1949). In both of these examples there was *an indirect tax on goods*. But most of all the tax was levied on, or with respect to, *goods*, the newspapers or the milk—and this is the mark of an excise duty, the kind of duty that a State cannot impose.

In the late 1960s various revenue-hungry States imposed a receipt duty or a tax simply on the receipt of money—any money. However, Hamersley Iron in Western Australia happened to have received its money from the sale of iron ore. Nevertheless, the High Court unearthed an excise duty even here. Strictly the duty was a tax on receipts or, at any rate, on receipt of money. Still, the High Court could see a tax "in effect" on the sale of *goods* for which the money was received and, therefore, a duty of excise (*Hamersley Iron* 1969). With the same liberalism, although certainly not from the States' angle, the High Court tested Queensland's *Stock Act* in 1977. The Act imposed a fee on the owners of livestock, say, cattle, sheep, pigs. The Court pointed out that the taxpayer before the Court was a grazing company, that its cattle, etc, would become beef, wool and ham, and that "in that sense" the State fee fell on articles of commerce and so was bad as an excise duty (*Logan Downs v Queensland*).

In the first Chapter on "general matters", No 5, I gave another example, a Victorian licence fee that was dressed up as a tax on the business of operating a pipeline. The High Court exposed the pipeline operation fee as a tax on the conveyed goods, hydrocarbons, "in practical operation" and "in substance" (*Hematite Petroleum* 1983).

By these High Court decisions the States are pushed further out of the market of taxation which is associated with goods.

And that has been happening in s 90 law—from the States' point of view, all too frequently. The States must tread very warily if they intend to impose a tax that is in some way associated with goods.

But take another example. Queensland once imposed a tax on the gross receipts taken by carriers. Suppose a transport company carried passengers only and no freight. Then the Queensland tax would not be an excise duty because there would be no tax *on goods*. Or take quite a different example. The Victorian Egg Marketing Board grades, stamps and packs eggs for Victorian poultry farmers, who are required by law to pay a fee to the Egg Board. The Egg Board is taking a payment for services rendered by it to the poultry farmers. Hence the egg levy is not a payment on goods, but a payment for *services*. In fact, a High Court challenge on the Victorian egg levy failed in 1966 (*Harper v Victoria*).

Another High Court challenge seemed at one stage to fail in 1974, only this time it was Tasmania's tobacco tax, as it was called. Strictly, as you can see, it could not have been a tobacco tax, a tax on goods, in the sense that I have used the phrase, otherwise it would have been bad. No, it was a tax on the consumption of tobacco, that is, a tax at the end of the process line and after the purchaser had received the goods. So at this stage the tax was in theory not an excise duty. However, in its actual operation the tax was designed to tax the purchaser as he purchased tobacco, rather like a sales tax. In the result, Tasmania's tobacco tax fell (*Dickenson's Arcade v Tasmania*).

On the same day and in the same case (now confirmed by *Philip Morris* 1989) Tasmania's licence fee for retailing tobacco was upheld. The fee was based on a retailer's turnover in a 12-month period that had ended about six months before he applied for his licence. The High Court described this fee as a payment for a *business franchise*, a payment for the privilege of being allowed to run a business at all in the taxing State, and not a payment that could be described as a tax on the goods in the business. And this is the modern origin of the State "business franchise" fee for running the business of dealing in liquor (as in *Dennis Hotels* 1960), tobacco or petrol. But in 1985 the High Court retreated somewhat. A New South Wales licence fee, based on animals slaughtered in a previous 12-month period, was an excise duty. Here the Court explained, the tax affected production, not sales (*Gosford Meats v NSW*).

And in 1993 the Court retreated more than somewhat. An Australian Capital Territory business franchise fee for selling X-rated videos was an excise duty, even though the fee (of 40% of the wholesale value) was based on a previous one-month period (*Capital Duplicators v ACT*). However, deferring to long-standing Commonwealth-State fiscal arrangements built on its decisions, the High Court allowed liquor, tobacco and petrol franchise fees to stand.

Thus, a State may not impose a tax on goods, for this is an excise duty; and such a tax is unearthed in unlikely places. But a State may exact a tax on the transport of passengers, or require a payment for services rendered to those who deal in goods, or impose a consumption tax, or a State may in certain circumstances require a licence fee for carrying on the business of selling liquor, tobacco, or petrol.

3. When Federal Parliament makes a law about the acquisition of property it must provide just terms

Federal Parliament can make a law with respect to the acquisition of property from a State or an individual—but it must give "just terms" or fair compensation to the State or individual. Otherwise, the Commonwealth law is not a law at all, and the State or individual takes back the property. Thus, the acquisition power in s 51(xxxi) of the Constitution does not only authorise the Commonwealth to acquire property or to make laws about the acquisition of property. It also guarantees just terms to the expropriated owner. I have already spoken of this guarantee to the State or the individual in the Chapter on "the powers of Federal Parliament", No 7 above.

4. The Commonwealth must not establish any religion, and it must not interfere with any religion

This is the nearest thing we have to a Bill of Rights provision in the Constitution. Not that it has incited such a raging dissension among Australians, as its United States counterpart, the 1st amendment, has among Americans. This guarantee in Constitution s 116 falls into four parts which can be set out as follows:

- no law for establishing any religion

- no law for imposing any religious observance

- no law for prohibiting the free exercise of any religion

- no religious test for Commonwealth office.

It is a give-and-take promise. Commonwealth Parliament will not help any religion. But at the same time Commonwealth Parliament will not interfere with any religion, either.

Until the *State aid* case—it began as long ago as 1973 and was finally disposed of only in 1981—the High Court had rarely been asked to speak on this provision. In that case the High Court read the non-establishment-of-religion clause as a prohibition against setting up or recognising a State religion, an official church for Australia. This meant that the clause did *not* prevent the Federal Government from continuing to fund, through the States, government and non-government schools. Some of the latter schools taught religion and were part of a religious sect. Hence the "State aid" argument that failed.

In 1943 the High Court dealt with Jehovah's Witnesses and that part of s 116 which protects the free exercise of religion. The teachings of this religious sect, if found anarchical or dangerous in a community engaged in World War II, would not be protected from practical and adequate Commonwealth laws, not even by invoking the freedom-of-religion clause (*Jehovah's Witnesses v The Commonwealth*).

> "The meaning and scope of s 116 must be determined, not as an isolated enactment, but as one of a number of sections intended to provide in their inter-relation a practical instrument of government, within the framework of which laws can be passed for organising the citizens of the Commonwealth in national affairs into a civilised community, not only enjoying religious tolerance, but also possessing adequate laws . . ."

Notice that the four prohibitions in the provision on religion bind only the Parliament of *the Commonwealth*. Whether the States can establish any religion, and the rest, will depend on the Constitutions of *the States*. In fact only the *Constitution Act* 1934 of Tasmania deals with religion; it prohibits any law interfering with religious freedom or imposing a religious test for office.

And so, we find once again that a citizen in the Australian Federation must always take into account two bodies.

- *The Commonwealth*, with its Parliament, its Government, its Courts, its Constitution.

- *The States*, with their Parliaments, their Governments, their Courts, their Constitutions.

How the Constitution was made

In a previous Chapter on "the States" I gave our earlier constitutional history. A short account there summarises what happened between 1770 (when Captain James Cook landed on the east coast of Australia) and the 1850s-1890s (when the Colonies evolved, growing into independence). The Colonies were now separate and independent—and Federation was the next stage. The present Chapter takes up this next stage in our constitutional history. This Chapter deals with the beginnings of the federal idea in the 19th century, the draftings of the constitutional document throughout the National Conventions of the 1890s, and the formal enactment of the Constitution by the Imperial Parliament in 1900.

In anticipation I will give a bird's-eye view of the coming-of-age of the Constitution and Federation in the 19th century.

• 1847—The Secretary of State called on the Colonies to legislate on "national" interests.

• 1850s—Constitutional Committees spoke of a General Assembly.

• 1880s—The Federal Council of Australasia was such a general assembly; but it was a loose arrangement. Besides, New South Wales kept out of it.

• 1890s—First, an exploratory Melbourne Conference was held in 1890. Second, the two National Conventions themselves met in 1891 and 1897-1898 to draft a bill on the Constitution. Third, the Premiers' conference in 1899 added some amendments.

• 1900—The Constitution was enacted in 1900, and Federation was established in 1901.

It was Earl Grey, British Secretary of State for the Colonies, who started it all in his 1847 Despatch to the Colonies. Grey encouraged "the creation of a central legislative authority for the whole of the Australian colonies"—to make laws, he suggested, on such "common interests" as customs and excise, postage, roads and railways. But nothing tangible came of this exhortation, other than pipe-dreams of a Federation at some future date.

237

By the middle of the 19th century, or a little later, the six Australian Colonies had separated as independent territories. And even at this early date, the 1850s, there were Constitutional Committees in New South Wales and in Victoria. These spoke of an overall "General Assembly" to legislate on matters of "intercolonial interest". The Wentworth Constitutional Committee, a Select Committee of the New South Wales Legislative Council in 1853, crystallised a definite list of federal subjects—tariffs and coastal trade, intercolonial roads and railways, beacons and lighthouses, postage, monetary regulations, a general court of appeal.

These rudimentary subjects are now found, more or less, in the Commonwealth catalogue of powers in the present Constitution of 1900. See s 51(i), (ii), (v), (vii), (xii) with s 115, s 71 and s 73.

Intercolonial Conferences between the 1860s and the 1880s— constituted by representatives of the Colonial Governments— mooted an Australasian Court of Appeal or encouraged uniform legislation, for instance, on defence, postage and telegraphic services, lighthouses and immigration. The latter legislation was especially concerned with uniform controls of Chinese immigrants who were undercutting labour on the gold fields in the 1880s.

At the 1867 Intercolonial Conference Sir Henry Parkes, the Premier from New South Wales, declaimed: "I think the time has arrived when these Colonies should be united by some federal bond of connection". And yet, throughout the whole period from the 1850s to the 1890s there was really a fair amount of resistance to Federation.

Border tariffs constituted the main obstacle to Federation in Australia—the customs and excise question.

That is, South Australia, Western Australia and especially Victoria wanted to protect their local industries, and safeguard against unemployment, by imposing customs duties on incoming goods. Moreover, Western Australia particularly, but the other Colonies also, thought they would be starved of revenue in a Federation where they must surrender their independent revenue sources—their customs duties at the borders. Apart from one Colony with its added source of income tax, the Colonies relied almost entirely on customs and excise duties as their source of revenue. And so, throughout the 1891 and the 1897-1898 debates, discussed below, the financial provisions that were to go into the Constitution were on the top of the agenda. The question was, what was to be done with customs and excise? (Federal income tax, the present revenue octopus, did not appear until 1915.) How much of the customs and excise revenue was to be surrendered to the new government? And how was the surplus to be distributed to the States?

Still, by the same token—the lines of Custom-houses at the borders—customs duties became in time a *cause* of Federation. The colonists, and not just the free-traders in New South Wales, grew impatient with their divisive barriers.

1. The Federal Council of Australasia

An Imperial law, the Federal Council of Australasia Act 1885, created a national assembly, a kind of supra-legislature for the early Colonies. The Act grew out of a local Bill drafted by the Colonies at a Convention in 1883; two years before this, in a memorandum to an Intercolonial Conference Parkes had suggested setting up a Federal Council. As a matter of fact, you will find the Council mentioned in the Constitution itself. Clause VII refers to its abolition and to the survival of its laws. Section 51(xxxviii) refers to the Federal Council's powers which a State can now ask the Commonwealth to exercise on behalf of the State.

Each of the six Colonies, as well as New Zealand and Fiji, could send along a couple of representatives to the Council; (we forget that from 1823 to 1840 New Zealand was associated with, even annexed to, New South Wales). As it happened, South Australia did not join until 1888. New Zealand stayed away—worse still, so did New South Wales. Perhaps New South Wales saw the Council as a Victorian institution under the presidency of James Service, the Premier of Victoria. But what New South Wales Premier Parkes (who now professed "maturer thoughts on the subject") actually said was: the Council would "impede the way for a sure and solid Federation".

However, when it was all boiled down, the Federal Council was only a law-making body. It had no central sanctions. On top of this, any member of the Council dissatisfied with the Council's proposals could simply secede.

The Council could make laws on Australasian relations with the Pacific islands, influx of criminals—possibly, French criminals transported to New Caledonia—fisheries in Australasian waters beyond territorial limits, inter-colonial service and execution of process, and extradition. At the request of two or more Colonies, the Council could also make laws on defence—the French and

Germans seemed to be coveting islands in the Pacific, such as New Guinea and the New Hebrides—quarantine, patents and copyrights, bills of exchange and promissory notes, weights and measures, recognition of marriage and divorce, naturalisation of aliens, the status of corporations, and any other matter referred by the Colonies to the Council.

You will still find each of these 15 powers in the present Constitution, or variants of them. In other words, these powers were thought to be then, and have remained, powers suitable for a central government. See s 51(vi), (ix), (x), (xv), (xvi), (xviii)-(xxii), (xxiv), (xxviii)-(xxx), (xxxvii).

The Federal Council of Australasia first met in Hobart, January 1886. It last met in Melbourne, January 1899. But, really, it was barely ever viable. The Imperial Act setting up the Council was repealed by clause VII of the Constitution.

2. The Melbourne Conference 1890

The Australasian Federation Conference was the next step. Strictly, I should not call this Melbourne Conference of 1890 the next step, because it began a separate stream. It did not flow out of the Federal Council of Australasia.

Sir Henry Parkes, the aging New South Wales Premier, and Duncan Gillies, the Premier of Victoria, were the organisers. Gillies wanted to build a federation out of the existing Federal Council of Australasia. But Parkes wanted to make a new beginning. Remember that New South Wales had opted out of the Federal Council experiment. Since Parkes triggered the series of conferences and conventions that were to result in a Constitution and a Federation, and since Parkes was the architect of the starting point of the Constitution Bill—the Resolutions of 1891—he is usually hailed as the Father of Federation.

But as long ago as the Intercolonial Conference of March 1867, as we have seen, Parkes was calling on the Colonies to "be united by some federal bond of connection". It was Parkes, too, who reminded the colonists of the parlous state of their separated defence forces in his famous speech on Federation in October 1889 at Tenterfield, New South Wales. For various British officers in the 1870s up to the 1890s visited the colonies to point out the need for an overall Australian defence force. The colonists, for their part, were already anxious about assumed German intentions in the direction of New Guinea. The audience at the School of Arts in

Tenterfield heard Parkes' exhortation "that the whole of their (armed) forces should be amalgamated" and that, therefore, they should create a "great national government for all Australia".

The "federal" defence of Australia, in other words, was one of the causes of Federation. Another cause I have already noticed: the invidious lines of Custom-houses at the borders.

Return to the Melbourne conference of 1890: the 13 delegates to the Conference came from the five member-Colonies of the existing Federal Council of Australasia and from New South Wales and New Zealand. They were politicians who included Government members and two Opposition leaders—Playford from South Australia and Griffith from Queensland. Notice that New Zealand might have become a seventh State of Australia had its delegates persisted throughout the Conventions. In fact, you will see New Zealand given as one of "The States" in clause VI of the Constitution. Even as late as July 1899 a Federation League was trying to stir up enthusiasm in Auckland.

For seven days, before the public and the press, the Conference discussed Federation, the powers of a central government, and the relative merits of Canadian federation and the United States federation.

- The Canadians gave too much power to the centre. The Dominion Parliament not only had a list of special subjects, it also had what was left after the Provinces took their list of special subjects. The Dominion Government could veto Provincial laws. And the Dominion Government also appointed Provincial Lieutenant-Governors and some Provincial Judges.

- The Americans left their States with more independence. The States had the residual powers, and their laws were not vetoed by Congress.

And so, the 1890 Melbourne Conference, jealous of Colonial powers and privileges, much preferred the United States style of federation which we still have. See ss 51 and 52 and, on the other hand, ss 106 and 107 of the Constitution.

"Much preferred" is an understatement, for some delegates asseverated that their Colonies would never federate on the "centralist" Canadian pattern. In fact, the Colonies—indeed, Western Australia and Queensland right up till the 11th hour— were really reluctant to federate at all.

241

At this Conference, too, James Service (he was a Victorian Premier before Gillies) isolated one of the most troublesome obstacles, to which I have already referred: "the lion in the way", that is, the selfish border tariff that each Colony clung to, the "hundred Custom-houses". Instead of this protective tariff, and source of revenue as well, Service preached a Federation with a "uniform fiscal policy".

In time there was to be just that. When the Federation was established the Commonwealth was to take over the collection of customs and excise (ss 69, 86); it alone was to impose these taxes (s 90); they were to be uniform (ss 51(ii) and 99); and they were to be uniform within two years of Federation (s 88).

But this Melbourne Conference of 1890 was exploratory only and not too formal. The Colonies, other than Parkes' New South Wales, were not altogether sold on the idea of a full-bodied national convention. The delegates did not bind their home Parliaments.

3. The National Convention 1891

The National Australasian Convention in 1891 in Sydney was the next step towards a Constitution and Federation.

Back from the Melbourne Conference of 1890, the members persuaded their Parliaments to appoint delegates to a National Convention. These were balloted out of the Upper and Lower Houses and included Opposition members. The six Colonies sent off seven delegates each, New Zealand sent three—observers, rather than delegates. So, in all 45 members. There were 16 or 17 lawyers in this Convention. They would be useful in drawing up a bill, a piece of legislation, which the Constitution was to become.

Then there was the President, Parkes, the Premier of the host Colony. And there was the Vice-President, Sir Samuel Griffith, the Premier of Queensland and the man who had drawn up the 1883 Federal Council of Australasia Bill. Griffith master-minded the 1891 Draft Bill on the Constitution which became practically *the Constitution*. Later he became Chief Justice of the Queensland Supreme Court in 1893, and even then his opinion on later drafts was sought. In 1903 Griffith was the first Chief Justice of the High Court of Australia.

The National Convention, sitting in Sydney between 2nd March and 9th April, say, six weeks, went through three stages, just as the later series did in 1897-1898.

First, half a dozen or so general federal Resolutions were voted on by the Convention.

Second, three Committees put these Resolutions into the form of a Bill. A Drafting Committee pulled together the work of the three Committees.

Third, the provisions of the Draft Bill were now voted on by the Convention.

In the first place, then, Parkes put seven Resolutions to the Convention, not that Parkes personally was enamoured of all seven Resolutions, especially the leading Resolutions on State permanence. But remember Parkes—as Reid later—came from New South Wales, a Colony more centrally minded than the other Colonies. Each delegate voted as an individual, that is, not as a member of a unit from his Colony. The leading Resolutions strongly protested that the powers, privileges and territorial rights of the existing Colonies "shall remain intact", except such powers, etc, as were surrendered to the central government. It was an American theme favouring the status quo—the States and their continued powers, as much as possible—not the Canadian theme, as I mentioned above.

Speaking of his 1897 Resolutions, which almost matched Parkes' 1891 Resolutions, Barton declared: "Those (Resolutions) under the first head are those which prescribe the principal conditions of Federation"—namely the survival of State powers, privileges and rights.

This declaration of State self-respect has persisted in ss 106-108 and s 123 of the Constitution. These provisions save a State's Constitution, powers, laws and boundaries as far as is compatible with the federal polity.

Two other Resolutions gave defence and customs to Federal Parliament. (Remember these were two of the "causes" of Federation.) Under another Resolution, trade and commerce were to be absolutely free—*hence, in time, s 51(vi) with s 114, s 90 and s 92 of the Constitution which immortalised these three Resolutions.* The remaining Resolutions foreshadowed a Parliament with

243

a States' House, that is, the Senate and a House of Representatives—a Judiciary with a Federal Supreme Court, constituting "a
high court of appeal for Australia"—and an Executive with a
Governor-General and his advisers, such persons sitting in
Parliament. That is, even at this embryonic stage a separation of
powers was introduced between the legislature, the Judiciary and
the Executive. But not entirely, because the chief members of the
Executive were required to sit in the legislature and depend on its
confidence.

Next, these seven broad Resolutions were handed over to three
Committees. On each Committee a Colony was represented. These
Committees comprised a Constitutional Committee (Griffith
especially), a Finance Committee, and a Judiciary Committee.

Inglis Clark who served on the Judiciary Committee was, like
Griffith, another key figure. He had moved swiftly to present to the
Convention a complete draft constitution. In fact, nearly all of his
thirty "Powers of Federal Parliament" are now found in ss 51, 52,
121, 123 and 124 of the Constitution. Clark was at the time the
Tasmanian Attorney-General and became a Supreme Court Judge
in Tasmania. Both Griffith and Clark (and later Barton) along with
the South Australian Attorney-General, Kingston, formed the
all-important Drafting Committee which pieced together the work
of the three head Committees.

The resulting bill was voted on, clause by clause, by the full
Convention. Thus, **the Draft Bill of 1891** came into being at this
National Convention in Sydney. For that matter, this Bill of 1891
practically became our Constitution of 1900.

What were the source books used by the vital Committee
members, Griffith, Clark, and the others? Particularly the United
States Constitution of 1789 with its special list of federal powers,
its general list of State residual powers . . . the Canadian
Constitution, that is, the British North America Act of 1867 (now
re-entitled the Constitution Act 1867), with its provisions on
responsible government and the Governor-General, and a few
federal legislative powers . . . the Federal Council of Australasia
Act of 1885 and the existing Colonial Constitutions.

In other words, the present Constitution of 1900 is an amalgam
of the United States Constitution, the Canadian Constitution, and
the rest—*but principally our Constitution is built on the United
States Constitution*. Remember the Colonial Premiers were none
too keen on the subservience of Canadian Provinces to the central
government. How things have changed under High Court law.

_____

244

Here are a few points of interest in the 1891 Draft Bill.

The **"Commonwealth of Australia"** was settled on—despite its Cromwellian overtones—not "United Australia", or "Federated States", or "Dominion". **"States"** as in United States, not "Provinces" as in Canada, was chosen. Both terms have persisted, as we well know. "The Commonwealth" looms large in clause III and in the Preamble to the Constitution. The Preamble recites the reason for the Colonies joining forces—viz, they "agreed to unite in one indissoluble Federal Commonwealth". So, there was to be a Federation of States, not a loose confederacy. And it was to be indissoluble; no State could later opt out or secede. In time, as a matter of fact, Western Australia did speak of seceding, in 1934. Indeed, in the 1973 Constitutional Convention delegates from Western Australia and Tasmania hinted at secession also. The latter were annoyed by the high-handed centralism at Canberra.

Many of Federal Parliament's existing powers are found in the 1891 Bill. There were omissions: no insurance power, no acquisition power, no arbitration power, as we now have in s 51(xiv), s 51(xxxi) and s 51(xxxv) of the Constitution. But there was a general power over shipping and navigation which has since disappeared: it would have given the Commonwealth power over shipping and navigation within a State, even in its ports and harbours; instead, see the merely descriptive provision in s 98 which is locked into the restrictions in s 51(i) of the Constitution. On the other hand, there was a limited power over "the status" of certain corporations which in time became widened to give the Commonwealth power simply over certain corporations without being restricted to their status: see s 51(xx) of the Constitution.

The Senate was emphatically a House to preserve State interests, even if the Colonies had decided to federate. See s 7 of the Constitution.

Therefore, to preserve each State's interests equally, the smaller States opposed proportional representation in the Senate based on the size of the population in each State. Instead, each State, large or small, had equal representation in the Senate, initially six senators for every State. See s 7 of the Constitution, preserving this equality. With party politics the Senate quickly ceased to be a States' House. Yet another distortion was created by the High Court in 1975: by a cliff-hanger 4:3 decision, four "senators" from the *Commonwealth's* territories were admitted through the doors of what had seemed to be a States' House (*Territorial Senators* case). Again, in this early Draft Bill of 1891, as in United States up till 1913, the State legislatures were to elect their Senators, not the people as now happens in s 7. In other words, the Senate was to have been an indirectly elected body, not an institution directly responsible to the people.

Money bills, the lifeline of government, had to originate in, and be amended by, the House of Representatives alone.

The small Colonies, led by Sir John Downer of South Australia, wanted the Senate to have the power to amend—the power to "veto in detail", as well as the power to "veto in bulk", as they argued. But Reid of New South Wales would only concede the latter power at the 1897 Adelaide session. Of course, the Senate could have the power to reject money bills, Reid said handsomely, "not as an antiquated power, never to be used, but as a real living power". And at the Melbourne session in 1898 Higgins, a later High Court Justice, insisted: "The Senate has full power to reject an ordinary Appropriation Bill". Why the Senate would want to refuse money to the government was explained in the 1891 debates by Griffith, later the first Chief Justice on the High Court: "Surely if the Senate wanted to stop the machinery of government the way to do that would be to throw out the Appropriation Bill"—"and the government would consult the electors", added Deakin in 1897.

Well, in time the Senate's power to withhold Supply became just that: "a real living power". In October 1975 the Senate deferred two Appropriation Bills until the Government came out to face the people. See the closing pages in the Chapter on "Federal Parliament machinery".

So much for the Senate's power to reject or defer money bills . . . Return now to the debate on the Senate's power to amend money bills. "The compromise of 1891" between the small States and the large States on the Senate's power to amend money bills allowed the Senate, if not to amend, then at least to request an amendment of money bills. And this compromise won the day at the 1897-1898 Convention. Otherwise the States' House, as the Senate was regarded in the coming Federation, had as much law-making power as the House of Representatives.

All of this has now been perpetuated in s 53 of the Constitution.

The Governor-General was to be above politics, and not elected as was proposed. Neither was he to be allowed to veto legislation. In other words, he was not to be a President, such as was found in United States. He was to be merely the formal Head of State representing the Crown in Australia—and so he has remained: see s 2 of the Constitution.

There might be **a Supreme Court of Australia,** as it was then called—"might", because the Bill left it to Parliament to set up the Court, if Parliament felt the need. The Court would be a national Court taking appeals from State Supreme Courts on general matters, like the Privy Council but unlike the United States Supreme Court. Appeals to the Privy Council were severely curtailed: none as of right; some by leave of the Queen, but only if "the public interests" of a part of the Dominions demanded it. In short, a new Supreme Court in Australia was to take the place of the former Final Court, the Privy Council in London. See now ss 71 and 73 on the High Court, s 74 on the Privy Council.

The delegates returned to their several Colonies, each with his copy of a "Draft of a Bill as adopted by the National Australasian Convention" held in Sydney in 1891. They were to ask their Parliaments to submit the Bill to a plebiscite in each Colony.

Back in the Colonies the 1891 Draft Bill never got off the ground. New South Wales was the vital Colony. Both Houses here let the Bill lapse. Queensland, Western Australia and New Zealand were not particularly interested. Their Parliaments did not consider the Bill. There were more important things than a highfalutin Federation, such as social legislation for the New South Wales Labor Party, or the survival of the Colonial tariffs for Western Australian agriculture and Victorian manufacture.

For the next few years grassroots federalism alone prevailed. Tired of the politicians' dithering around, the Australian Natives' Association organised branches of federal activists throughout the Colonies. Founded in 1871 the Association promoted the federal cause through publicists, conferences, meetings. Federation Leagues and Border Leagues joined the crusade; (the border areas were especially disadvantaged by customs duties).

Politicians again entered the scene, at the Premiers' Conference in Hobart in 1895. The Premiers solemnly avowed that Federation was "the great and pressing question of Australasian politics"— and went off to arrange another National Convention. So, between 1895 and 1896 the five Colonies (Queensland did not join in) passed Enabling Acts. And they decided to send ten representatives from each Colony for the next Constitutional Convention of 1897-1898.

4. The National Convention 1897-1898

The National Australasian Convention of 1897-1898 actually consisted of a series of three sessions: at Adelaide in 1897, at Sydney in the same year, and at Melbourne in 1898. The press and public were admitted to the Convention.

There was a peculiarity about this Convention, absent in the 1891 Convention. The Colonies, other than Western Australia, held popular elections for Convention representatives. Thus, the delegates at the 1897-1898 National Convention were directly chosen by the people themselves, not by the politicians. (The 1986-1988 Constitutional Commission consisted of government appointees; this may explain why it was largely ineffectual.) You will also notice later that at various steps a referendum of the people was called to vote on the Bill.

That is, the people were involved in making the Constitution at this stage, 1897-1898.

Tickets were run by the "Prudent Federalists", the Labor Party, the "Age", the "Argus". In the event, the delegates were mostly parliamentarians, Government and Opposition. Five non parliamentarians were also elected. Each of the five Colonies sent ten delegates. Even Western Australia sent its representatives, but Queensland stood aloof.

The Vice-President, the man who piloted the Bill through this Convention, was Edmund Barton. A New South Wales lawyer-politician, Barton became Australia's first Prime Minister and in 1903 a High Court Justice. Barton was to the 1897-1898 Convention and Bill what Griffith was to the 1891 Convention and Bill. By this time Griffith had become Chief Justice of the Queensland Supreme Court (in 1893), although his advice was still sought subsequently.

Adelaide Session 1897

The first session of the National Convention met in Adelaide. The popularly elected delegates were determined to be an authentic popular expression. So they drew up their own Draft Bill. That is, the new Convention did not merely build on the 1891 Bill. But, of course, much of the earlier Bill of 1891 simply flowed into the 1897 Draft.

Again the general Resolutions of high principles: Barton's 1897 Resolutions almost matched Parkes' 1891 Resolutions . . . Again the Constitutional Committee, the Finance Committee and the Judiciary Committee . . . Again the Drafting Committee.

Barton, O'Connor and Isaacs (the Victorian Attorney-General) served on the Constitutional Committee. They all became High Court Justices in time. Indeed, Isaacs later became the Chief Justice in 1930 and then went on to become the first Australian Governor-General in 1931. Higgins, another High Court Justice, served on the Judiciary Committee with the invaluable Inglis Clark. The Drafting Committee, consisting of the ever-present Barton with O'Connor and Downer, drew up the 1897 Draft Bill itself. The Secretary to this overall Drafting Committee was Robert Garran, later the Solicitor-General for the Commonwealth and co-author (with Quick) of the first text on the new Constitution. Then, as before, the Drafting Committee recommended the Bill to the full Convention for its perusal and vote.

Here are some examples of the provisions that arose in the 1897 Convention in Adelaide.

Federal Parliament acquired powers over telephones and other like services (s 51 (v)), insurance (s 51 (xiv)), corporations without the 1891 limit to "status" (s 51 (xx)).

The Senate, or "The States Assembly" as it was called then ("to preserve the individuality of the several States") was to be directly elected by the people, as it is now: see s 7 of the Constitution. And the numbers in the House of Representatives were tied in a 2:1 ratio with the numbers in the Senate—"*the nexus*", as it is called: see s 24 of the Constitution. Various reasons were given for this tie, such as the expense of Parliament, or the protection of the Senators, the State's representatives, in a joint sitting in s 57.

Ministerial responsibility—or the answerability of the Government to the Parliament—was catered for at this Adelaide Convention. Ministers were required to sit in one or other House of Parliament. Despite criticism, the Founding Fathers combined the system of responsible government (familiar to them in their own Colonies and in Great Britain) with the system of a federation, although United States had not made this combination. See s 64 of the Constitution, making provision for federal Ministers of State and directing them to sit in one of either House of Parliament.

The High Court of Australia appeared for the first time under this familiar title. And it was established by the very Constitution itself, s 71, not left to the good offices of Commonwealth Parliament as it had been in the 1891 Convention. Thus, not beholden to the central Parliament, the High Court was to be the arbiter between central interests and State interests. Indeed, the delegates rather thought of the High Court as the protector of State rights against encroachment from the new central government. (How bitterly disillusioned the States have become in modern times.)

Another important judicial provision appeared only in the 1897 Draft Bill—the existing State courts could be used by Commonwealth Parliament in federal matters. This was a novel device not found in the United States Constitution, which had expressly authorised instead a tier of lower federal courts. But the Founding Fathers in Australia shied away from the expense. See s 77(iii) of our Constitution, making State courts available as the judicial agents of the Commonwealth.

Appeals to the Privy Council were still very limited: none by right and few by the Queen's leave in special circumstances: see s 74.

"The lion in the way", or the mischief of colonial border tariffs, was to be removed within two years of the founding of the Federation: see s 88.

Any amendment to the Constitution was to be initiated by Federal Parliament, and then ratified directly by the people in a referendum, not indirectly by State conventions, as had been required in the 1891 Bill. The earlier double-majority rule stipulated in the 1891 Bill remained, namely, a successful referendum must be carried by a majority of States and by a majority of the overall electorate. See s 128 of the Constitution, still leaving the initiative with Federal Parliament and fixing the double-majority rule.

Once again the delegates (none from Queensland) returned home to the five participating Colonies with copies of the Draft Bill. In these Colonies the Parliaments suggested amendments, nearly 300 as a matter of fact.

Sydney Session 1897

Five months after the Adelaide Convention, and after the Colonial legislatures had seen the Draft Bill, the National Convention held its second session, only this time it met in Sydney in 1897. The same representatives, with some replacements for Western Australia, arrived from the various Colonies. Again Queensland did not attend. The Drafting Committee still consisted

250

of Barton, O'Connor and Downer. The Convention got to work on the 1897 Draft Bill plus the 286 amendments that had come in from the Colonial legislatures.

This particular Convention—with confirmation at Melbourne in 1898, but with an absolute majority rule (instead of a three-fifths rule) substituted at the 1899 Premiers' Conference—settled the double dissolution provision, now s 57. Deadlocks between the two federal Houses were to be resolved by a simultaneous dissolution of both Houses, not by a dissolution of the House of Representatives and then by the Senate, as had been proposed, or by a nationwide referendum of the people independently of the legislative process.

Melbourne Session 1898

The third and last session of the National Australasian Convention 1897-1898 was held in Melbourne in January 1898.

Here the Drafting Committee, still composed of Barton, Downer and O'Connor, undertook the gigantic task of handling hundreds of amendments. The committee set out to overhaul and finalise the Bill on the Constitution.

Federal Parliament at this late stage acquired two odd powers for a national government of those times—the power over invalid and old age pensions, and the power over conciliation and arbitration for the prevention and settlement of industrial disputes extending beyond the limits of any one State. I did describe these powers as "odd" national powers. But perhaps they were not unexpected in the 1890s context of hard times and Australia-wide shearing and shipping industrial disputes. Back in 1891 Kingston failed to introduce federal conciliation and arbitration "courts" into the Constitution. And now another radical, Higgins, twice fought for the arbitration power, in Adelaide in 1897 and in Melbourne in 1898—Higgins referred to the intercolonial disputes in the shearing and shipping industry. He succeeded at this Melbourne session in having the present arbitration power inserted in the Constitution. Later Higgins became the second President of the Commonwealth Court of Conciliation and Arbitration. A third power, a power to acquire property compulsorily, even State property, was also given to the national Parliament at this Melbourne Convention.

All three powers have persisted in the Constitution. See the invalid and old age pensions power, the acquisition power and the arbitration power in s 51(xxiii), s 51(xxxi) and s 51(xxxv).

251

At this Melbourne Conference, too, Isaacs protested against the vagueness in what was to become s 92 which insists that interstate trade and travelling shall be "absolutely free". But Reid, New South Wales Premier, retorted that the provision touched "the vital point for which we are federating"—true enough—and offhandedly: "It is a little bit of layman's language which comes in here very well". There has been a good deal of lawyer's language on the section for 80 years now, in fact something like 145 court cases.

Since those days the vagaries, because of the vagueness, of s 92 have persisted.

Ever since 1891 the members had been searching for financial guarantees in the new Federation. They were particularly jealous of their customs and excise revenues. But it was not until the 1898 Melbourne Conference that a device was hit upon. The Tasmanian Premier, Braddon, proposed that the Federal Government should distribute to the States three quarters of the customs and excise duties collected—whence, with an amendment in 1899 (the ten-year sunset clause), the "Braddon clause" which is now found in s 87 of the Constitution.

Following the usual pattern, the Draft Bill of 1897-1898 was put to the electors in four Colonies, New South Wales, Victoria, South Australia and Tasmania—and was accepted only in the last three Colonies. New South Wales did not reach the number of votes laid down by its Parliament. The Western Australian Parliament had yet to look at the Bill. Queensland just watched the results. Because of differences at home, it had not attended the 1897-1898 Convention. Besides, Brisbane and the Premier, Nelson, were not won over to the federal cause.

The Premiers' Conference 1899 was next. New South Wales proposed amendments and its Premier, Reid, called for a Premiers' Conference. The Premiers met in Melbourne in January-February 1899. All six Premiers, even Queensland's Mr Dickson (now), attended to think about the New South Wales amendments and to approve some of these amendments.

At this Premiers' Conference two fiscal provisions were settled—both with a view to flexibility in Commonwealth-State financial arrangements. First, a ten-year time limit was put to the Braddon clause because of New South Wales' protest. Thereafter Parliament could try some other scheme. Second, during this ten-year period Parliament could adjust Commonwealth-State

252

financial relations by making ad hoc grants to the States, especially those that were not doing so well out of the distribution under the Braddon clause, for instance, Tasmania.

This temporising and incidental States-grants provision became s 96 of the Constitution, the central government's strongest weapon to subject money-starved States to Federal dictates.

The other alteration effected by the 1899 Premiers' Conference was given above: the lesser absolute majority rule (instead of the three-fifths rule) to resolve parliamentary deadlocks.

After this, a people's referendum on the amended Bill was held, and carried, in five Colonies, New South Wales, Victoria, South Australia, Queensland and Tasmania. Hence these are the only five Colonies mentioned in the Preamble to the Constitution. Hence, too, Western Australia is assumed in clause III of the Constitution to have only one way open to it: simply to accept the Constitution as it had already been agreed to by the other five Colonies. Similarly, ss 26 and 95 suggest that Western Australia might yet become an "Original State" within clause VI. Section 7 makes the same suggestion about Queensland; you remember its lack of enthusiasm for the 1897-1898 Convention.

5. The Constitution and the Federation

The Commonwealth Bill was next presented to the Imperial Parliament for enactment, under the watching eyes of six Colonial delegates. Western Australia had now joined the movement—in interest, but not as a party.

When the Bill came into the Imperial Parliament the "Appeals to the Queen-in-Council" section, s 74, was not there. At the 1898 Melbourne session s 74 had stopped all appeals as of right to the Privy Council. It allowed the Queen to grant her special leave only if the matter did *not* involve the interpretation of the Commonwealth Constitution or the Constitution of any State. In other words, the Convention delegates had resolved to supplant the overseas Privy Council by the local High Court of Australia. The Privy Council might retain its special prerogative to grant appeals—but even here constitutional cases were not to be taken by the Privy Council.

Yet in the Imperial Parliament the Bill appeared without these limitations on the Queen's prerogative. Instead, clause V of the Bill in the Imperial Parliament insisted that the Queen could grant leave to appeal from any High Court or Supreme Court decision. When the Australian delegates protested, the Secretary of State, Chamberlain, and his Law Officers agreed to a compromise.

This compromise appears in the present s 74, which requires a High Court certificate before certain constitutional cases, "inter se questions", can go to the Privy Council.

And so it came about that the Commonwealth of Australia Constitution Act 1900 (Imp.), 63 & 64 Vic c 12, was eventually passed by the House of Commons and the House of Lords, and assented to by the Queen on 9 July 1900.

Western Australia, as I said, was not a party at this stage. Chamberlain had exhorted her by telegraph to join back in April. Then, at a late hour on 31 July, Western Australia held and carried a referendum in favour of Federation and the new Constitution. Throughout she had feared the lack of tariff to protect her agriculture. Besides, she needed the money, especially this revenue from the customs duties at her borders. For this reason you will read a concession to Western Australia in s 95 of the Constitution: for the first five years of Federation Western Australia was allowed to continue her customs duties until they were phased out. Now that Western Australia had "agreed thereto", as clause III puts it, the Queen proclaimed 1 January 1901 as the date for the establishment of the Federation. Hence the disparity:

We speak of the Constitution Act of 1900 because it was passed on 9 July 1900.

But we say that Federation began in 1901 because Federation was established on 1 January 1901.

Changing the Constitution

A talkfest on the Constitution is not new. Now, the talking suggests that something must be done about the Constitution, that it is fossilised. And yet, something has been done. Despite the agitation for reform, our constitutional law has changed almost beyond recognition since the 1920s, and grows steadily—like a living organism. Indeed, one might debate whether the Constitution really is "badly in need of reform".

There have been innumerable gatherings to change the Constitution. In the 1920s, the 1930s and the 1940s national conventions, more or less defined, ran. In 1927-1929 the Royal Commission on the Constitution talked and reported, as did the Parliamentary Joint Committee on Constitutional Review in 1956-1959. Again between 1973 and 1985—that is, for 12 years—Constitutional Conventions met, no fewer than six. The Constitutional Commission of 1986-1988 came and went.

And now a series of memorials, commemorating Federation staging posts, has been held or will be held in 1990, 1991, 1993, 1997-1998, 2001. In April 1992 the Constitutional Centenary Foundation was publicly launched to promote public awareness of "the Australian constitutional system".

The output: say 1200 pages from the 1973-1985 Conventions, the same from the 1986-1988 Commission, and more besides. The cost: huge. The result in changes to the Constitution: little.

Referendums are no better. Between 1906 and 1988 there have been 18 referendum days, 42 Constitution Alteration Bills with 50 odd proposals. The result: eight referendums carried, with nine amendments to the Constitution, only two of any moment, possibly three. It may be apathy. It may be suspicion born of ignorance. It may be going by the rule on the farm, "if the pump works, don't fix it". Whatever the cause of Australian referendum malaise, there's no denying this malaise over the last 80 to 90 years. Why should tomorrow be any different?

And yet, Australia is *not* a "frozen continent" constitutionally. Changes have taken place, and will continue to take place, because of three influences

- the High Court of Australia
- Commonwealth-State cooperative federalism

• the substance behind the form.

The High Court of Australia is continually up-dating the Commonwealth Constitution.

What the Federal Parliament at Canberra can do now under its seemingly limited powers differs—almost unrecognisably—from what the Parliament seemed to be able to do in 1901. Because of High Court law, Federal Parliament under its postal power controls broadcasting and television; under its trading corporations power, controls football clubs or Tasmania's Hydro-Electric Commission's attempt to build a dam; under its financial corporations power, controls Victoria's State Superannuation Board's mortgage loans; under its marriage power controls, not just the ceremony of marriage, but the institution of marriage, that is, controls such matters as matrimonial property, children and maintenance; under its arbitration power, controls about half the Australian work force; under its external affairs power, controls . . . well, there seems to be no limit: under this power Canberra now controls civil rights, environment, war crimes in Europe just because they were crimes in Europe, New Zealand custody orders, intrastate air navigation as much as interstate air navigation.

This nationalisation of power in Australia has grown in other aspects of Commonwealth-State relations, especially financial.

The High Court permitted Commonwealth surplus revenue, that the Constitution seemed to promise the States, to be squirrelled away in Commonwealth trust funds. The Commonwealth scheme to monopolise income tax was upheld by the High Court twice. The many State attempts to scrape up revenue from taxes in some way associated with goods—by sales taxes or receipt duties or inspection fees—are repeatedly foiled in the High Court. Whence our present Commonwealth-State fiscal imbalance.

Here is a different kind of High Court case, not about Commonwealth expansionist powers or Commonwealth fiscal dominance, but about the prohibition in s 92 of the Constitution against interference with interstate trade. Yet it is the same High Court exercise of modernising the Constitution. In 1988 the Commonwealth and all six States pleaded with the Court for an agreeable interpretation of s 92, one that would give their legislators greater control of interstate traders. So the High Court constructed a new test out of the existing parts of s 92 for the 1990s.

And that's the point. If you look at early constitutional law and then constitutional law of the 1990s, you see quantum leaps. Yet the document itself, the Constitution of 1900, has not changed in these areas one iota.

One last example. The Constitution has no comprehensive Bill of Rights, only a scatter of rights. Yet the High Court, increasingly, is adding rights to the bare bones of the Constitution.

For instance, the rule of law is assumed by the Constitution, the High Court explained as far back as 1951. So associates of communists could not be penalised just because of that association and not because of specific criminal acts. The Rhodesian information centre in Sydney could not be denied postal and telephone services, for its officer also had committed no breach of the law. Neither could a foreign deserter, similarly blameless, be deprived of his liberty.

In September 1992 the High Court read in the Constitution two implied freedoms—one, a freedom of political discourse (eg the Commonwealth or a State cannot ban political advertising), the other, a freedom of criticism of government institutions (eg the Commonwealth cannot stop criticism of its Industrial Relations Commission).

Commonwealth-State cooperative federalism has made good where the High Court has failed to "reform" the Constitution.

When the High Court decided that the Constitution barred State law from Commonwealth places, such as RAAF bases, the Commonwealth with the States made use of Commonwealth-adopted State law for those enclaves in 1970. When the High Court found that the Constitution stopped the States from imposing receipt duties, the Commonwealth obliged by vacating the field of payroll tax for a State takeover in 1971. When the High Court declared that the territorial sea beside a coastal State was beyond State jurisdiction, the Commonwealth on State request authorised the use of State powers, and conceded State title, in those waters in 1980. When the High Court allowed the Federal Court of Australia to take on board only so much jurisdiction in a State matter as was closely associated with a federal matter already in the Federal Court, the Commonwealth and States liberally cross-vested jurisdiction in each other's courts in 1988. Finally, when the High Court interpreted the corporations power as insufficient to support the Commonwealth's Corporations Act, the Commonwealth and States cooperated to substitute a joint Corporations Law in 1990.

And then the High Court itself has blessed a Commonwealth-State joint venture, as it did in 1983 for the Commonwealth-New South Wales Coal Industry Tribunal. In 1988 the High Court hinted that national Commonwealth-State collective marketing arrangements are not likely to be thwarted by the High Court's newly found version of the freedom-of-trade clause.

There are other possibilities of Commonwealth-State cooperation to get around or "reform" the Constitution. From 1986 to 1990 the States referred to the Commonwealth certain matters relating to children, even children outside the marriage circle, where the Commonwealth's marriage power would stumble. In March 1993 the Commonwealth with a State or Territory participating jurisdiction facilitated an Australia-wide mutual recognition: under the Commonwealth Act one State or Territory will recognise the standards of goods or occupations of another State or Territory. In 1985-1986 the States requested the Commonwealth, and the Commonwealth agreed, to pass the kind of law for them that the United Kingdom Parliament alone in 1901 could have enacted—viz, the Australia Act, which gives the States legislative, executive and judicial autonomy. These two existing powers, the State reference power and the look-alike 1901 United Kingdom power, can be tools of Commonwealth-State cooperative federalism to "reform" the Constitution.

The fact is, Commonwealth and State politicians can do a lot for themselves before bothering us with referendums, which are expensive and, almost always, futile.

The substance behind the form may effect constitutional changes that the unchanging form gives no hint of.

However the formal terms of the Constitution may read, the substance is: for years now we have had an independent Australia and an independent resident head of State, a Governor-General who is more like a de facto President than a representative of a foreign potentate. When I come to discuss the republican question below, I will supply the details.

Descend from these lofty notions to roads and rails—and descend again from form to substance. Technically, the Commonwealth has no power in the Constitution to plan a national road and rail system, but it can do so in effect. The Commonwealth can use tied grants to cajole the States to fall in with a national plan, and not only for roads and rails, but for education, health, housing. Formally, too, the Commonwealth has no power in the Constitution, for instance, over the environment of Fraser Island or over cultural property. But in substance the Commonwealth can safeguard both by prohibiting overseas trade in environmentally damaging products or in movable cultural property. Formally, the

Commonwealth has no power over State utilities, like water, gas, electricity, but it can twist its taxation power to bribe investors into these State markets; the Commonwealth has no formal power over employee training either, but it can "threaten" employers with taxation if they do not pay for that training.

And so it goes on, the substance continually outwitting the form.

The reformers are no doubt aware of these indirect processes of constitutional reform. Obviously they find them unsatisfactory. What can be done?

To begin, there are inescapable developments. Nations are becoming internationally orientated. Certain matters are now regarded globally, not just environment, but human rights as well, corporate regulation, consumer protection, cultural and natural heritage, to name but a few. There is international competitiveness. There is need for strong national control because there is now an integrated Australian economy. There is a call for Australia-wide uniformity, say in defamation laws, labour relations, court jurisdictions.

This conglomerate of advances incites a shift of power to the centre and a national unity. In the first place, you can see from what I have written above that the High Court serves the Commonwealth well here. Secondly, the reformers are less likely to fail on this front because the amendment machinery is started by the interested party, the Commonwealth.

On the other hand, there are still hankerings after local autonomy, here and abroad (for instance, in United States, Canada and even in the nascent European Community). In Australia some may think that the shift of power to the centre has gone far enough under High Court law, and that a federal political system, such as we have, has the virtue of decentralising government regulation. Hence some reformers may want to buttress the States, especially on the financial side.

Once again High Court law assists already, although not much. As for the reformers' own efforts, they will have less success here because, as I said, the amendment process cannot be initiated by the States. As a self-help, the States may unite in a Council of the Federation to wrest revenue from the Commonwealth, or refuse to join in Commonwealth plans unless the States are given greater input or the Commonwealth meets the cost from its favoured coffers.

The relation between Parliament and the Executive is another issue for the reformers, a pivotal issue in our parliamentary democracy, for the centre of power has moved from Parliament that represents the people to the Executive. The Executive or, worse still, a cabal of Ministers seeks to run Parliament—an inversion of parliamentary government.

At the outset there's a Catch 22. A political party that likes to govern Parliament is not going to institute reforms that make Parliament govern.

All that can be said is that the Senate which differs in tenure, electoral basis and times from the Lower House is one factor that may influence changes here. It is because of these differences that in the sixties and seventies and since 1981, we have been blessed with a "hostile Senate". It was such a Senate that was able to introduce one of those changes outside the sheer terms of the Constitution that I keep emphasising. In 1970 the Senate created standing committees to probe government. It was not until 17 years later that the conscience of the Lower House was jolted. In the early 1990s it was another "hostile Senate" that disciplined question time, by increasing the number of questions to be slotted into question time and by shortening the time allowed for answers.

Other factors that may reintroduce parliamentary democracy are a stronger committee system that scrutinises bills as they arise and that oversees the Executive and the government departments, the election of Independents, a Speaker who pays more regard to the Standing Orders than to the political party that put him there, and an impartial parliamentary press gallery.

Away from Commonwealth-State relations and government, some reformers are talking about a tablet of distinct rights, unbreakable by the Commonwealth and the States—a Bill of Rights in place of the few rights in the Commonwealth Constitution, the near absence of rights in the State Constitutions.

The safest path for those reformers is through the Commonwealth's external affairs corridor. The Commonwealth itself used this part of the existing Constitution to bring about changes. In 1975 it passed the Racial Discrimination Act, and in 1984 the Sex Discrimination Act. That is a surer way than recourse to the people since the people said "No" to enshrined rights in their 1944 referendum, "No" in 1974 and "No" in 1988.

The last paragraph miniaturises this Chapter. Without disturbing existing structures, changes are most certainly taking place in Australian constitutional law—more changes than those achieved by talking and referendums.

A republic in Australia was called for as far back as 1850 when John Dunmore Lang started a republican Australia League. Looking to the United States of America in 1852, he wrote on "Freedom and Independence for the Golden Lands of Australia". So his concern was to cut the apron strings, as there were in those days (but not now).

Latter day republicans appeared during the aftermath of the events of October and November 1975. Then the Governor-General followed up the Senate's deferral of Supply by dismissing the Government and arranging an election; (see the account in the Chapter on "Federal Parliament machinery"). So the concern of the post 1975 republicans extended to—and for some republicans still extends to—the abolition of the Senate's power to refuse Supply and the Governor-General's power to dismiss a Government.

For the time being, some republicans will settle for a minimum: the substitution of a new head of State for the Queen and the Governor-General. In April 1993 the Prime Minister announced a Republic Advisory Committee, chaired by Malcolm Turnbull, to construct an options paper around the objective, "to replace the hereditary monarchy with a non hereditary head of State". Nothing more.

A non hereditary head of State, commonly called a President, often elected by the people, and in whom rests supreme power but a power that is exercised on the people's behalf . . . these are the elements in a democratic republic.

So in October 1993 the Committee delivered its report of 151 pages, listing options rather than recommendations. Nevertheless, you get the impression that the Committee has preferences. My impression is given.

To begin, the Committee supported the office of a head of State, a President or whatever name is settled on. He/she would be a non partisan figure representing the nation. Such a figure was seen as part of our institutional checks and balances and able to untie parliamentary deadlocks.

Now for the two sticking points in the republican debate: *the appointment* (and qualifications) of a new head of State and *the powers* of the head of State.

The Committee seemed to prefer an appointment (or dismissal) of the head of State by a two-thirds majority vote in a joint sitting of the two Houses at Canberra. Strange that. Public surveys opposed political involvement. The Committee countered with the argument that two popularly elected heads (of State and of government) could lead to conflict. The appointee would be a sole nominee. The simple qualifications would be an adult Australian citizen who does not hold another paid office and (again contrary to current polls) might be a former politician.

The powers of the head of State would be codified in detail in the Constitution to clear away uncertainty, and to dispel apprehension about their abuse by the new figure. Those powers would be patterned on the existing gubernatorial powers. The usual powers would be summoning Parliament, assenting to bills, issuing writs for elections, appointing Ministers or judges, and so on. The reserve powers, according to the Committee, would be appointing or dismissing a Prime Minister along with the government, refusing a Prime Minister's request to dissolve Parliament, forcing a dissolution of Parliament when Supply has been refused and the Prime Minister will neither resign nor advise an election. You notice that the new head of State would retain some reserve or discretionary powers. This accords with the Committee's minimalist dictate to change form, not substance.

For the future, a Cabinet working party will produce an issues paper sometime in 1994. The Committee will assist by monitoring the progress.

Before starting out on the republican quest, it is well to recall the realities.

Whatever the formal opening clauses in the Commonwealth Constitution imply, and the State Constitutions imply, Australia and the States are now, in Realpolitik, autonomous political entities. The United Kingdom Parliament acknowledged in the Statute of Westminster of 1931 what had been a political reality since the 1926-1930 Imperial Conferences—the independence of the Commonwealth of Australia. Later in the Australia Act of 1986 the United Kingdom Government abandoned the States to their own affairs, and the United Kingdom Parliament completely surrendered any power to make laws for us, the Commonwealth, the States, the Territories.

In September 1993 the Prime Minister spoke to the Queen at Balmoral Castle about our republican stirrings. What was made public stated the obvious: *Australia is independent here and now*. "Her Majesty authorised me (Mr Keating) to say that she would, of course, act on the advice of her Australian Ministers, as she always has, and on any decision made by the Australian people".

Under the formal terms of the Constitution we owe allegiance to a monarch abroad with a local representative, a Governor-General, who is appointed by that monarch. But in the 1990s the monarch has a status presence only, occasionally opening Federal Parliament. In the 1990s also (in fact as far back as Casey in 1965) the Governor-General is an Australian recommended—in substance appointed—by the Prime Minister of Australia, as each vacancy arises. The Governor-General is his own man, not answerable to the monarch abroad, as Sir John Kerr showed in November 1975 with the monarch's official imprimatur *after the event*. The Governor-General liaises with the Commonwealth Government, not with some overseas authority. Similarly, under the Australia Act of 1986 the Queen now appoints a State Governor on the advice of the State Premier, and this Governor is likely to be an Australian; New South Wales has had Australian Governors since 1946. Under the Australia Act the Queen gave up any colonial powers she had to the State Governor. The Governor liaises with the State Government, again not with some overseas authority.

The monarch is only a shadow over a de facto republic. The Governor-General is a de facto President appointed by an elected Prime Minister, and answerable to this Prime Minister, almost invariably acting on his advice (that is, the Governor-General may see himself, in most exceptional circumstances, answerable to the nation). The same kind of remarks can be made about a State Governor and a State Premier.

The Australianisation of the Crown is now complete. The Governor-General or the Governor has become in substance an Australian institution.

Not only that. Because of the method of appointment, the incumbent and the independence of the office, this Australian Crown is less like a monarch than a President, while still standing aloof from politics.

If the Governor-General is in substance a de facto President then, the republicans may well argue, why not match the form with the substance? On this argument the present role of the Governor-General would persist, as well as the present powers, since only the form would be changed.

(You can put aside an argument about the pursuit of a national identity and the attainment of a maturity, unless you write off New Zealanders and Canadians, who cling to a constitutional monarchy, as confused minors.)

The present role of the Governor-General was explained in the Chapter on "the Federal Government"—a role as the authentic spokesman for the nation as a whole, a role with duties in connection with the Federal Parliament, and a role with duties in connection with the Federal Government.

Here are some examples of how the office has served Australia in practice.

In New South Wales, May 1932, Governor Sir Philip Game did not act on the advice of his Ministers, believing that the Lang Government breached Commonwealth law. Neither did Sir John Kerr in October-November 1975, calling in the people when faced with a parliamentary impasse ("Fraser's" Senate deferred Supply, and Prime Minister Whitlam would neither resign, nor go to the people). In Queensland, November 1987, Governor Sir Walter Campbell seemed likely to refuse Premier Bjelke-Petersen's request for a new commission to cobble together a second ministry (whose chances of retaining the confidence of the Assembly were doubtful). In Tasmania, June 1989, after the general elections Governor Sir Phillip Bennett was faced with former Premier Gray's conservative minority party and Field's Labor minority; the Governor first discussed the predicament with the Green Independents; he then accepted a kind of coalition built on the Field-Greens' accord—not that this was what the former Premier wanted. In New South Wales, March 1991, Governor Rear Admiral Peter Sinclair waited on Premier Greiner's minority conservative coalition to reach agreement with the Independents. If the coalition lost the support of the Independents, the Governor had a further role: to call on the Labor opposition to form a government.

This parade of Governors-General and Governors reveals a useful institution in the governance of the State, an institution that is more than a mere ceremonial appurtenance.

But notice also it is because the institution has authority and standing in the community and operates outside politics, and it is because of the kind of incumbents in the office, that the institution can act as a respected mediator between Government and Opposition, counselling the belligerents to talk through their political crises. It may even become a fail-safe mechanism letting in the wishes of the electorate if normal processes break down.

Would the institution in the new form of a President serve the Australian community in the same way as the former institution? And would the office holder command the same respect and deference in a political crisis?

Tradition has delivered Governors-General or Governors who act outside politics, and who act almost with reluctance in political crises. An elected head of State, propelled by different machinery with its own power source, will be outside this tradition. Furthermore, an elected head of State, if politics intrude in the election, may compete with the elected head of government, the Prime Minister, and cause friction. Still, if there is to be a new head of State, it may be possible to define a class of eligible candidates by reference to the existing class and to exclude political nominees—and hope for a continuity of the tradition of political aloofness and restraint.

The present principles, conventions or what you will that steer a Governor-General (or a Governor) into a particular course include a principle which requires a Governor-General to commission that Ministry which can marshal a majority vote in the lower House. Another principle dictates that a Governor-General, almost invariably, follow the advice of such a Ministry (which is answerable through Parliament to the electors). A countervailing principle suggests that, where a Prime Minister would like to dissolve the House of Representatives to get over a political crisis, a Governor-General will first exhaust the possibility of the House itself untangling the crisis.

But the overriding principle is the primacy of the will of the electorate. In most exceptional circumstances a Governor-General may try to open the doors to the people to let them decide, say, where the Government thwarts Parliament (which, for instance, refuses Supply) and the courts cannot intervene. In those extreme circumstances the Governor-General may be the only institution left to secure parliamentary democracy.

To the extent that the principles are uncertain, or their application uncertain, a Governor-General is left with a personal discretion, guided because of tradition by a political aloofness and restraint and, because of authority and standing, by sagacity. In fact, ad hoc judgments may even be desirable, given the unique political crises that can arise. Principles set in a legal document are rigid and do not anticipate unforeseen situations and, when it comes to a challenge, invite judges into the pragmatic affairs of State.

Once again, would a new head of State be guided by the principles we have come to accept as serving the ultimate norm: not the politicians, but the people?

265

Quotations used in the text

("Lane Cases" refers to P H Lane, *A Digest of Australian Constitutional Cases*, 4th ed, Sydney, Law Book Co Ltd, 1992. It summarises and gives extracts from many of the cases before the Privy Council and the High Court which are reported in the Commonwealth Law Reports, here cited as "CLR".)

p 2 *Attorney-General (Cth) v Colonial Sugar Refining Co Ltd (Royal Commissions)* (1913) 17 CLR 644 at 653-654 (Lane Cases 1).

p 6 *Australian National Airways Pty Ltd v The Commonwealth* (1945) 71 CLR 29 at 81, 85 (Lane Cases 34).

p 12 *State of South Australia v The Commonwealth (First Uniform Tax Case)* (1942) 65 CLR 373 at 424-425 (Lane Cases 55).

p 30 *Amalgamated Society of Engineers v Adelaide Steamship Co Ltd (The Engineers case)* (1920) 28 CLR 129 at 154 (Lane Cases 468).

p 33 *Ex parte McLean* (1930) 43 CLR 472 at 483 (Lane Cases 417).

p 37 *State of Victoria v The Commonwealth (Second Uniform Tax Case)* (1957) 99 CLR 575 at 610 (Lane Cases 58).

p 87 *Airlines of New South Wales Pty Ltd v State of New South Wales (No 2)* (1965) 113 CLR 54 at 78 (Lane Cases 22).

p 89 *R v Barger* (1908) 6 CLR 41 (Lane Cases 68)—esp the dissenting judgments of Isaacs and Higgins JJ.

p 93 *Australian Communist Party v The Commonwealth* (1951) 83 CLR 1 at 255 (Lane Cases 74).

p 95 *Strickland v Rocla Concrete Pipes Ltd* (1971) 124 CLR 468 at 489, 511, 525 (Lane Cases 101).

p 99 *Ex p Walsh and Johnson; in re Yates* (1925) 37 CLR 36 at 137, 138.

p 102 *R v Burgess; ex parte Henry* (1936) 55 CLR 608 at 682, 687-688 (Lane Cases 152).

p 103 *The Commonwealth v State of Tasmania (Tasmanian Dam case)* (1983) 158 CLR 1 at 123, 124 (Lane Cases 136).

p 105 *Grace Bros Pty Ltd v The Commonwealth* (1946) 72 CLR 269 at 291 (Lane Cases 168).

p 105 *Re Dohnert Muller Schmidt & Co; Attorney-General (Cth) v Schmidt* (1961) 105 CLR 361 at 372 (Lane Cases 160).

p 108 *R v Kelly; ex parte Victoria* (1950) 81 CLR 64 at 80, 82 (Lane Cases 182).

p 117 *Lamshed v Lake* (1958) 99 CLR 132 at 148 (Lane Cases 433).

p 118 *State of Victoria v The Commonwealth (Australian Assistance Plan)* (1975) 134 CLR 338 at 367, 419 (Lane Cases 3).

p 132 The quotation is adapted from Dicey, *Law of the Constitution*, 10th ed, 1959, 431.

p 135 *Victorian Stevedoring and General Contracting Co Pty Ltd and Meakes v Dignan* (1931) 46 CLR 73 at 100 (Lane Cases 215).

p 136 *Shell Co of Australia Ltd v Federal Commissioner of Taxation* (1930) 44 CLR 530 at 544 (Lane Cases 241).

p 146 The quotations are adapted from Dicey, *Law of the Constitution*, 10th ed, 1959, 156, 470.

p 161 *R v Bevan; ex p Elias and Gordon* (1942) 66 CLR 452 at 464-465 (Lane Cases 263).

p 186 *Le Mesurier v Connor* (1929) 42 CLR 481 at 495 (Lane Cases 315).

p 186 *Lorenzo v Carey* (1921) 29 CLR 243 at 252 (Lane Cases 318).

p 188 *James v The Commonwealth* (1936) 55 CLR 1 at 41, 60.

p 228 *Cole v Whitfield (Crayfish case)* (1988) 165 CLR 360 at 393, 404 (Lane Cases 359).

p 232 *Dennis Hotels Pty Ltd v State of Victoria (Liquor Licence case)* (1960) 104 CLR 529 at 587, 588, 589 (Lane Cases 342).

p 236 *Adelaide Company of Jehovah's Witnesses Inc v The Commonwealth* (1943) CLR 116 at 159.

COMMONWEALTH OF AUSTRALIA
CONSTITUTION ACT, 1900
with Amendments to the Constitution made by
CONSTITUTION ALTERATION
(SENATE ELECTIONS) 1906
(No. 1 of 1907),
CONSTITUTION ALTERATION (STATE DEBTS) 1909
(No. 3 of 1910),
CONSTITUTION ALTERATION (STATE DEBTS) 1928
(No. 1 of 1929),
CONSTITUTION ALTERATION (SOCIAL SERVICES) 1946
(No. 81 of 1946),
CONSTITUTION ALTERATION (ABORIGINALS) 1967
(No. 55 of 1967),
CONSTITUTION ALTERATION (SENATE CASUAL VACANCIES) 1977
(No. 82 of 1977),
CONSTITUTION ALTERATION (RETIREMENT OF JUDGES) 1977
(No. 83 of 1977),
CONSTITUTION ALTERATION (REFERENDUMS) 1977
(No. 84 of 1977)

COMMONWEALTH OF AUSTRALIA
CONSTITUTION ACT

(63 & 64 VICTORIA, CHAPTER 12.)
An Act to constitute the Commonwealth of Australia

(9th July, 1900[1].)

WHEREAS the people of New South Wales, Victoria, South Australia, Queensland and Tasmania, humbly relying on the blessing of Almighty God, have agreed to unite in one indissoluble Federal Commonwealth under the Crown of the United Kingdom of Great Britain and Ireland, and under the Constitution hereby established:

And whereas it is expedient to provide for the admission into the Commonwealth of other Australasian Colonies and possessions of the Queen:

Be it therefore enacted by the Queen's Most Excellent Majesty, by and with the advice and consent of the Lords Spiritual and Temporal, and Commons, in this present Parliament assembled, and by the authority of the same, as follows:

1. Short title   This Act be cited as the Commonwealth of Australia Constitution Act.

2. Act to extend to the Queen's successors   The provisions of this Act referring to the Queen shall extend to Her Majesty's heirs and successors in the sovereignty of the United Kingdom.

3. Proclamation of Commonwealth   It shall be lawful for the Queen, with the advice of the Privy Council, to declare by proclamation that, on and after a day therein appointed, not being later than one year after the passing of this Act, the

---

1 This copy of the Constitution Act contains all the alterations of the Constitution up to the date of publication of this book. Marginal notes have been inserted in **bold type** at the beginning of each section.

people of New South Wales, Victoria, South Australia, Queensland and Tasmania, and also, if Her Majesty is satisfied that the people of Western Australia have agreed thereto, of Western Australia, shall be united in a Federal Commonwealth under the name of the Commonwealth of Australia.[2] But the Queen may, at any time after the proclamation appoint a Governor-General for the Commonwealth.

4. Commencement of Act   The Commonwealth shall be established and the Constitution of the Commonwealth shall take effect, on and after the day so appointed. But the Parliaments of the several colonies may at any time after the passing of this Act make any such laws, to come into operation on the day so appointed, as they might have made if the Constitution had taken effect at the passing of this Act.

5. Operation of the Constitution and laws   This Act, and all laws made by the Parliament of the Commonwealth under the Constitution, shall be binding on the courts, judges, and people of every State and of every part of the Commonwealth, notwithstanding anything in the laws of any State; and the laws of the Commonwealth shall be in force on all British ships, the Queen's ships of war excepted, whose first port of clearance and whose port of destination are in the Commonwealth.

6. Definitions   "The Commonwealth" shall mean the Commonwealth of Australia as established under this Act

"The States" shall mean such of the colonies of New South Wales, New Zealand, Queensland, Tasmania, Victoria, Western Australia, and South Australia, including the northern territory of South Australia, as for the time being are parts of the Commonwealth, and such colonies or territories as may be admitted into or established by the Commonwealth as States; and each of such parts of the Commonwealth shall be called "a State".

"Original States" shall mean such States as are parts of the Commonwealth at its establishment.

7. Repeal of Federal Council Act, 48 & 49 Vict. c. 60   The Federal Council of Australasia Act, 1885, is hereby repealed, but so as not to affect any laws passed by the Federal Council of Australasia and in force at the establishment of the Commonwealth.

Any such law may be repealed as to any State by the Parliament of the Commonwealth, or as to any colony not being a State by the Parliament thereof.

8. Application of Colonial Boundaries Act, 58 & 59 Vict. c. 34   After the passing of this Act the Colonial Boundaries Act, 1895, shall not apply to any colony which becomes a state of the Commonwealth; but the Commonwealth shall be taken to be a self-governing colony for the purposes of that Act.

9. Constitution   The Constitution of the Commonwealth shall be as follows:—

THE CONSTITUTION

This Constitution is divided as follows:—

Chapter   I.—The Parliament:
Part   I.—General:
Part   II.—The Senate:
Part   III.—The House of Representatives:

---

2 The day appointed by proclamation was 1st January, 1901. Western Australia on that day, along with the other five States, became part of the Commonwealth of Australia.

CHAPTER I.—THE PARLIAMENT.

PART I.—GENERAL.

1. Legislative power   The legislative power of the Commonwealth shall be vested in a Federal Parliament, which shall consist of the Queen, a Senate, and a House of Representatives, and which is hereinafter called "The Parliament", or "The Parliament of the Commonwealth".

2. Governor-General   A Governor-General appointed by the Queen shall be Her Majesty's representative in the Commonwealth, and shall have and may exercise in the Commonwealth during the Queen's pleasure, but subject to this Constitution, such powers and functions of the Queen as Her Majesty may be pleased to assign to him.

3. Salary of Governor-General   There shall be payable to the Queen out of the Consolidated Revenue Fund of the Commonwealth, for the salary of the Governor-General, an annual sum which, until the Parliament otherwise provides, shall be ten thousand pounds.

The salary of a Governor-General shall not be altered during his continuance in office.

4. Provisions relating to Governor-General   The provisions of this Constitution relating to the Governor-General extend and apply to the Governor-General for the time being, or such person as the Queen may appoint to administer the Government of the Commonwealth; but no such person shall be entitled to receive any salary from the Commonwealth in respect of any other office during his administration of the Government of the Commonwealth.

5. Sessions of Parliament, Prorogation and Dissolution   The Governor-General may appoint such times for holding the sessions of Parliament as he thinks fit, and may also from time to time, by Proclamation or otherwise, prorogue the Parliament, and may in like manner dissolve the House of Representatives.

Summoning Parliament   After any general election the Parliament shall be summoned to meet not later than thirty days after the day appointed for the return of the writs.

First Session   The Parliament shall be summoned to meet not later than six months after the establishment of the Commonwealth.

6. Yearly session of Parliament   There shall be a session of the Parliament once at least in every year, so that twelve months shall not intervene between the last sitting of the Parliament in one session and its first sitting in the next session.

PART II.—THE SENATE.

7. The Senate The Senate shall be composed of senators for each State, directly chosen by the people of the State, voting, until the Parliament otherwise provides, as one electorate.

But until the Parliament of the Commonwealth otherwise provides, the Parliament of the State of Queensland, if that State be an Original State, may make laws dividing the State into divisions and determining the number of senators to be chosen for each division, and in the absence of such provision the State shall be one electorate.

Until the Parliament otherwise provides there shall be six senators for each Original State. The Parliament may make laws increasing or diminishing the number of senators for each State, but so that equal representation of the several Original States shall be maintained and that no Original State shall have less than six senators.

The senators shall be chosen for a term of six years, and the names of the senators chosen for each State shall be certified by the Governor to the Governor-General.

8. Qualification of electors The qualification of electors of senators shall be in each State that which is prescribed by this Constitution, or by the Parliament, as the qualification for electors of members of the House of Representatives; but in the choosing of senators each elector shall vote only once.

9. Method of election of senators The Parliament of the Commonwealth may make laws prescribing the method of choosing senators, but so that the method shall be uniform for all the States. Subject to any law, the Parliament of each State may make laws prescribing the method of choosing the senators for that State.

Times and places The Parliament of a State may make laws for determining the times and places of elections of senators for the State.

10. Application of State laws Until the Parliament otherwise provides, but subject to this Constitution, the laws in force in each State, for the time being, relating to elections for the more numerous House of Parliament of the State shall, as nearly as practicable, apply to elections of senators for the State.

11. Failure to choose senators The Senate may proceed to the despatch of business, notwithstanding the failure of any State to provide for its representation in the Senate.

12. Issue of writs The Governor of any State may cause writs to be issued for elections of senators for the state. In case of the dissolution of the Senate the writs shall be issued within ten days from the proclamation of such dissolution.

13.[3] Rotation of senators As soon as may be after the Senate first meets, and after each first meeting of the Senate following a dissolution thereof, the Senate shall divide the senators chosen for each State into two classes, as nearly equal in number as practicable; and the places of the senators of the first class shall become vacant at the expiration of three years, and the places of those of the second class at the expiration of six years, from the beginning of their term of service; and afterwards the places of senators shall become vacant at the expiration of six years from the beginning of their term of service.

The election to fill vacant places shall be made within one year before the places are to become vacant.

For the purposes of this section the term of service of a senator shall be taken to begin on the first day of July following the day of his election, except in the cases of the first election and of the election next after any dissolution of the Senate, when it shall be taken to begin on the first day of July preceding the day of his election.

---

3 As amended by No. 1, 1907, s. 2.

14. Further provision for rotation   Whenever the number of senators for a State is increased or diminished, the Parliament of the Commonwealth may make such provision for the vacating of the places of senators for the State as it deems necessary to maintain regularity in the rotation.

15.[4] Casual vacancies   If the place of a senator becomes vacant before the expiration of his term of service, the Houses of Parliament of the State for which he was chosen, sitting and voting together, or, if there is only one House of that Parliament, that House, shall choose a person to hold the place until the expiration of the term. But if the Parliament of the State is not in session when the vacancy is notified, the Governor of the State, with the advice of the Executive Council thereof, may appoint a person to hold the place until the expiration of fourteen days from the beginning of the next session of the Parliament of the State or the expiration of the term, whichever first happens.

Where a vacancy has at any time occurred in the place of a senator chosen by the people of a State and, at the time when he was so chosen, he was publicly recognized by a particular political party as being an endorsed candidate of that party and publicly represented himself to be such a candidate, a person chosen or appointed under this section in consequence of that vacancy, or in consequence of that vacancy and a subsequent vacancy or vacancies, shall, unless there is no member of that party available to be chosen or appointed, be a member of that party.

Where—

   (a)   in accordance with the last preceding paragraph, a member of a particular political party is chosen or appointed to hold the place of a senator whose place had become vacant; and.

   (b)   before taking his seat he ceases to be a member of that party (otherwise than by reason of the party having ceased to exist);

he shall be deemed not to have been so chosen or appointed and the vacancy shall be again notified in accordance with section twenty-one of this Constitution.

The name of any senator chosen or appointed under this section shall be certified by the Governor of the State to the Governor-General.

If the place of a senator chosen by the people of a State at the election of senators last held before the commencement of the *Constitution Alteration (Senate Casual Vacancies)* 1977 became vacant before that commencement and, at that commencement, no person chosen by the House or Houses of Parliament of the State, or appointed by the Governor of the State, in consequence of that vacancy, or in consequence of that vacancy and a subsequent vacancy or vacancies, held office, this section applies as if the place of the senator chosen by the people of the State had become vacant after that commencement.

A senator holding office at the commencement of the *Constitution Alteration (Senate Casual Vacancies)* 1977, being a senator appointed by the Governor of a State in consequence of a vacancy that had at any time occurred in the place of a senator chosen by the people of the State, shall be deemed to have been appointed to hold the place until the expiration of fourteen days after the beginning of the next session of the Parliament of the State that commenced or commences after he was appointed and further action under this section shall be taken as if the vacancy in the place of the senator chosen by the people of the State had occurred after that commencement.

---

4 Inserted by No. 82, 1977.

Subject to the next succeeding paragraph, a senator holding office at the commencement of the *Constitution Alteration (Senate Casual Vacancies)* 1977 who was chosen by the House or Houses of Parliament of a State in consequence of a vacancy that had at any time occurred in the place of a senator chosen by the people of the State shall be deemed to have been chosen to hold office until the expiration of the term of service of the senator elected by the people of the State.

If, at or before the commencement of the *Constitution Alteration (Senate Casual Vacancies)* 1977, a law to alter the Constitution entitled "*Constitution Alteration (Simultaneous Elections)* 1977" came into operation, a senator holding office at the commencement of that law who was chosen by the House or Houses of Parliament of a State in consequence of a vacancy that had at any time occurred in the place of a senator chosen by the people of the State shall be deemed to have chosen to hold office—

(a) if the senator elected by the people of the State had a term of service expiring on the thirtieth day of June, One thousand nine hundred and seventy-eight—until the expiration or dissolution of the first House of Representatives to expire or be dissolved after that law came into operation; or

(b) if the senator elected by the people of the State had a term of service expiring on the thirtieth day of June, One thousand nine hundred and eighty-one—until the expiration or dissolution of the second House of Representatives to expire or be dissolved after that law came into operation or, if there is an earlier dissolution of the Senate, until that dissolution.

16. Qualifications of senator The qualification of a senator shall be the same as those of a member of the House of Representatives.

17. Election of a President The Senate shall, before proceeding to the despatch of any other business, choose a senator to be the President of the Senate; and as often as the office of President becomes vacant the Senate shall again choose a senator to be the President.

The President shall cease to hold his office if he ceases to be a senator. He may be removed from office by a vote of the Senate, or he may resign his office or his seat by writing addressed to the Governor-General.

18. Absence of President Before or during any absence of the President, the Senate may choose a senator to perform his duties in his absence.

19. Resignation of senator A senator may, by writing addressed to the President, or to the Governor-General if there is no President or if the President is absent from the Commonwealth, resign his place, which thereupon shall become vacant.

20. Vacancy by absence The place of a senator shall become vacant if for two consecutive months of any session of the Parliament he, without the permission of the senate, fails to attend the Senate.

21. Vacancy to be notified Whenever a vacancy happens in the Senate, the President, or if there is no President or if the President is absent from the Commonwealth the Governor-General, shall notify the same to the Governor of the State in the representation of which the vacancy has happened.

22. Quorum Until the Parliament otherwise provides, the presence of at least one-third of the whole number of the senators shall be necessary to constitute a meeting of the Senate for the exercise of its powers.

23. Voting in Senate Questions arising in the Senate shall be determined by a majority of votes, and each senator shall have one vote. The President shall in all cases be entitled to a vote; and when the votes are equal the question shall pass in the negative.

PART III.—THE HOUSE OF REPRESENTATIVES.

24. Constitution of House of Representatives The House of Representatives shall be composed of members directly chosen by the people of the Commonwealth, and the number of such members shall be, as nearly as practicable, twice the number of the senators.

The number of members chosen in the several States shall be in proportion to the respective numbers of their people, and shall, until the Parliament otherwise provides, be determined, whenever necessary, in the following manner:—

- (i.) A quota shall be ascertained by dividing the number of the people of the Commonwealth, as shown by the latest statistics of the Commonwealth, by twice the number of the senators:

- (ii.) The number of members to be chosen in each State shall be determined by dividing the number of the people of the State, as shown by the latest statistics of the Commonwealth, by the quota; and if on such division there is a remainder greater than one-half of the quota, one more member shall be chosen in the State.

But notwithstanding anything in this section, five members at least shall be chosen in each Original State.

25. Provision as to races disqualified from voting For the purposes of the last section, if by the law of any State all persons of any race are disqualified from voting at elections for the more numerous House of the Parliament of the State, then, in reckoning the number of the people of the State or of the Commonwealth, persons of that race resident in that State shall not be counted.

26. Representatives in first Parliament Notwithstanding anything in section twenty-four, the number of members to be chosen in each State at the first election shall be as follows:—

New South Wales .... twenty-three;
Victoria .... twenty;
Queensland .... eight;
South Australia .... six;
Tasmania .... five.

Provided that if Western Australia is an Original State, the numbers shall be as follows:—

New South Wales .... twenty-six;
Victoria .... twenty-three;
Queensland .... nine;
South Australia .... seven;
Western Australia .... five;
Tasmania .... five.

27. Alteration of numbers of members Subject to this Constitution, the Parliament may make laws for increasing or diminishing the number of the members of the House of Representatives.

28. Duration of House of Representatives Every House of Representatives shall continue for three years from the first meeting of the House, and no longer, but may be sooner dissolved by the Governor-General.

29. Electoral divisions   Until the Parliament of the Commonwealth otherwise provides, the Parliament of any State may make laws for determining the divisions in each State for which members of the House of Representatives may be chosen, and the number of members to be chosen for each division. A division shall not be formed out of parts of different States.

In the absence of other provisions, each State shall be one electorate.

30. Qualification of electors   Until the Parliament otherwise provides, the qualification of electors of members of the House of Representatives shall be in each State that which is prescribed by the law of the State as the qualification of electors of the more numerous House of Parliament of the State; but in the choosing of members each elector shall vote only once.

31. Application of State laws   Until the Parliament otherwise provides, but subject to the Constitution, the laws in force in each State for the time being relating to elections for the more numerous House of Parliament of the State shall, as nearly as practicable, apply to elections in the State of members of the House of Representatives.

32. Writs for general election   The Governor-General in Council may cause writs to be issued for general elections of members of the House of Representatives.

After the first general election, the writs shall be issued within ten days from the expiry of a House of Representatives or from the proclamation of a dissolution thereof.

33. Writs for vacancies   Whenever a vacancy happens in the House of Representatives, the Speaker shall issue his writ for the election of a new member, or if there is no Speaker or if he is absent from the Commonwealth the Governor-General in Council may issue the writ.

34. Qualifications of members   Until the Parliament otherwise provides, the qualifications of a member of the House of Representatives shall be as follows:—

(i.)   He must be the full age of twenty-one years, and must be an elector entitled to vote at the election of members of the House of Representatives, or a person qualified to become such elector, and must have been for three years at least a resident within the limits of the Commonwealth as existing at the time when he is chosen:

(ii.)   He must be a subject of the Queen, either natural-born or for at least five years naturalized under a law of the United Kingdom, or of a Colony which has become or becomes a State, or of the Commonwealth, or of a State.

35. Election of Speaker   The House of Representatives shall, before proceeding to the despatch of any other business, choose a member to be the Speaker of the House, and as often as the office of Speaker becomes vacant the House shall again choose a member to be the Speaker.

The Speaker shall cease to hold his office if he ceases to be a member. He may be removed from office by a vote of the House, or he may resign his office or seat by writing addressed to the Governor-General.

36. Absence of Speaker   Before or during any absence of the Speaker, the House of Representatives may choose a member to perform his duties in his absence.

37. Resignation of member   A member may by writing addressed to the Speaker, or to the Governor-General if there is no Speaker or if the Speaker is absent from the Commonwealth, resign his place, which thereupon shall become vacant.

38. Vacancy by absence   The place of a member shall become vacant if for two consecutive months of any session of the Parliament he, without the permission of the House, fails to attend the House.

39. Quorum   Until the Parliament otherwise provides, the presence of at least one-third of the whole number of the members of the House of Representatives shall be necessary to constitute a meeting of the House for the exercise of its powers.

40. Voting in House of Representatives   Questions arising in the House of Representatives shall be determined by a majority of votes other than that of the Speaker. The Speaker shall not vote unless the numbers are equal, and then he shall have a casting vote.

PART IV.—BOTH HOUSES OF THE PARLIAMENT.

41. Right of electors of States   No adult person who has or acquires a right to vote at elections for the more numerous House of the Parliament of a State shall, while the right continues, be prevented by any of the Commonwealth from voting at elections for either House of the Parliament of the Commonwealth.

42. Oath or affirmation of allegiance   Every senator and every member of the House of Representatives shall before taking his seat make and subscribe before the Governor-General, or some person authorized by him, an oath or affirmation of allegiance in the form set forth in the schedule to this Constitution.

43. Member of one House ineligible for other   A member of either House of Parliament shall be incapable of being chosen or of sitting as a member of the other House.

44. Disqualification   Any person who—

    (i.)   Is under any acknowledgment of allegiance, obedience, or adherence to a foreign power, or is a subject or a citizen or entitled to the rights or privileges of a subject or a citizen of a foreign power: or

    (ii.)   Is attained of treason, or has been convicted and is under sentence, or subject to be sentenced, for any offence punishable under the law of the Commonwealth or of a State by imprisonment for one year or longer: or

    (iii.)   Is an undischarged bankrupt or insolvent: or

    (iv.)   Holds any office of profit under the Crown, or any pension payable during the pleasure of the Crown out of any of the revenues of the Commonwealth: or

    (v.)   Has any direct pecuniary interest in any agreement with the Public Service of the Commonwealth otherwise than as a member and in common with the other members of an incorporated company consisting of more than twenty-five persons:

shall be incapable of being chosen or of sitting as a senator or a member of the House of Representatives.

But sub-section (iv.) does not apply to the office of any of the Queen's Ministers of State for the Commonwealth, or of any of the Queen's Ministers for a State, or to the receipt of pay, half-pay, or a pension by any person as an officer or member of the Queen's navy or army, or to the receipt of pay as an officer or member of the naval or military forces of the Commonwealth by any person whose services are not wholly employed by the Commonwealth.

45. Vacancy on happening of disqualification   If a senator or member of the House of Representatives—

(i.)   Becomes subject to any of the disabilities mentioned in the last preceding section: or

(ii.)   Takes the benefit, whether by assignment, composition, or otherwise, of any law relating to bankrupt or insolvent debtors: or

(iii.)   Directly or indirectly takes or agrees to take any fee or honorarium for services rendered to the Commonwealth, or for services rendered in the Parliament to any person or State:

his place shall thereupon become vacant.

46. Penalty for sitting when disqualified   Until the Parliament otherwise provides, any person declared by this Constitution to be incapable of sitting as a senator or as a member of the House of Representatives shall, for every day on which he so sits, be liable to pay the sum of one hundred pounds to any person who sues for it in any court of competent jurisdiction.

47. Disputed elections   Until the Parliament otherwise provides, any question respecting the qualification of a senator or of a member of the House of Representatives, or respecting a vacancy in either House of the Parliament, and any question of a disputed election to either House, shall be determined by the House in which the question arises.

48. Allowance to members   Until the Parliament otherwise provides, each senator and each member of the House of Representatives shall receive an allowance of four hundred pounds a year, to be reckoned from the day on which he takes his seat.

49. Privileges, &c., of Houses   The powers, privileges, and immunities of the Senate and the House of Representatives, and of the members and the committees of each House, shall be such as are declared by the Parliament, and until declared shall be those of the Commons House of Parliament of the United Kingdom, and of its members and committees, at the establishment of the Commonwealth.

50. Rules and orders   Each House of Parliament may make rules and orders with respect to—

(i.)   The mode in which its powers, privileges, and immunities may be exercised and upheld:

(ii.)   The order and conduct of its business and proceedings either separately or jointly with the other House.

PART V.—POWERS OF THE PARLIAMENT.

51. Legislative powers of the Parliament   The Parliament shall, subject to this Constitution, have power to make laws for the peace, order, and good government of the Commonwealth with respect to:

(i.)   Trade and commerce with other countries, and among the States:

(ii.)   Taxation; but so as not to discriminate between States or parts of States:

(iii.)   Bounties on the production or export of goods, but so that such bounties shall be uniform throughout the Commonwealth:

(iv.)   Borrowing money on the public credit of the Commonwealth:

(v.)   Postal, telegraphic, telephonic, and other like services:

(vi.) The naval and military defence of the Commonwealth and of the several States, and the control of the forces to execute and maintain the laws of the Commonwealth:

(vii.) Lighthouses, lightships, beacons and buoys:

(viii.) Astronomical and meteorological observations:

(ix.) Quarantine:

(x.) Fisheries in Australian waters beyond territorial limits:

(xi.) Census and statistics:

(xii.) Currency, coinage, and legal tender:

(xiii.) Banking, other than State banking; also State banking extending beyond the limits of the State concerned, the incorporation of banks, and the issue of paper money:

(xiv.) Insurance, other than State insurance; also State insurance extending beyond the limits of the State concerned:

(xv.) Weights and measures:

(xvi.) Bills of exchange and promissory notes:

(xvii.) Bankruptcy and insolvency:

(xviii.) Copyrights, patents of inventions and designs, and trade marks:

(xix.) Naturalization and aliens:

(xx.) Foreign corporations, and trading or financial corporations formed within the limits of the Commonwealth:

(xxi.) Marriage:

(xxii.) Divorce and matrimonial causes; and in relation thereto, parental rights, and the custody and guardianship of infants:

(xxiii.) Invalid and old-age pensions:

(xxiiiA.)[5] The provision of maternity allowances, widows' pensions, child endowment, unemployment, pharmaceutical, sickness and hospital benefits, medical and dental services (but not so as to authorize any form of civil conscription), benefits to students and family allowances:

(xxiv.) The service and execution throughout the Commonwealth of the civil and criminal process and the judgments of the courts of the States:

(xxv.) The recognition throughout the Commonwealth of the laws, the public Acts and records, and the judicial proceedings of the States:

(xxvi.)[6] The people of any race for whom it is deemed necessary to make special laws:

(xxvii.) Immigration and emigration:

(xxviii.) The influx of criminals:

(xxix.) External affairs:

(xxx.) The relations of the Commonwealth with the islands of the Pacific:

(xxxi.) The acquisition of property on just terms from any State or person for any purpose in respect of which the Parliament has power to make laws:

(xxxii.) The control of railways with respect to transport for the naval and military purposes of the Commonwealth:

(xxxiii.) The acquisition, with the consent of a State, of any railways of the State on terms arranged between the Commonwealth and the State:

(xxxiv.) Railway construction and extension in any State with the consent of that State:

(xxxv.) Conciliation and arbitration for the prevention and settlement of industrial disputes extending beyond the limits of any one State:

---

5 Inserted by No. 81, 1946, s. 2.

6 As amended by No. 55, 1967, s. 2.

(xxxvi.) Matters in respect of which this Constitution makes provision until the Parliament otherwise provides:

(xxxvii.) Matters referred to the Parliament of the Commonwealth by the Parliament or Parliaments of any State or States, but so that the law shall extend only to States by whose Parliaments the matter is referred, or which afterwards adopt the law:

(xxxviii.) The exercise within the Commonwealth, at the request or with the concurrence of the Parliaments of all the States directly concerned, of any power which can at the establishment of this Constitution be exercised only by the Parliament of the United Kingdom or by the Federal Council of Australasia:

(xxxix.) Matters incidental to the execution of any power vested by this Constitution in the Parliament or in either House thereof, or in the Government of the Commonwealth, or in the Federal Judicature, or in any department or officer of the Commonwealth.

52. Exclusive powers of the Parliament The Parliament shall, subject to this Constitution, have exclusive power to make laws for the peace, order, and good government of the Commonwealth with respect to—

(i.) The seat of government of the Commonwealth, and all places acquired by the Commonwealth for public purposes:

(ii.) Matters relating to any department of the public service the control of which is by this Constitution transferred to the Executive Government of the Commonwealth:

(iii.) Other matters declared by this Constitution to be within the exclusive power of the Parliament.

53. Powers of the Houses in respect of legislation Proposed laws appropriating revenue or moneys, or imposing taxation, shall not originate in the Senate. But a proposed law shall not be taken to appropriate revenue or moneys, or to impose taxation, by reason only of its containing provisions for the imposition or appropriation of fines or other pecuniary penalties, or for the demand or payment or appropriation of fees for licences, or fees for services under the proposed law.

The Senate may not amend proposed laws imposing taxation, or proposed laws appropriating revenue or moneys for the ordinary annual services of the Government.

The Senate may not amend any proposed law so as to increase any proposed charge or burden on the people.

The Senate may at any stage return to the House of Representatives any proposed law which the Senate may not amend, requesting, by message, the omission or amendment of any items or provisions therein. And the House of Representatives may, if it thinks fit, make any of such omissions or amendments, with or without modifications.

Except as provided in this section, the Senate shall have equal power with the House of Representatives in respect of all proposed laws.

54. Appropriation Bills The proposed law which appropriates revenue or moneys for the ordinary annual services of the Government shall deal only with such appropriation.

55. Tax Bill Laws imposing taxation shall deal only with the imposition of taxation, and any provisions therein dealing with any other matter shall be of no effect.

Laws imposing taxation, except laws imposing duties of customs or of excise, shall deal with one subject of taxation only; but laws imposing duties of customs shall deal with duties of customs only, and laws imposing duties of excise shall deal with duties of excise only.

56. Recommendation of money votes   A vote, resolution, or proposed law for the appropriation of revenue or moneys shall not be passed unless the purpose of the appropriation has in the same session been recommended by message of the Governor-General to the House in which the proposal originated.

57. Disagreement between the Houses   If the House of Representatives passes any proposed law, and the Senate rejects or fails to pass it, or passes it with amendments to which the House of Representatives will not agree, and if after an interval of three months the House of Representatives, in the same or the next session, again passes the proposed law with or without any amendments which have been made, suggested, or agreed to by the Senate, and the Senate rejects or fails to pass it, or passes it with amendments to which the House of Representatives will not agree, the Governor-General may dissolve the Senate and the House of Representatives simultaneously. But such dissolution shall not take place within six months before the date of the expiry of the House of Representatives by effluxion of time.

If after such dissolution the House of Representatives again passes the proposed law, with or without any amendments which have been made, suggested, or agreed to by the Senate, and the Senate rejects or fails to pass it, or passes it with amendments to which the House of Representatives will not agree, the Governor-General may convene a joint sitting of the members of the Senate and of the House of Representatives.

The members present at the joint sitting may deliberate and shall vote together upon the proposed law as last proposed by the House of Representatives, and upon amendments, if any, which have been made therein by one House and not agreed to by the other, and any such amendments which are affirmed by an absolute majority of the total number of the members of the Senate and House of Representatives shall be taken to have been carried, and if the proposed law, with the amendments, if any, so carried is affirmed by an absolute majority of the total number of the members of the Senate and the House of Representatives, it shall be taken to have been duly passed by both Houses of the Parliament, and shall be presented to the Governor-General for the Queen's assent.

58. Royal assent to Bills   When a proposed law passed by both Houses of the Parliament is presented to the Governor-General for the Queen's assent, he shall declare, according to his discretion, but subject to this Constitution, that he assents in the Queen's name, or that he withholds assent, or that he reserves the law for the Queen's pleasure.

Recommendations by Governor-General   The Governor-General may return to the House in which it originated any proposed law so presented to him, and may transmit therewith any amendments which he may recommend, and the Houses may deal with the recommendation.

59. Disallowance by the Queen   The Queen may disallow any law within one year from the Governor-General's assent, and such disallowance on being made known by the Governor-General by speech or message to each of the Houses of the Parliament, or by Proclamation, shall annul the law from the day when the disallowance is so made known.

60. Signification of Queen's pleasure on Bills reserved A proposed law reserved for the Queen's pleasure shall not have any force unless and until within two years from the day on which it was presented to the Governor-General for the Queen's assent the Governor-General makes known, by speech or message to each of the Houses of Parliament, or by Proclamation, that it has received the Queen's assent.

CHAPTER II.—THE EXECUTIVE GOVERNMENT.

61. Executive power The executive power of the Commonwealth is vested in the Queen and is exercisable by the Governor-General as the Queen's representative, and extends to the execution and maintenance of this Constitution, and of the laws of the Commonwealth.

62. Federal Executive Council There shall be a Federal Executive Council to advise the Governor-General in the government of the Commonwealth, and the members of the Council shall be chosen and summoned by the Governor-General and sworn as Executive Councillors, and shall hold office during his pleasure.

63. Provisions referring to Governor-General The provisions of this Constitution referring to the Governor-General in Council shall be construed as referring to the Governor-General acting with the advice of the Federal Executive Council.

64. Ministers of State The Governor-General may appoint officers to administer such departments of State of the Commonwealth as the Governor-General in Council may establish.

Such officers shall hold office during the pleasure of the Governor-General. They shall be members of the Federal Executive Council, and shall be the Queen's Ministers of State for the Commonwealth.

Ministers to sit in Parliament After the first general election no Minister of State shall hold office for a longer period than three months unless he is or becomes a senator or a member of the House of Representatives.

65. Number of Ministers Until the Parliament otherwise provides, the Ministers of State shall not exceed seven in number, and shall hold such offices as the Parliament prescribes, or, in the absence of provision, as the Governor-General directs.

66. Salaries of Ministers There shall be payable to the Queen, out of the Consolidated Revenue Fund of the Commonwealth, for the salaries of the Ministers of State, an annual sum which, until the Parliament otherwise provides, shall not exceed twelve thousand pounds a year.

67. Appointment of civil servants Until the Parliament otherwise provides, the appointment and removal of all other officers of the Executive Government of the Commonwealth shall be vested in the Governor-General in Council, unless the appointment is delegated by the Governor-General in Council or by a law of the Commonwealth to some other authority.

68. Command of naval and military forces The commander in chief of the naval and military forces of the Commonwealth is vested in the Governor-General as the Queen's representative.

69. Transfer of certain departments   On a date or dates to be proclaimed by the Governor-General after the establishment of the Commonwealth the following departments of the public service in each State shall become transferred to the Commonwealth:

> Posts, telegraphs, and telephones:
> Naval and military defence:
> Lighthouses, lightships, beacons, and buoys:
> Quarantine.

But the departments of customs and excise in each State shall become transferred to the Commonwealth on its establishment.

70. Certain powers of Governors to vest in Governor-General   In respect of matters which, under this Constitution, pass to the Executive Government of the Commonwealth, all powers and functions which at the establishment of the Commonwealth are vested in the Governor of a Colony, or in the Governor of a Colony with the advice of his Executive Council, or in any authority of a Colony, shall vest in the Governor-General, or in the Governor-General in Council, or in the authority exercising similar powers under the Commonwealth, as the case requires.

CHAPTER III.—THE JUDICATURE.

71. Judicial power and Courts   The judicial power of the Commonwealth shall be vested in a Federal Supreme Court, to be called the High Court of Australia, and in such other federal courts as the Parliament creates, and in such other courts as it invests with federal jurisdiction. The High Court shall consist of a Chief Justice, and so many other Justices, not less than two, as the Parliament prescribes.

72.[7] Judges' appointment, tenure, and remuneration   The Justices of the High Court and of other courts created by the Parliament—

   (i.)   Shall be appointed by the Governor-General in Council:

   (ii.)   Shall not be removed except by the Governor-General in Council, on an address from both Houses of the Parliament in the same session, praying for such removal on the ground of proved misbehaviour or incapacity:

   (iii.)   Shall receive such remuneration as the Parliament may fix; but the remuneration shall not be diminished during their continuance in office.

The appointment of a Justice of the High Court shall be for a term expiring upon his attaining the age of seventy years, and a person shall not be appointed as a Justice of the High Court if he has attained that age.

The appointment of a Justice of a court created by the Parliament shall be for a term expiring upon his attaining the age that is, at the time of his appointment, the maximum age for Justices of that court and a person shall not be appointed as a Justice of such a court if he has attained the age that is for the time being the maximum age for Justices of that court.

Subject to this section, the maximum age for Justices of any court created by the Parliament is seventy years.

---

7 As amended by No. 83, 1977.

The Parliament may make a law fixing an age that is less than seventy years as the maximum age for Justices of a court created by the Parliament and may at any time repeal or amend such a law, but any such repeal or amendment does not affect the term of office of a Justice under an appointment made before the repeal or amendment.

A Justice of the High Court or of a court created by the Parliament may resign his office by writing under his hand delivered to the Governor-General.

Nothing in the provisions added to this section by the *Constitution Alteration (Retirement of Judges)* 1977 affects the continuance of a person in office as a Justice of a court under an appointment made before the commencement of those provisions.

A reference in this section to the appointment of a Justice of the High Court or of a court created by the Parliament shall be read as including a reference to the appointment of a person who holds office as a Justice of the High Court or of a court created by the Parliament to another office of Justice of the same court having a different status or designation.

73. Appellate jurisdiction of High Court The High Court shall have jurisdiction, with such exceptions and subject to such regulations as the Parliament prescribes, to hear and determine appeals from all judgments, decrees, orders, and sentences—

- (i.) Of any Justice or Justices exercising the original jurisdiction of the High Court:
- (ii.) Of any other federal court, or court exercising federal jurisdiction; or of the Supreme Court of any State, or of any other court of any State from which at the establishment of the Commonwealth an appeal lies to the Queen in Council:
- (iii.) Of the Inter-State Commission, but as to questions of law only:

and the judgment of the High Court in all such cases shall be final and conclusive.

But no exception or regulation prescribed by the Parliament shall prevent the High Court from hearing and determining any appeal from the Supreme Court of a State in any matter in which at the establishment of the Commonwealth an appeal lies from such Supreme Court to the Queen in Council.

Until the Parliament otherwise provides, the conditions of and restrictions on appeals to the Queen in Council from the Supreme Courts of the several States shall be applicable to appeals from them to the High Court.

74. Appeal to Queen in Council No appeal shall be permitted to the Queen in Council from a decision of the High Court upon question, howsoever arising, as to the limits inter se of the Constitutional powers of the Commonwealth and those of any State or States, or as to the limits inter se of the Constitutional powers of any two or more States, unless the High Court shall certify that the question is one which ought to be determined by Her Majesty in Council.

The High Court may so certify if satisfied that for any special reason the certificate should be granted, and thereupon an appeal shall lie to Her Majesty in Council on the question without further leave.

Except as provided in this section, this Constitution shall not impair any right which the Queen may be pleased to exercise by virtue of Her Royal prerogative to grant special leave of appeal from the High Court to Her Majesty in Council. The Parliament may make laws limiting the matters in which such leave may be asked, but proposed laws containing any such limitation shall be reserved by the Governor-General for Her Majesty's pleasure.

283

75. Original jurisdiction of High Court In all matters—

(i.) Arising under any treaty:

(ii.) Affecting consuls or other representatives of other countries:

(iii.) In which the Commonwealth, or a person suing or being sued on behalf of the Commonwealth, is a party:

(iv.) Between States, or between residents of different States, or between a State and a resident of another State:

(v.) In which a writ of Mandamus or prohibition or an injunction is sought against an officer of the Commonwealth:

the High Court shall have original jurisdiction.

76. Additional original jurisdiction The Parliament may make laws conferring original jurisdiction on the High Court in any matter—

(i.) Arising under this Constitution, or involving its interpretation:

(ii.) Arising under any laws made by the Parliament:

(iii.) Of Admiralty and maritime jurisdiction:

(iv.) Relating to the same subject-matter claimed under the laws of different States.

77. Power to define jurisdiction With respect to any of the matters mentioned in the last two sections the Parliament may make laws—

(i.) Defining the jurisdiction of any federal court other than the High Court:

(ii.) Defining the extent to which the jurisdiction of any federal court shall be exclusive of that which belongs to or is vested in the courts of the States:

(iii.) Investing any court of a State with federal jurisdiction.

78. Proceedings against Commonwealth or State The Parliament may make laws conferring rights to proceed against the Commonwealth or a State in respect of matters within the limits of the judicial power.

79. Number of judges The federal jurisdiction of any court may be exercised by such number of judges as the Parliament prescribes.

80. Trial by jury The trial on indictment of any offence against any law of the Commonwealth shall be by jury, and every trial shall be held in the State where the offence was committed, and if the offence was not committed within any State the trial shall be held at such place or places as the Parliament prescribes.

CHAPTER IV.—FINANCE AND TRADE.

81. Consolidated Revenue Fund All revenues or moneys raised or received by the Executive Government of the Commonwealth shall form one Consolidated Revenue Fund, to be appropriated for the purposes of the Commonwealth in the manner and subject to the charges and liabilities imposed by this Constitution.

82. Expenditure charged thereon The costs, charges, and expenses incident to the collection, management, and receipt of the Consolidated Revenue Fund shall form the first charge thereon; and the revenue of the Commonwealth shall in the first instance be applied to the payment of the expenditure of the Commonwealth.

83. Money to be appropriated by law No money shall be drawn from the Treasury of the Commonwealth except under appropriation made by law.

But until the expiration of one month after the first meeting of the Parliament the Governor-General in Council may draw from the Treasury and expend such moneys as may be necessary for the maintenance of any department transferred to the Commonwealth and for the holding of the first elections for the Parliament.

84. Transfer of officers   When any department of the public service of a State becomes transferred to the Commonwealth, all officers of the department shall become subject to the control of the Executive Government of the Commonwealth.

Any such officer who is not retained in the service of the Commonwealth shall, unless he is appointed to some other office of equal emolument in the public service of the State, be entitled to receive from the State any pension, gratuity, or other compensation, payable under the law of the State on the abolition of his office.

Any such officer who is retained in the service of the Commonwealth shall preserve all his existing and accruing rights, and shall be entitled to retire from office at the time, and on the pension or retiring allowance, which would have been permitted by the law of the State if his service with the Commonwealth were a continuation of his service with the State. Such pension or retiring allowance shall be paid to him by the Commonwealth; but the State shall pay to the Commonwealth a part thereof, to be calculated on the proportion which his term of service with the State bears to his whole term of service, and for the purpose of the calculation his salary shall be taken to be that paid to him by the State at the time of the transfer.

Any officer who is, at the establishment of the Commonwealth, in the public service of a State, and who is, by consent of the Governor of the State with the advice of the Executive Council thereof, transferred to the public service of the Commonwealth, shall have the same rights as if he had been an officer of a department transferred to the Commonwealth and were retained in the service of the Commonwealth.

85. Transfer of property of State   When any department of the public service of a State is transferred to the Commonwealth—

(i.)   All property of the State of any kind, used exclusively in connexion with the department, shall become vested in the Commonwealth; but, in the case of the departments controlling customs and excise and bounties, for such time only as the Governor-General in Council may declare to be necessary:

(ii.)   The Commonwealth may acquire any property of the State, of any kind used, but not exclusively used in connexion with the department; the value thereof shall, if no agreement can be made, be ascertained in, as nearly as may be, the manner in which the value of land, or of an interest in land, taken by the State for public purposes is ascertained under the law of the State in force at the establishment of the Commonwealth:

(iii.)   The Commonwealth shall compensate the State for the value of any property passing to the Commonwealth under this section; if no agreement can be made as to the mode of compensation, it shall be determined under laws to be made by the Parliament:

(iv.)   The Commonwealth shall, at the date of the transfer, assume the current obligations of the State in respect of the department transferred.

86. On the establishment of the Commonwealth, the collection and control of duties of customs and of excise, and the control of the payment of bounties, shall pass to the Executive Government of the Commonwealth.

285

87. During a period of ten years after the establishment of the Commonwealth and thereafter until the Parliament otherwise provides, of the net revenue of the Commonwealth from duties of customs and of excise not more than one-fourth shall be applied annually by the Commonwealth towards its expenditure.

The balance shall, in accordance with this Constitution, be paid to the several States, or applied towards the payment of interest on debts of the several States taken over by the Commonwealth.

88. Uniform duties of customs Uniform duties of customs shall be imposed within two years after the establishment of the Commonwealth.

89. Payment to States before uniform duties Until the imposition of uniform duties of customs—

    (i.) The Commonwealth shall credit to each State the revenues collected therein by the Commonwealth:

    (ii.) The Commonwealth shall debit to each State—

        (*a*) The expenditure therein of the Commonwealth incurred solely for the maintenance or continuance, as at the time of transfer, of any department transferred from the State to the Commonwealth:

        (*b*) The proportion of the State, according to the number of its people, in the other expenditure of the Commonwealth.

    (iii.) The Commonwealth shall pay to each State month by month the balance (if any) in favour of the State.

90. Exclusive power over customs, excise, and bounties On the imposition of uniform duties of customs the power of the Parliament to impose duties of customs and of excise, and to grant bounties on the production or export of goods, shall become exclusive.

On the imposition of uniform duties of customs all laws of the several States imposing duties of customs or of excise, or offering bounties on the production of export of goods, shall cease to have effect, but any grant of or agreement for any such bounty lawfully made by or under the authority of the Government of any State shall be taken to be good if made before the thirtieth day of June, one thousand eight hundred and ninety-eight, and not otherwise.

91. Exceptions as to bounties Nothing in this Constitution prohibits a State from granting any aid to or bounty on mining for gold, silver, or other metals, nor from granting, with the consent of both Houses of the Parliament of the Commonwealth expressed by resolution, any aid to or bounty on the production or export of goods.

92. Trade within the Commonwealth to be free On the imposition of uniform duties of customs, trade, commerce, and intercourse among the States, whether by means of internal carriage or ocean navigation, shall be absolutely free.

But notwithstanding anything in this Constitution, goods imported before the imposition of uniform duties of customs into any State, or into any Colony which, whilst the goods remain therein, becomes a State, shall, on thence passing into another State within two years after the imposition of such duties, be liable to any duty chargeable on the importation of such goods into the Commonwealth, less any duty paid in respect of the goods on their importation.

93. Payment to States for five years after uniform Tariffs During the first five years after the imposition of uniform duties of customs, and thereafter until the Parliament otherwise provides—

(i.) The duties of customs chargeable on goods imported into a State and afterwards passing into another State for consumption, and the duties of excise paid on goods produced or manufactured in a State and afterwards passing into another State for consumption, shall be taken to have been collected not in the former but in the latter State:

(ii.) Subject to the last subsection, the Commonwealth shall credit revenue, debit expenditure, and pay balance to the several States as prescribed for the period preceding the imposition of uniform duties of customs.

94. Distribution of surplus After five years from the imposition of uniform duties of customs, the Parliament may provide, on such basis as it deems fair, for the monthly payment to the several States of all surplus revenue of the Commonwealth.

95. Customs duties of Western Australia Notwithstanding anything in this Constitution, the Parliament of the State of Western Australia, if that State be an original State, may, during the first five years after the imposition of uniform duties of customs, impose duties of customs on goods passing into that State and not originally imposed from beyond the limits of the Commonwealth; and such duties shall be collected by the Commonwealth.

But any duty so imposed on any goods shall not exceed during the first of such years the duty chargeable on the goods under the law of Western Australia in force at the imposition of uniform duties, and shall not exceed during the second, third, fourth, and fifth of such years respectively, four-fifths, three-fifths, two-fifths and one-fifth of such latter duty, and all duties imposed under this section shall cease at the expiration of the fifth year after the imposition of uniform duties.

If at any time during the five years the duty on any goods under this section is higher than the duty imposed by the Commonwealth on the importation of the like goods, then such higher duty shall be collected on the goods when imported into Western Australia from beyond the limits of the Commonwealth.

96. Financial assistance to States During a period of ten years after the establishment of the Commonwealth and thereafter until the Parliament otherwise provides, the Parliament may grant financial assistance to any State on such terms and conditions as the Parliament thinks fit.

97. Audit Until the Parliament otherwise provides, the laws in force in any Colony which has become or becomes a State with respect to the receipt of revenue and the expenditure of money on account of the Government of the Colony, and the review and audit of such receipt and expenditure, shall apply to the receipt of revenue and the expenditure of money on account of the Commonwealth in the State in the same manner as if the Commonwealth, or the Government or an officer of the Commonwealth, were mentioned whenever the Colony, or the Government or an officer of the Colony, is mentioned.

98. Trade and commerce includes navigation and State railways The power of the Parliament to make laws with respect to trade and commerce extends to navigation and shipping, and to railways the property of any State.

99. Commonwealth not to give preference The Commonwealth shall not, by any law or regulation of trade, commerce, or revenue, give preference to one State or any part thereof over another State or any part thereof.

100. Nor abridge right to use water The Commonwealth shall not, by any law or regulation of trade or commerce, abridge the right of a State or of the residents therein to the reasonable use of the waters of rivers for conservation or irrigation.

101. Inter-State Commission There shall be an Inter-State Commission, with such powers of adjudication and administration as the Parliament deems necessary for the execution and maintenance, within the Commonwealth, of the provisions of this Constitution, relating to trade and commerce, and of all laws made thereunder.

102. Parliament may forbid preferences by State The Parliament may by any law with respect to trade or commerce forbid, as to railways, any preference or discrimination by any State, or by any authority constituted under a State, if such preference or discrimination is undue and unreasonable, or unjust to any State; due regard being had to the financial responsibilities incurred by any State in connexion with the construction and maintenance of its railways. But no preference or discrimination shall, within the meaning of this section, be taken to be undue and unreasonable, or unjust to any State, unless so adjudged by the Inter-State Commission.

103. Commissioners' appointment, tenure, and remuneration The members of the Inter-State Commission—

    (i.)   Shall be appointed by the Governor-General in Council:

    (ii.) Shall hold office for seven years, but may be removed within that time by the Governor-General in Council, on an address from both Houses of the Parliament in the same session praying for such removal on the ground or proved misbehaviour or incapacity:

    (iii.) Shall receive remuneration as the Parliament may fix; but such remuneration shall not be diminished during their continuance in office.

104. Saving of certain rates Nothing in this Constitution shall render unlawful any rate for the carriage of goods upon a railway the property of a State, if the rate is deemed by the Inter-State Commission to be necessary for the development of the territory of the State, and if the rate applies equally to goods within the State and to goods passing into the State from other States.

105.[8] Taking over public debts of States The Parliament may take over from the States their public debts or a proportion thereof according to the respective numbers of their people as shown by the latest statistics of the Commonwealth, and may convert, renew, or consolidate such debts, or any part thereof; and the States shall indemnify the Commonwealth in respect of the debts taken over, and thereafter the interest payable in respect of the debts shall be deducted and retained from the portions of the surplus revenue of the Commonwealth payable to the several States, or if such surplus is insufficient, or if there is no surplus, then the deficiency or the whole amount shall be paid by the several States.

105A.[9] Agreements with respect to State debts (1) The Commonwealth may make agreements with the States with respect to the public debts of the States, including—

    (*a*) the taking over of such debts by the Commonwealth;

    (*b*) the management of such debts;

    (*c*) the payment of interest and the provision and management of sinking funds in respect of such debts;

    (*d*) the consolidation, renewal, conversion, and redemption of such debts;

    (*e*) the indemnification of the Commonwealth by the States in respect of debts taken over by the Commonwealth; and

    (*f*) the borrowing of money by the States or by the Commonwealth, or by the Commonwealth for the States.

---

8 As amended by No. 3, 1910, s. 2.
9 Inserted by No. 1, 1929, s. 2.

(2) The Parliament may make laws for validating any such agreement made before the commencement of this section.

(3) The Parliament may make laws for the carrying out by the parties thereto of any such agreement.

(4) Any such agreement may be varied or rescinded by the parties thereto.

(5) Every such agreement and any such variation thereof shall be binding upon the Commonwealth and the States parties thereto notwithstanding anything contained in this Constitution or the Constitution of the several States or in any law of the Parliament of the Commonwealth or of any State.

(6) The powers conferred by this section shall not be construed as being limited in any way by the provisions of section one hundred and five of this Constitution.

CHAPTER V.—THE STATES.

106. Saving of Constitutions The Constitution of each State of the Commonwealth shall, subject to this Constitution, continue as at the establishment of the Commonwealth, or as at the admission or establishment of the State, as the case may be, until altered in accordance with the Constitution of the State.

107. Saving of power of State Parliaments Every power of the Parliament of a Colony which has become or becomes a State, shall, unless it is by this Constitution exclusively vested in the Parliament of the Commonwealth or withdrawn from the Parliament of the State, continue as at the establishment of the Commonwealth, or as at the admission or establishment of the State, as the case may be.

108. Saving of State laws Every law in force in a Colony which has become or becomes a State, and relating to any matter within the powers of the Parliament of the Commonwealth, shall, subject to this Constitution, continue in force in the State: and, until provision is made in that behalf by the Parliament of the Commonwealth, the Parliament of the State shall have such powers of alteration and of appeal in respect of any such law as the Parliament of the Colony had until the Colony became a State.

109. Inconsistency of laws When a law of a State is inconsistent with a law of the Commonwealth, the latter shall prevail, and the former shall, to the extent of the inconsistency, be invalid.

110. Provisions referring to Governor The provisions of this Constitution relating to the Governor of a State extend and apply to the Governor for the time being of the State, or other chief executive officer or administrator of the government of the State.

111. States may surrender territory The Parliament of a State may surrender any part of the State to the Commonwealth; and upon such surrender, and the acceptance thereof by the Commonwealth, such part of the State shall become subject to the exclusive jurisdiction of the Commonwealth.

112. States may levy charges for inspection laws After uniform duties of customs have been imposed, a State may levy on imports or exports, or on goods passing into or out of the State, such charges as may be necessary for executing the inspection laws of the State; but the net produce of all charges so levied shall be for the use of the Commonwealth; and any such inspection laws may be annulled by the Parliament of the Commonwealth.

113. Intoxicating liquids   All fermented, distilled, or other intoxicating liquids passing into any State or remaining therein for use, consumption, sale, or storage, shall be subject to the laws of the State as if such liquids had been produced in the State.

114. States may not raise forces. Taxation of property of Commonwealth or State   A State shall not, without the consent of the Parliament of the Commonwealth, raise or maintain any naval or military force, or impose any tax on property of any kind belonging to the Commonwealth, nor shall the Commonwealth impose any tax on property of any kind belonging to a State.

115. States not to coin money   A State shall not coin money, nor make anything but gold and silver coin legal tender in payment of debts.

116. Commonwealth not to legislate in respect of religion   The Commonwealth shall not make any law for establishing any religion, or for imposing any religious observance, or for prohibiting the free exercise of any religion, and no religious test shall be required as a qualification for any office or public trust under the Commonwealth.

117. Rights of residents in States   A subject of the Queen, resident in any State, shall not be subject in any other State to any disability or discrimination which would not be equally applicable to him if he were a subject of the Queen resident in such other State.

118. Recognition of laws, &c. of States   Full faith and credit shall be given, throughout the Commonwealth, to the laws, the public Acts and records, and the judicial proceedings of every State.

119. Protection of States from invasion and violence   The Commonwealth shall protect every State against invasion and, on the application of the Executive Government of the State, against domestic violence.

120. Custody of offenders against laws of the Commonwealth   Every State shall make provision for the detention in its prisons of persons accused or convicted of offences against the laws of the Commonwealth, and for the punishment of persons convicted of such offences, and the Parliament of the Commonwealth may make laws to give effect to this provision.

CHAPTER VI.—NEW STATES.

121. New States may be admitted or established   The Parliament may admit to the Commonwealth or established new States, and may upon such admission or establishment make or impose such terms and conditions, including the extent of representation in either House of the Parliament, as it thinks fit.

122. Government of territories   The Parliament may make laws for the government of any territory surrendered by any State to and accepted by the Commonwealth, or of any Territory placed by the Queen under the authority of and acceptance by the Commonwealth, or otherwise acquired by the Commonwealth, and may allow the representation of such territory in either House of the Parliament to the extent and on the terms which it thinks fit.

123. Alteration of limits of States   The Parliament of the Commonwealth may, with the consent of the Parliament of a State, and the approval of the majority of the electors of the State voting upon the question, increase, diminish, or otherwise alter the limits of the State, upon such terms and conditions as may be agreed on, and may, with the like consent, make provision respecting the effect and operation of any increase or diminution or alteration of territory in relation to any State affected.

124. Formation of new States   A new State may be formed by separation of territory from a State, but only with the consent of the Parliament thereof, and a new State may be formed by the union of two or more States or parts of States, but only with the consent of the Parliaments of the States affected.

CHAPTER VII.—MISCELLANEOUS.

125. Seat of Government   The seat of Government of the Commonwealth shall be determined by the Parliament, and shall be within territory which shall have been granted to or acquired by the Commonwealth, and shall be vested in and belong to the Commonwealth, and shall be in the State of New South Wales, and be distant not less than one hundred miles from Sydney.

Such territory shall contain an area of not less than one hundred square miles, and such portion thereof as shall consist of Crown lands shall be granted to the Commonwealth without any payment therefor.

The Parliament shall sit at Melbourne until it meet at the seat of Government.

126. Power to Her Majesty to authorize Governor-General to appoint deputies   The Queen may authorize the Governor-General to appoint any person, or any persons jointly or severally, to be his deputy or deputies within any part of the Commonwealth, and in that capacity to exercise during the pleasure of the Governor-General such powers and functions of the Governor-General as he thinks fit to assign to such deputy or deputies, subject to any limitations expressed or directions given by the Queen; but the appointment of such deputy or deputies shall not affect the exercise by the Governor-General himself of any power or function.

127.[10]

CHAPTER VIII.—ALTERATION OF THE CONSTITUTION.[11]

128.[12] **Mode of altering the Constitution**   This Constitution shall not be altered except in the following manner:

The proposed law for the alteration thereof must be passed by an absolute majority of each House of the Parliament, and not less than two nor more than six months after its passage through both Houses the proposed law shall be submitted in each State and Territory, to the electors qualified to vote for the election of members of the House of Representatives.

---

10 Repealed by No. 55, 1967, s. 3.
11 The eight Acts amending the Constitution have been listed at the beginning of this copy of the Constitution.
12 As amended by No. 84, 1977.

But if either House passes any such proposed law by an absolute majority, and the other House rejects or fails to pass it or passes it with any amendment to which the first-mentioned House will not agree, and if after an interval of three months the first-mentioned House in the same or the next session again passes the proposed law by an absolute majority with or without any amendment which has been made or agreed to by the other House, and such other House rejects or fails to pass it or passes it with any amendment to which the first-mentioned House will not agree, the Governor-General may submit the proposed law as last proposed by the first-mentioned House, and either with or without any amendments subsequently agreed to by both Houses, to the electors in each State and Territory qualified to vote for the election of the House of Representatives.

When a proposed law is submitted to the electors the vote shall be taken in such manner as the Parliament prescribes. But until the qualification of electors of members of the House of Representatives becomes uniform throughout the Commonwealth, only one half the electors voting for and against the proposed law shall be counted in any State in which adult suffrage prevails.

And if in a majority of the States a majority of the electors voting approve the proposed law, and if a majority of all the electors voting also approve the proposed law, it shall be presented to the Governor-General for the Queen's assent.

No alteration diminishing the proportionate representation of any State in either House of the Parliament, or the minimum number of representatives of a State in the House of Representatives, or increasing, diminishing, or otherwise altering the limits of the State, or in any manner affecting the provisions of the Constitution in relation thereto, shall become law unless the majority of the electors voting in that State approve the proposed law.

In this section, "Territory" means any Territory referred to in section one hundred and twenty-two of this Constitution in respect of which there is in force a law allowing its representation in the House of Representatives.

SCHEDULE

OATH

I, *A.B.*, do swear that I will be faithful and bear true allegiance to Her Majesty Queen Victoria, Her heirs and successors according to law, So HELP ME GOD!

AFFIRMATION

I, *A.B.*, do solemnly and sincerely affirm and declare that I will be faithful and bear true allegiance to Her Majesty Queen Victoria, Her heirs and successors according to law.

(NOTE—*The name of the King or Queen of the United Kingdom of Great Britain and Ireland for the time being is to be substituted from time to time.*).

AUSTRALIA ACT 1986

No 142 of 1985

An Act to bring constitutional arrangements affecting the Commonwealth and the States into conformity with the status of the Commonwealth of Australia as a sovereign, independent and federal nation.

[Assented to 4 December 1985]

WHEREAS the Prime Minister of the Commonwealth and the Premiers of the States at conferences held in Canberra on 24 and 25 June 1982 and 21 June 1984 agreed on the taking of certain measures to bring constitutional arrangements affecting the Commonwealth and the States into conformity with the status of the Commonwealth of Australia as a sovereign, independent and federal nation:

AND WHEREAS in pursuance of paragraph 51(xxxviii) of the Constitution the Parliaments of all the States have requested the Parliament of the Commonwealth to enact an Act in the terms of this Act:

BE IT THEREFORE ENACTED by the Queen, and the Senate and the House of Representatives of the Commonwealth of Australia, as follows:

Termination of power of Parliament of United Kingdom to legislate for Australia

1. No Act of the Parliament of the United Kingdom passed after the commencement of this Act shall extend, or be deemed to extend, to the Commonwealth, to a State or to a Territory as part of the law of the Commonwealth, of the State or of the Territory.

Legislative powers of Parliaments of States

2. (1) It is hereby declared and enacted that the legislative powers of the Parliament of each State include full power to make laws for the peace, order and good government of that State that have extra-territorial operation.

(2) It is hereby further declared and enacted that the legislative powers of the Parliament of each State include all legislative powers that the Parliament of the United Kingdom might have exercised before the commencement of this Act for the peace, order and good government of that State but nothing in this subsection confers on a State any capacity that the State did not have immediately before the commencement of this Act to engage in relations with countries outside Australia.

Termination of restrictions on legislative powers of Parliaments of States

3. (1) The Act of the Parliament of the United Kingdom known as the Colonial Laws Validity Act 1865 shall not apply to any law made after the commencement of this Act by the Parliament of a State.

(2) No law and no provision of any law made after the commencement of this Act by the Parliament of a State shall be void or inoperative on the ground that it is repugnant to the law of England, or to the provisions of any existing or future Act of the Parliament of the United Kingdom, or to any order, rule or regulation made under any such Act, and the powers of the Parliament of a State shall include the power to repeal or amend any such Act, order, rule or regulation in so far as it is part of the law of the State.

Powers of State Parliaments in relation to merchant shipping

4. Section 735 and 736 of the Act of the Parliament of the United Kingdom known as the Merchant Shipping Act 1894, in so far as they are part of the law of a State, are hereby repealed.

Commonwealth Constitution, Constitution Act and Statute of Westminister not affected

5. Sections 2 and 3(2) above—

(a) are subject to the Commonwealth of Australia Constitution Act and to the Constitutuon of the Commonwealth; and

(b) do not operate so as to give any force or effect to a provision of an Act of the Parliament of a State that would repeal, amend or be repugnant to this Act, the Commonwealth of Australia Constitution Act, the Constitution of the Commonwealth or the Statute of Westminster 1931 as amended and in force from time to time.

Manner and form of making certain State laws

6. Notwithstanding sections 2 and 3(2) above, a law made after the commencement of this Act by the Parliament of a State respecting the constitution, powers or procedure of the Parliament of the State shall be of no force or effect unless it is made in such manner and form as may from time to time be required by a law made by that Parliament, whether made before or after the commencement of this Act.

Powers and functions of Her Majesty and Governors in respect of States

7. (1) Her Majesty's representative in each State shall be the Governor.

(2) Subject to subsections (3) and (4) below, all powers and functions of Her Majesty in respect of a State are exercisable only by the Governor of the State.

(3) Subjection (2) above does not apply in relation to the power to appoint, and the power to terminate the appointment of, the Governor of a State.

(4) While Her Majesty is personally present in a State, Her Majesty is not precluded from exercising any of Her powers and functions in respect of the State that are the subject of subsection (2) above.

(5) The advice to Her Majesty in relation to the exercise of the powers and functions of Her Majesty in respect of a State shall be tendered by the Premier of the State.

State laws not subject to disallowance or suspension of operation

8. An Act of the Parliament of a State that has been assented to by the Governor of the State shall not, after the commencement of this Act, be subject to disallowance by Her Majesty, nor shall its operation be suspended pending the signification of Her Majesty's pleasure thereon.

State laws not subject to withholding of assent or reservation

9. (1) No law or instrument shall be of any force or effect in so far as it purports to require the Governor of a State to withhold assent from any Bill for an Act of the State that has been passed in such manner and form as may from time to time be required by a law made by the Parliament of the State.

(2) No law or instrument shall be of any force or effect in so far as it purports to require the reservation of any Bill for an Act of a State for the signification of Her Majesty's pleasure thereon.

Termination of responsibility of United Kingdom Government in relation to State matters

10. After the commencement of this Act Her Majesty's Government in the United Kingdom shall have no responsibility for the government of any State.

Termination of appeals to Her Majesty in Council

11. (1) Subject to subsection (4) below, no appeal to Her Majesty in Council lies or shall be brought, whether by leave or special leave of any court or of Her Majesty in Council or otherwise, and whether by virtue of any Act of the Parliament of the United Kingdom, the Royal Prerogative or otherwise, from or in respect of any decision of an Australian court.

(2) Subject to subsection (4) below—

(a) the enactments specified in subsection (3) below and any orders, rules, regulations or other instruments made under, or for the purposes of, those enactments; and

(b) any other provisions of Acts of the Parliament of the United Kingdom in force immediately before the commencement of this Act that make provision for or in relation to appeals to Her Majesty in Council from or in respect of decisions of courts, and any orders, rules, regulations or other instruments made under, or for the purposes of, any such provisions,

in so far as they are part of the law of the Commonwealth, of a State or of a Territory, are hereby repealed.

(3) The enactments referred to in subsection (2)(a) above are the following Acts of the Parliament of the United Kingdom or provisions of such Acts:

The Australian Courts Act 1828, section 15

The Judicial Committee Act 1833

The Judicial Committee Act 1844

The Australian Constitutions Act 1850, section 28

The Colonial Courts of Admiralty Act 1890, section 6.

(4) Nothing in the foregoing provisions of this Section—

(a) affects an appeal instituted before the commencement of this Act to Her Majesty in Council from or in respect of a decision of an Australian court; or

(b) precludes the institution after that commencement of an appeal to Her Majesty in Council from or in respect of such a decision where the appeal is instituted—

(i) pursuant to leave granted by an Australian court on an application made before that commencement; or

(ii) pursuant to special leave granted by Her Majesty in Council on a petition presented before that commencement,

but this subsection shall not be construed as permitting or enabling an appeal to Her Majesty in Council to be instituted or continued that could not have been instituted or continued if this section had not been enacted.

Australia Act, 1986

Amendment of Statute of Westminster

12. Sections 4, 9(2) and (3) and 10(2) of the Statute of Westminster 1931, in so far as they are part of the law of the Commonwealth, of a State or of a Territory, are hereby repealed.

Amendment of Constitution Act of Queensland

13. (1) The Constitution Act 1867-1978 of the State of Queensland is in this section referred to as the Principal Act.

(2) Section 11A of the Principal Act is amended in subsection (3)—

(a) by omitting from paragraph (a)—

  (i) "and Signet"; and

  (ii) "constituted under Letters Patent under the Great Seal of the United Kingdom"; and

(b) by omitting from paragraph (b)—

  (i) "and Signet"; and

  (ii) "whenever and so long as the office of Governor is vacant or the Governor is incapable of discharging the duties of administration or has departed from Queensland".

(3) Section 11B of the Principal Act is amended—

(a) by omitting "Governor to conform to instructions" and substituting "Definition of Royal Sign Manual";

(b) by omitting subsection (1); and

(c) by omitting from subsection (2)—

  (i) "(2)";

  (ii) "this section and in"; and

  (iii) "and the expression 'Signet' means the seal commonly used for the sign manual of the Sovereign or the seal with which documents are sealed by the Secretary of State in the United Kingdom on behalf of the Sovereign".

(4) Section 14 of the Principal Act is amended in subsection (2) by omitting ", subject to his performing his duty prescribed by section 11B,".

Amendment of Constitution Act of Western Australia

14. (1) The Constitution Act 1889 of the State of Western Australia is in this section referred to as the Principal Act.

(2) Section 50 of the Principal Act is amended in subsection (3)—

(a) by omitting from paragraph (a)—

  (i) "and Signet"; and

  (ii) "constituted under Letters Patent under the Great Seal of the United Kingdom";

(b) by omitting from paragraph (b)—

  (i) "and Signet"; and

  (ii) "whenever and so long as the office of Governor is vacant or the Governor is incapable of discharging the duties of administration or has departed from Western Australia"; and

(c) by omitting from paragraph (c)—

    (i) "under the Great Seal of the United Kingdom"; and

    (ii) "during a temporary absence of the Governor for a short period from the seat of Government or from the State".

(3) Section 51 of the Principal Act is amended—

(a) by omitting subsection (1); and

(b) by omitting from subsection (2)—

    (i) "(2)";

    (ii) "this section and in"; and

    (iii) "and the expression 'Signet' means the seal commonly used for the sign manual of the Sovereign or the seal with which documents are sealed by the Secretary of State in the United Kingdom on behalf of the Sovereign".

Method of repeal or amendment of this Act or Statute of Westminster

15. (1) This Act or the Statute of Westminster 1931, as amended and in force from time to time, in so far as it is part of the law of the Commonwealth, of a State or of a Territory, may be repealed or amended by an Act of the Parliament of the Commonwealth passed at the request or with the concurrence of the Parliaments of all the States and, subject to subsection (3) below, only in that manner.

(2) For the purposes of subsection (1) above, an Act of the Parliament of the Commonwealth that is repugnant to this Act or the Statute of Westminster 1931, as amended and in force from time to time, or to any provision of this Act or of that Statute as so amended and in force, shall, to the extent of the repugnancy, be deemed an Act to repeal or amend the Act, Statute or provision to which it is repugnant.

(3) Nothing in subsection (1) above limits or prevents the exercise by the Parliament of the Commonwealth of any powers that may be conferred upon that Parliament by any alteration to the Constitution of the Commonwealth made in accordance with section 128 of the Constitution of the Commonwealth after the commencement of this Act.

Interpretation

16. (1) In this Act, unless the contrary intention appears—

"appeal" includes a petition of appeal, and a complaint in the nature of an appeal;

"appeal to Her Majesty in Council" includes any appeal to Her Majesty;

"Australian court" means a court of a State or any other court of Australia or of a Territory other than the High Court;

"court" includes a judge, judicial officer or other person acting judicially;

"decision" includes determination, judgment, decree, order or sentence;

"Governor", in relation to a State, includes any person for the time being administering the government of the State;

"State" means a State of the Commonwealth and includes a new State;

"the Commonwealth of Australia Constitution Act" means the Act of the Parliament of the United Kingdom known as the Commonwealth of Australia Constitution Act;

"the Constitution of the Commonwealth" means the Constitution of the Commonwealth set forth in section 9 of the Commonwealth of Australia Constitution Act, being that Constitution as altered and in force from time to time;

"the Statute of Westminster 1931" means the Act of the Parliament of the United Kingdom known as the Statute of Westminster 1931.

(2) The expression "a law made by that Parliament" in section 6 above and the expression "a law made by the Parliament" in section 9 above include, in relation to the State of Western Australia, the Constitution Act 1889 of that State.

(3) A reference in this Act to the Parliament of a State includes, in relation to the State of New South Wales, a reference to the legislature of that State as constituted from time to time in accordance with the Constitution Act, 1902, or any other Act of that State, whether or not, in relation to any particular legislative act, the consent of the Legislative Council of that State is necessary.

Short title and commencement

17. (1) This Act may be cited as the *Australia Act 1986*.

(2) This Act shall come into operation on a day and at a time to be fixed by Proclamation.[1]

---

1. The day appointed by proclamation was 3 March 1986.

AUSTRALIA ACT 1986 (UK)

The United Kingdom Parliament passed its Australia Act 1986 as a fail-safe if the Commonwealth Parliament's Act failed for validity.

So, the United Kingdom Act is identical with the Commonwealth Act (even in the numbering of the sections), save for the following slight differences:

AUSTRALIA ACT 1986

1986 Chapter 2

An Act to give effect to a request by the Parliament and Government of the Commonwealth of Australia.

[17th February 1986]

Wheras the Parliament and Government of the Commonwealth of Australia have, with the concurrence of the States of Australia, requested and consented to the enactment of an Act of the Parliament of the United Kingdom in the terms hereinafter set forth:

Be it therefore enacted by the Queen's most Excellent Majesty, by and with the advice and consent of the Lords Spiritual and Temporal, and Commons, in this present Parliament assembled, and by the authority of the same, as follows:—

. . .

16. (1) In this Act—

"appeal" includes a petition of appeal, and a complaint in the nature of an appeal;

"appeal to Her Majesty in Council" includes an appeal to Her Majesty;

"Australian court" means a court of a State or any other court of Australia or of a Territory other than the High Court of Australia;

"the Commonwealth" means the Commonwealth of Australia as established under the Commonwealth of Australia Constitution Act;

"the Constitution of the Commonwealth" means the Constitution of the Commonwealth set forth in section 9 of the Commonwealth of Australia Constitution Act, being that Constitution as altered and in force from time to time;

"court" includes a judge, judicial officer or other person acting judicially;

"decision" includes determination, judgment, decree, order or sentence;

"Governor", in relation to a State, includes any person for the time being administering the government of the State;

"State" means a State of the Commonwealth and includes a new State;

"Territory" means a territory referred to in section 122 of the Constitution of the Commonwealth;

(2) The expression "a law made by that Parliament" in section 6 above and the expression "a law made by the Parliament" in section 9 above, include, in relation to the State of Western Australia, the Constitution Act 1889 of that State.

299

(3) A reference in this Act to the Parliament of a State includes, in relation to the State of New South Wales, a reference to the legislature of that State as constituted from time to time in accordance with the Constitution Act, 1902, or any other Act of that State, whether or not, in relation to any particular legislative act, the consent of the Legislative Council of that State is necessary.

17. (1) . . .

(2) This Act shall come into force on such day and at such time as the Secretary of State may by order made by statutory instrument appoint.[1]

---

1. The day appointed was 3 March 1986.

Index

The section numbers **in bold type** refer to the Commonwealth Constitution, a copy of which appears in front of this Index.

A

C

G

Index